COMPUTER SCIENCE FROM SCRATCH

COMPUTER SCIENCE FROM SCRATCH

Building Interpreters, Art, Emulators, and ML in Python

by David Kopec

no starch press®

San Francisco

Printed in the United States of America

First printing

29 28 27 26 25   1 2 3 4 5

ISBN-13: 978-1-7185-0430-1 (print)
ISBN-13: 978-1-7185-0431-8 (ebook)

 Published by No Starch Press®, Inc.
245 8th Street, San Francisco, CA 94103
phone: +1.415.863.9900
www.nostarch.com; info@nostarch.com

Publisher: William Pollock
Managing Editor: Jill Franklin
Production Manager: Sabrina Plomitallo-González
Production Editor: Jennifer Kepler
Developmental Editor: Nathan Heidelberger
Cover Illustrator: Josh Kemble
Interior Design: Octopod Studios
Technical Reviewer: Michael Kennedy
Copyeditor: Audrey Doyle
Proofreader: Céline Parent

The following images are reproduced with permission: Figures 6-2, 6-4, 6-5, and 6-6 were created by user Damian Yerrick of nesdev.org. Figure 6-7 was created by user Persune of nesdev.org. All the information on nesdev.org is released into the public domain.

Library of Congress Control Number: 2025016217

For customer service inquiries, please contact info@nostarch.com. For information on distribution, bulk sales, corporate sales, or translations: sales@nostarch.com. For permission to translate this work: rights@nostarch.com. To report counterfeit copies or piracy: counterfeit@nostarch.com. The authorized representative in the EU for product safety and compliance is EU Compliance Partner, Pärnu mnt. 139b-14, 11317 Tallinn, Estonia, hello@eucompliancepartner.com, +3375690241.

To my mother, Sylvia, who has celebrated every win with me,
and helped me with every loss.

About the Author

David Kopec is an associate professor of computer science at Albright College. He joined academia in 2016 after working as a software developer, with a concentration in iOS app development. He's the author of four previous technical books, including *Classic Computer Science Problems in Python*, which has been translated into eight languages and published around the world. An avid app developer and podcaster, Kopec lives with his wife and three children in Wyomissing, Pennsylvania.

About the Technical Reviewer

Michael Kennedy is well known in the Python space through his work at the *Talk Python to Me* and *Python Bytes* podcasts, which have covered important topics and news in the Python community for almost 10 years. He's the founder of Talk Python Training, which offers many developer courses online, and is a Python Software Foundation Fellow. Kennedy is based in Portland, Oregon. When he's not programming or enjoying time with his family, you might find him exploring the local mountains on his motorcycle.

BRIEF CONTENTS

CONTENTS IN DETAIL

PART II: COMPUTATIONAL ART　　　61

3
RETRO IMAGE PROCESSING　　　63

4
A STOCHASTIC PAINTING ALGORITHM　　　89

PART III: EMULATORS　　　113

5
BUILDING A CHIP-8 VIRTUAL MACHINE　　　115

8
REGRESSION WITH K-NEAREST NEIGHBORS 221

AFTERWORD 231

APPENDIX: BITWISE OPERATIONS 237

INDEX 245

ACKNOWLEDGMENTS

Most importantly, I would like to thank you, the reader, for purchasing this book. You probably could have found online tutorials for most of the topics in this book, but it's unlikely they would have been as vetted, as cohesive, or as well put together. At least I think so, and that's why I wrote this book. By purchasing it, you supported not only its development but also the continued existence of an industry that produces other books like it.

Next, I would like to thank Champlain College, which provided me with a sabbatical after seven years of service. There are very few remaining industries that give people time off for the better part of a year to pursue their own work-related interests and pay them to do it. Sometimes something wonderful comes out of that time and space. Completing this book was my sabbatical project.

I would like to thank my family who supported me in pursuing this project, especially my mom, Sylvia, and my wife, Rebecca. My kids, Daniel, Vera, and Lucille, are too young to really understand what it means to write a technical book, but I couldn't have written it if Rebecca wasn't taking care of them, so instead of thanking them, I'll thank her a second time.

I would like to thank No Starch Press for believing in this book. I came to them with a fully written draft manuscript, which is a bit unusual for a technical book, and they believed in its contents enough to put the resources into refining it for your consumption. In particular, I would like to thank Nathan Heidelberger, my developmental editor, who took the time to empathetically put himself in the shoes of the reader and found ways both large and small to improve the book. And, of course, I'd like to thank the rest of the team at No Starch Press who helped bring the book through development and production. I would also like to thank my technical reviewer, Michael Kennedy, for his good suggestions.

Last but not least, I want to thank all of the folks who publicly reviewed my prior books. If you hadn't reacted positively to my prior books and taken the time to record that, this book would never have had the fuel to take off. If you're reading this, please take the time to review this book too!

INTRODUCTION

How does a programming language work? How is a simple computer organized? I'm the type of person who likes to learn new subjects from first principles, in a hands-on way. I want more than just high-level overviews. If you're that type of learner too, then you've found the right resource. Through the seven Python projects in this book, you'll build an understanding of some fundamental ideas from the realm of computer science.

Who This Book Is For

This book is for intermediate and advanced Python programmers. If you're a beginning programmer, you should probably come back to this book at a later point. Throughout the text, I assume the reader knows the syntax and semantics of Python, is comfortable writing programs of moderate complexity, knows how to install Python libraries, and understands basic data structures like lists, sets, and dictionaries.

While I do assume readers will have some programming experience, I don't assume readers' knowledge of computer science or advanced mathematics. This book is designed for those who either lack a formal computer science education or want to fill in some gaps in their knowledge. For example, if you have an interest in writing your own programming language but you never took a course on compilers, this book is a great starting point. If you want to write a video game console emulator, this book will show you how. It even has a very digestible introduction to machine learning.

The exact projects in the book may not themselves be your end goal, but that's not the point. Think of them as a means to unlock deeper knowledge about algorithmic thinking and how software works, and as a jumping-off point for your own explorations.

What's in the Book

Each chapter constitutes one complete project, except for Chapters 7 and 8, which together make up one project. The seven projects in the book range from easy (the Brainfuck interpreter in Chapter 1) to difficult (the NES emulator in Chapter 6), but since all the source code is provided, you'll never get stuck and be unable to proceed.

Each project begins with some theory—just enough to understand what we'll be implementing, without getting bogged down in the details—and then walks through the code. The chapters also include stories about how I personally got interested in the subject, a discussion of how the implemented algorithms or computational techniques are used in the real world, and challenges for the reader to extend the provided code.

The book is divided into four parts. In Part I, we'll explore the world of interpreters by creating implementations of two simple programming languages.

Chapter 1: The Smallest Possible Programming Language Brainfuck is a minimal programming language often used for educational purposes because of its simplicity—the whole language consists of just eight characters. We'll learn how a very simple interpreter works by implementing one that can run any Brainfuck program. We'll also learn what it means for a language to be Turing-complete.

Chapter 2: Writing a BASIC Interpreter The BASIC programming language and its pared-down dialect, Tiny BASIC, were popular during the PC revolution of the late 1970s. We'll implement an interpreter for a slightly simplified variant of Tiny BASIC called NanoBASIC. Doing so will demonstrate the constituent parts of more sophisticated interpreters, including a tokenizer, parser, and runtime environment.

In Part II, we'll get into the vibrant world of computational art.

Chapter 3: Retro Image Processing When display technology was simpler, dithering algorithms were necessary to adapt images for devices that used a limited color palette. We'll implement a dithering algorithm capable of displaying modern color photos on the black-and-white screen of an original Macintosh. Then, we'll convert the dithered images to a format compatible with the classic MacPaint application, using the run-length encoding compression algorithm in the process. The images we output can be displayed on actual 1980s Macintosh hardware.

Chapter 4: A Stochastic Painting Algorithm   Can a relatively simple algorithm create sophisticated abstract art? We'll use a stochastic technique to generate "impressions" of existing images by matching random shapes to the underlying image, and we'll see how a hill-climbing algorithm can help optimize the results.

Part III is all about emulators—programs that allow one type of computer to pretend to be another type of computer.

Chapter 5: Building a CHIP-8 Virtual Machine   CHIP-8 is a virtual machine (VM) specification that was originally used for developing video games in the 1970s. Building a CHIP-8 VM is often considered the best first step into the world of emulation: it's relatively simple but still involves all the steps necessary to create an emulator. Our CHIP-8 VM will be capable of playing all the CHIP-8 games that ran on machines in the 1970s.

Chapter 6: Emulating the NES Game Console   The NES was one of the best-selling video game consoles of all time. We'll create an emulator that can play real NES games. It will have no sound, be rather slow, and not be completely accurate or universally compatible, but it will still be a great way to learn not just about emulators but also about how computers work at a low level.

Finally, Part IV is a very gentle introduction to the world of machine learning using the *k*-nearest neighbors (KNN) algorithm.

Chapter 7: Classification with K-Nearest Neighbors   We'll learn KNN, perhaps the simplest algorithm in machine learning (ML), and use it as a gateway to understand some introductory ML topics. We'll use KNN to classify fish as well as images of handwritten digits. Amazingly, it will complete the latter task with 98 percent accuracy.

Chapter 8: Regression with K-Nearest Neighbors   We'll take KNN to the next level by using it not just to classify items into categories but also to predict unknown attributes of data points. In the chapter finale, we'll use it to predict the missing pixels from an image of a digit that the user draws.

Beyond the main chapters, the afterword features some suggested resources for learning more about the topics in this book, and the appendix covers the basics of low-level bit manipulation in Python, an essential component of several projects.

This Book's Approach

I try to keep my books as succinct as possible. I value your time. I use a tutorial-like, code-centric format to teach, and where possible, I let the code speak for itself.

This is not a textbook. You'll find some theory, especially at the beginning of each chapter, but it will never be too long before we get to some code. There's just enough information to help you understand how each of the projects works, and enough pointers so that you know where to look next if you want to dive deeper into any of the covered topics.

I'm not claiming to be an expert on interpreters, computational art, emulators, or machine learning. That may sound weird coming from the author of a book on those topics, but it's true. I'm not an expert; I'm a teacher. I've worked as a software developer, and I've worked as computer science faculty at a teaching college. My claim is that I'm able to write clean code and explain that code to you in an exceptionally comprehensible manner. And since I'm not an expert, I won't be talking down to you. I'll be treating you like my peer as we go on this journey together. This is the guide I wish I had as I tried doing projects in these areas on my own.

About the Code

All the source code in this book is available on the companion GitHub repository at *https://github.com/davecom/ComputerScienceFromScratch*. The code was created and tested against Python versions 3.12 and 3.13. Because some type hint–related features of Python 3.12 are utilized, some of the code won't work with earlier versions of Python (but will likely work with any new version of Python in the foreseeable future). However, if you remove the type hints, the vast majority of the code will work with Python version 3.10 and later.

I've used Python type hints (or "type annotations") throughout the source code because I believe they increase readability by telling you a function's parameter and return types without you needing to scrutinize the code or the comments. If you don't like them, you can ignore them; they don't change anything about how the code works. I've tried not to overuse type hints, as some find them to be too verbose. For example, I rarely use them within function bodies, but I do use them in every function signature. I type-checked all the source code against the contemporary version of Pyright at the time of the book's writing.

Several of the projects in this book use external libraries. You should have Pygame, NumPy, and Pillow installed in the virtual environment you create for the book's source code or in your system Python interpreter. For most readers, installing them should be as simple as running `pip install pygame, numpy, pillow`. A *requirements.txt* file that pip can use is included in the book's source code repository.

Corrections and Comments

The book's GitHub repository is a great place to open an issue if you think you found a mistake. You're also welcome to reach out to me by email at *csfromscratch@oaksnow.com* or via X @davekopec. I welcome your feedback, both positive and negative. If you enjoy the book, please also consider leaving a review on Amazon or wherever you purchased it.

PART I

INTERPRETERS

1

THE SMALLEST POSSIBLE PROGRAMMING LANGUAGE

What's the smallest possible programming language that can still be used to solve real problems? Certainly, a candidate for that prize would be Brainfuck, an esoteric programming language developed by Urban Müller in 1993. In this chapter, we'll develop a Brainfuck interpreter. Brainfuck is perhaps the easiest possible programming language to write an interpreter for—you'll be amazed at how succinct ours is. By the end of the chapter, you'll have learned not only how Brainfuck works but also the core tenets of any interpreter.

What Is Brainfuck?

Brainfuck has only eight commands (+, -, ., ,, >, <, [,]), and every command is a single character. Here's "Hello World!" in Brainfuck:[1]

```
++++++++[>++++[>++>+++>+++>+<<<<-]>+>+>->>+[<]<-]>>.>---.+++++++..+++.>>.<-.<.
+++.------.-----\---.>>+.>++.
```

It may look strange, but that's an actual program. Brainfuck's exotic syntax and minimal feature set make it unsuitable for any practical purpose. Instead, it's a toy that's useful as an educational model. But it's a Turing-complete toy!

What Makes a Language Turing-Complete?

A programming language is considered *Turing-complete* if it can simulate a *Turing machine*, an abstract model of a machine that can implement any computer algorithm.[2] To picture a Turing machine, imagine a tape of unlimited length, split into cells that either are blank or have a character on them. Then, imagine a head that can read or write the character in a cell, including erasing it. Imagine that the head can move left or right one cell at a time. Finally, imagine that it can write or move based on the value read—that is, that it can *branch*. In other words, the head follows some simple rules, which can be thought of as a program that essentially says, "If this value is read, write this other value. If that value is read, move left one cell."

That's it. That's enough to be able to implement any computing algorithm. By extension, any programming language that can simulate this functionality—even a simple language like Brainfuck—can be used to solve real problems. Figure 1-1 illustrates a hypothetical Turing machine.

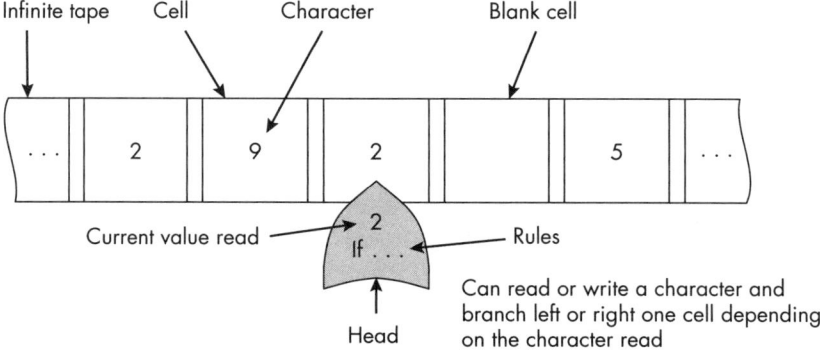

Figure 1-1: A hypothetical Turing machine, including infinite tape, cells, and a head that follows rules

What features does a programming language need to be Turing-complete? As Allen Tucker and Robert Noonan explain in their book *Programming Languages: Principles and Paradigms*, it doesn't take much:

> A programming language is said to be Turing complete if it contains integer variables, values, and operations and has assignment statements and the control constructs of statement sequencing, conditionals, and branching statements. All other statement forms (while and for loops, case selections, procedure declarations and calls, etc.) and data types (strings, floating point values, etc.) are provided in modern languages only to enhance the ease of programming various complex applications.[3]

Let me reduce that description further using simpler language. A programming language needs integer variables, a way to change the values associated with those variables, something like an if statement, and something like a goto statement (a "jump") to be Turing-complete. That's not much. And if you think about it, you can imagine how those simple constructs can map to the elements of a Turing machine. The integer variables are the characters on the cells, changing the variables is the head writing on the cells, and the if and goto statements represent the head branching.

Any programming language that's Turing-complete can implement the same algorithms as any other programming language that's Turing-complete. You can implement Quicksort in C, but you can also implement Quicksort in Brainfuck. You can write a JSON parser in Python, but you could also write a JSON parser in Brainfuck. In this sense, although Brainfuck is a "toy" programming language, it's also a "real" programming language.

How Brainfuck Works

The main state in a Brainfuck program is an array of integers. Each of the slots in the array is called a *cell*. The array of cells can be thought of as analogous to the tape in a Turing machine. Instead of characters being read or written on a cell, it's integers. The commands in Brainfuck allow the programmer to move forward one cell (>), move backward one cell (<), increment a cell's value (+), decrement a cell's value (-), output a cell (.), input data to a cell (,), and loop while a particular cell is nonzero ([and]). Several of these operations map directly to the operations of a Turing machine, so Brainfuck is Turing-complete.

In Python, we'll need two variables to contain the cells' states: a list of all the cells (cells) and an integer representing the index of the current cell (cell_index). In addition, we'll need to keep track of where we are in the Brainfuck source file. We'll handle this with another integer, called instruction_index.

Table 1-1 is based on a table from a 2017 talk by Müller describing the commands that each character represents.[4] I've translated the C descriptions to Python using the variable names just discussed.

Table 1-1: Brainfuck Commands

Command	Python equivalent	Description
>	cell_index += 1	Move one cell to the right.
<	cell_index -= 1	Move one cell to the left.
+	cells[cell_index] += 1	Increment current cell.
-	cells[cell_index] -= 1	Decrement current cell.
.	print(chr(cells[cell_index]), end='', flush=True)	Print ASCII value of current cell.
,	cells[cell_index] = int(input())	Read value for current cell.
[	if cells[cell_index] == 0: instruction_index = self.find_bracket_match(instruction_index, True)	If the cell is zero, move to the corresponding closing bracket.
]	if cells[cell_index] != 0: instruction_index = self.find_bracket_match(instruction_index, False)	If the cell is nonzero, move to the corresponding opening bracket.

Using Table 1-1, we have enough information to step through a Brainfuck program and understand what it's doing. We'll consider a simple program that outputs a user-specified single character a user-specified number of times. Here's the whole program, with each command labeled with an index so that we can refer to it later (you can find this program in the book's source code repository, in *Brainfuck/Examples/repeat.bf*):

```
,>,[<.>-]
012345678
```

Let's talk about this program one command at a time. We'll describe how each command works and illustrate its effect on the program state using a table. The program requires only two cells, plus a cell index and an instruction index. The table initially looks like this:

Cell 0	Cell 1	Cell index	Instruction index
0	0	0	0

Here's the first command (for clarity, we'll precede each command with its instruction index and a colon):

```
0: ,
```

User input is retrieved and stored in cell 0 because the cell index is initially 0. For our example, imagine the user entered 88 (the ASCII character code for the capital letter X). After the command is run, the instruction index is incremented.

Cell 0	Cell 1	Cell index	Instruction index
88	0	0	1

```
1: >
```

The cell index is incremented, and then the instruction index is incremented.

Cell 0	Cell 1	Cell index	Instruction index
88	0	1	2

```
2: ,
```

User input is entered into cell 1. Let's say the user entered 10. Then, the instruction index is incremented.

Cell 0	Cell 1	Cell index	Instruction index
88	10	1	3

```
3: [
```

A loop is potentially started. Since the value at the current cell index isn't 0 (it's 10), instead of jumping to the matching closing bracket, we simply increment the instruction index by 1 to go to the next command.

Cell 0	Cell 1	Cell index	Instruction index
88	10	1	4

4: <

The cell index is decremented. The instruction index is then incremented.

Cell 0	Cell 1	Cell index	Instruction index
88	10	0	5

5: .

The ASCII value of the cell at the current cell index is output to the console—in this case, an *X*. Then, the instruction index is incremented.

Cell 0	Cell 1	Cell index	Instruction index
88	10	0	6

6: >

The cell index is incremented. Then, the instruction index is incremented.

Cell 0	Cell 1	Cell index	Instruction index
88	10	1	7

7: -

The value at the current cell index is decremented. The instruction index is incremented.

Cell 0	Cell 1	Cell index	Instruction index
88	9	1	8

8:]

If the value at the current cell index is nonzero, we jump to the matching opening bracket. In this case, cell 1 is 9, so we jump, meaning the instruction index becomes 3.

Cell 0	Cell 1	Cell index	Instruction index
88	9	1	3

Now we're through the first iteration of a loop that will repeat nine times to print a total of 10 *X*s. Instructions 3 through 8 will repeat those nine times until cell 1 is 0, in which case the check at the closing bracket (index 8) will end the repeats and the program will be over.

To provide some closure on this program, let's jump ahead and actually run it through our interpreter:

```
% python3 -m Brainfuck Brainfuck/Examples/repeat.bf
88
10
XXXXXXXXXX
```

Our Brainfuck interpreter accepts only integers as input. These integers can correspond to ASCII character codes, and 88 is the ASCII character code for *X*. Therefore, the expected output is 10 *X*s. After you complete the chapter, you'll be able to run the program yourself, as well as any other Brainfuck program.

The Structure of an Interpreter

Interpreters generally have at least three parts:

- A *tokenizer* (sometimes known as a *lexer*) that takes the original source code and divides it into the smallest recognizable constructs allowed in the programming language. These are known as *tokens*. For the code a + 2, the tokens may be a, +, and 2.

- A *parser* that takes tokens that are next to each other and figures out their meaning (that is, the expressions or statements they form). Parsers typically produce a tree of nodes representing the relative relationships between expressions, statements, and literal values. This tree is called the *abstract syntax tree (AST)*. For example, if a Python interpreter saw the token a followed by the token + followed by the token 2, it may construct an arithmetic expression node and connect it to nodes for the a and the 2.

- A *runtime environment* that walks through the nodes of the AST and runs the appropriate operations to execute the meaning inherent in them. For our a + 2 arithmetic expression node, this would mean looking up the value represented by a and adding 2 to it.

The beautiful thing about Brainfuck is that every statement is just a single symbol, so all we need to do to get a token is just read a single character from the source file. And each of those tokens on its own already represents a node of meaning. That makes writing an interpreter for Brainfuck easier than writing one for almost any other programming language. We can combine the tokenizer, the parser, and the runtime into a single loop that merges the three concepts together.

We'll come back to the idea of a separate tokenizer, parser, and runtime in Chapter 2, where we will build an interpreter for a slightly more complicated language called NanoBASIC. It will be illustrative to see how the pieces that are fused together in our Brainfuck interpreter get broken apart for our NanoBASIC interpreter.

Brainfuck interpreters are not only easy to write but also very compact. Inspired by another esoteric language, called FALSE, Müller's goal with Brainfuck was to produce a minimal language, and he certainly accomplished that. His original interpreter for his language with just eight commands was just 240 bytes. More impressive still, there's a Brainfuck interpreter written in x86 assembly that's just 69 bytes.[5] We won't get to 69 bytes, but the core of our Python Brainfuck interpreter will be just 25 lines of code and a couple of helper functions. And those 25 lines will be capable of running any Brainfuck program, and therefore any computer algorithm.

Müller's original Brainfuck implementation had some limitations that we'll repeat in our interpreter. Instead of an unlimited tape, like in a Turing machine, the original Brainfuck was limited to 30,000 cells. And each of those cells could hold just an 8-bit unsigned integer.

Implementing Brainfuck in Python

Before we get into the main interpreter implementation, let's do a bit of housekeeping. Every project we do in this book will be structured as a Python package. Each package will live in its own folder with a *__main__.py* file that kicks off execution when the project is run from the command line. You can find all the code on the book's GitHub repository at *https:// github.com/davecom/ComputerScienceFromScratch*. However, you'll also find all the necessary code directly in this book, unless otherwise noted. Each code listing appears with the name of the Python file it's associated with, so you can locate the code in the book's repository.

Getting the Source File

Our *__main__.py* file is responsible for taking in the command line argument that contains the path of a Brainfuck source file and passing it to the main interpreter:

```
# Brainfuck/__main__.py
from argparse import ArgumentParser
from Brainfuck.brainfuck import Brainfuck

if __name__ == "__main__":
    # Parse the file argument
    file_parser = ArgumentParser("Brainfuck")
    file_parser.add_argument("brainfuck_file",
                        help="A file containing Brainfuck source code.")
    arguments = file_parser.parse_args()
    Brainfuck(arguments.brainfuck_file).execute()
```

The `ArgumentParser` standard library class makes handling command line arguments easy. We'll use it in every project in the book. In this snippet, we create a single command line argument, `brainfuck_file`, which represents the path of the file we want to load the Brainfuck source from. The default type of the argument is a string, so we'll ultimately be passing a string of the path to our `Brainfuck` class, which will be responsible for reading its contents.

NOTE   *To learn more about* `ArgumentParser`, *see the official argparse documentation at* https://docs.python.org/3/library/argparse.html.

Writing the Interpreter

Our interpreter is responsible for maintaining Brainfuck state (the `cells`, `cell_index`, and `instruction_index`). It also needs to read each valid Brainfuck command in the source file and change the state or complete an input/output operation based on that command. Because Brainfuck commands are just a single character, reading them is trivial. And the actual "what to do" with each character is pretty much identical to Table 1-1. That's how we end up with just a single function (execute()) of 25 lines of code.

```python
# Brainfuck/brainfuck.py
from pathlib import Path

class Brainfuck:
    def __init__(self, file_name: str | Path):
        # Open text file and store in instance variable
        with open(file_name, "r") as text_file:
            self.source_code: str = text_file.read()

    def execute(self):
        # Setup state
        cells: list[int] = [0] * 30000
        cell_index = 0
        instruction_index = 0
        # Keep going as long as there are potential instructions left
        while instruction_index < len(self.source_code):
            instruction = self.source_code[instruction_index]
            match instruction:
                case ">":
                    cell_index += 1
                case "<":
                    cell_index -= 1
                case "+":
                    cells[cell_index] = clamp0_255_wraparound(cells[cell_index] + 1)
                case "-":
                    cells[cell_index] = clamp0_255_wraparound(cells[cell_index] - 1)
                case ".":
                    print(chr(cells[cell_index]), end='', flush=True)
                case ",":
                    cells[cell_index] = clamp0_255_wraparound(int(input()))
```

```
        case "[":
            if cells[cell_index] == 0:
                instruction_index = self.find_bracket_match(instruction_index, True)
        case "]":
            if cells[cell_index] != 0:
                instruction_index = self.find_bracket_match(instruction_index, False)
instruction_index += 1
```

The implementation of each command is straight from Table 1-1 and consists of simple manipulations of the three state variables. For those of you who haven't been keeping up with the latest versions of Python, the match statement was added in Python 3.10 and can be thought of as a powerful version of a switch statement from other languages. It executes the code section (or case) that matches the value in the variable being matched. In our program, the cases correspond to the possible values of instruction.

TYPE HINTS

You probably noticed my use of type hints on some of the local variables. I'll do that in this book where I think it adds clarity, but I won't be religious about it. For example, I think clarifying that cells is a list[int] makes sense because some people may not remember the list initialization syntax I used. But it's obvious that instruction is going to be a str based on the context, so I didn't provide a type hint for it. The other thing type hints allow me to do is run a static type checker to aid in verifying the correctness of all the code in the book. I always find that helpful.

A quick note on the type hint syntax file_name: str | Path used in the signature of __init__(): the syntax means that the supplied argument is expected to be of either the str type or the Path type. Both types are acceptable. Our ArgumentParser provides filepaths as strings, while our unit tests will supply them as Path objects. The open() function that uses the path in __init__() can accept either.

Missing from Table 1-1 are two helper functions: find_bracket_match() and clamp0_255_wraparound(). First, let's look at find_bracket_match(), which helps jump from one if statement–like bracket command to its partner. This function is implemented as a method on the Brainfuck class since it needs to access self.source_code:

```
# Find the location of the corresponding bracket to the one at *start*.
# If *forward* is true go to the right looking for a matching "]".
# Otherwise do the reverse.
def find_bracket_match(self, start: int, forward: bool) -> int:
    in_between_brackets = 0
 ❶ direction = 1 if forward else -1
    location = start + direction
    start_bracket = "[" if forward else "]"
```

```
        end_bracket = "]" if forward else "["
        while 0 <= location < len(self.source_code):
          ❷ if self.source_code[location] == end_bracket:
                if in_between_brackets == 0:
                    return location
                in_between_brackets -= 1
          ❸ elif self.source_code[location] == start_bracket:
                in_between_brackets += 1
            location += direction
        # Didn't find a match
        print(f"Error: could not find match for {start_bracket} at {start}.")
        return start
```

To find a matching bracket, we perform a linear search through the Brainfuck source code, looking at each subsequent character one at a time. We search to the right if forward is True or to the left if forward is False. The direction variable becomes a proxy for forward, either incrementing or decrementing location to go to the right or to the left ❶.

The confounding factor when searching for a matching bracket is the *in-between brackets*, sets of brackets that occur between the starting bracket and the bracket we want. For example, say we're searching for the matching bracket of the first bracket in this Brainfuck snippet (I've labeled the characters with indices for clarity):

```
[++[--]<<]
0123456789
```

The match for the opening bracket at index 0 is the closing bracket at index 9. If we naively accept the first closing bracket we find, however, our search will conclude that the match for index 0 is the closing bracket at index 6. In fact, that closing bracket matches the opening bracket at index 3.

The solution is simply to count the in-between brackets. Every time we encounter the start of an in-between pair of brackets, we increment the in_between_brackets counter ❸. Every time we encounter the end of an in-between pair of brackets, we decrement in_between_brackets, unless in_between_brackets is 0, meaning there are no more in-between brackets and the destination bracket has been found ❷.

A BRACKET-FINDING ALTERNATIVE

Another way to solve the in-between brackets problem is to use a stack. Every time a start bracket is encountered, its location is pushed to the stack. Every time an end bracket is encountered, the stack is popped. The two bracket locations that result (the locations of the encountered end bracket and the popped start bracket) are a pair.

(continued)

Using this method, you can run through all the source code at once and find all the bracket pairs easily. The bracket pairs' locations can then be cached to improve the interpreter's performance. Instead of running a linear search as in find_bracket_match() every time a jump is required, finding the other bracket (the jump-to location) just becomes a lookup from the cache.

The other helper function, clamp0_255_wraparound(), simulates the original Brainfuck by limiting cell values to 8-bit unsigned integers. We need this function because Python's int type is of arbitrary precision, meaning it can accommodate integers as large as you want without overflow (instead, more bytes are grabbed as needed). A true 8-bit unsigned integer would wrap around to 0 once it exceeded 255 by 1, and it would wrap back to 255 if it was at 0 and was decremented by 1. We simulate this behavior in clamp0_255_wraparound() with some simple conditionals:

```
# Simulate a 1-byte unsigned integer
def clamp0_255_wraparound(num: int) -> int:
    if num > 255:
        return 0
    elif num < 0:
        return 255
    else:
        return num
```

Because Brainfuck can't change a cell by more than 1 at a time, we don't need to worry about cases where we add more than 1 to a cell that's 255 or subtract more than 1 from a cell that's 0. The num > 255 and num < 0 tests are therefore sufficient.

With these two helper functions, our implementation of a Brainfuck interpreter is complete. It really doesn't take much to implement a Turing-complete language.

Running the Interpreter

Let's try running some Brainfuck code. The *Brainfuck* folder in this book's repository has an *Examples* subfolder with some sample programs to interpret, including *fibonacci.bf* to generate the first several members of the Fibonacci sequence and *hello_world_verbose.bf* containing the "Hello World!" program shown earlier in the chapter. Here, I'm running those programs from the main directory of the repository:

```
% python3 -m Brainfuck Brainfuck/Examples/fibonacci.bf
1, 1, 2, 3, 5, 8, 13, 21, 34, 55, 89
% python3 -m Brainfuck Brainfuck/Examples/hello_world_verbose.bf
Hello World!
```

You must execute these commands with the -m option indicating Brainfuck should be understood to be a module. If you don't, you'll receive import errors. Note also that the way Python is accessed from the shell will differ by operating system and the kind of Python installation. On my system, the Python interpreter has the alias python3 and paths use a forward slash. Your system may use python and backslashes (Windows style).

It looks like our interpreter works, but we should create some tests to be sure.

Testing the Interpreter

Let's write some tests to ensure our interpreter works correctly. We could start by writing some *unit tests* to confirm each individual command of the interpreter functions as expected. Does + work correctly? Does . work correctly? However, for the sake of brevity (and because the interpreter is so simple), we'll instead write some *integration tests*. These tests examine whether whole Brainfuck programs run correctly through the interpreter, producing the expected output.

To make continuous integration a little simpler to set up, the tests for the entire book live in their own folder within the main repository's root, called *tests*. Our tests for Brainfuck will run entire Brainfuck programs through the interpreter, capture their textual output, and compare that output to the known expected output.

tests/test _brainfuck.py
```
import unittest
import sys
from pathlib import Path
from io import StringIO
from Brainfuck.brainfuck import Brainfuck

# Tokenizes, parses, and interprets a Brainfuck
# program; stores the output in a string and returns it
def run(file_name: str | Path) -> str:
    output_holder = StringIO()
    sys.stdout = output_holder
    Brainfuck(file_name).execute()
    return output_holder.getvalue()
```

The run() function initializes the Brainfuck class with a file located at file_name. It also uses output_holder to capture and return stdout, meaning that instead of output from the run program going to the console, it will be assigned to a variable. This lets us programmatically compare the actual output with the expected output after calling run() in each of our tests:

```
class BrainfuckTestCase(unittest.TestCase):
    def setUp(self) -> None:
        self.example_folder = (Path(__file__).resolve().parent.parent
                               / 'Brainfuck' / 'Examples')
```

```
def test_hello_world(self):
    program_output = run(self.example_folder / "hello_world_verbose.bf")
    expected = "Hello World!\n"
    self.assertEqual(program_output, expected)

def test_fibonacci(self):
    program_output = run(self.example_folder / "fibonacci.bf")
    expected = "1, 1, 2, 3, 5, 8, 13, 21, 34, 55, 89"
    self.assertEqual(program_output, expected)

def test_cell_size(self):
    program_output = run(self.example_folder / "cell_size.bf")
    expected = "8 bit cells\n"
    self.assertEqual(program_output, expected)

def test_beer(self):
    program_output = run(self.example_folder / "beer.bf")
    with open(self.example_folder / "beer.out", "r") as text_file:
        expected = text_file.read()
        self.assertEqual(program_output, expected)

if __name__ == "__main__":
    unittest.main()
```

Each test takes a Brainfuck program in the *Examples* directory, uses run() to execute it, and compares the final output to some expected output via assertEqual(). Let's try running all the tests from the repository's main directory:

```
% python3 -m tests.test_brainfuck
....
----------------------------------------------------------------------
Ran 4 tests in 0.689s
OK
```

If our Brainfuck interpreter can successfully run four programs that are quite different from one another, there's a good chance it's working. In the online repository for this book, I've set up continuous integration so that these tests automatically run anytime the code is changed. Most of the chapters in this book have unit or integration tests that also run automatically.

CODE MEETS LIFE

I first heard of Brainfuck a long time ago as a curiosity, but I became really interested in it in 2018 when preparing to teach a class called Emerging Languages at Champlain College. It's a programming language theory class with a twist: we use languages that, in 2018, were just becoming relevant in industry—namely, Go, Swift, and Clojure—to illustrate programmatic ideas.

I developed the course with a colleague named Josh Auerbach. I created the Go and Swift portions of the class, and Josh developed the Clojure portion.

We both liked the idea of doing a Brainfuck assignment, because it's such a great educational tool for understanding how a simple interpreter works. Josh had the idea of using part of the Brainfuck assignment to teach Clojure macros. We used a Clojure macro to elucidate the idea of *homoiconicity* in a Lisp (Clojure is a dialect of Lisp)—that is, the concept that "code is data." In a Clojure macro, you can manipulate code before it runs, treating it like any other data in a Clojure program. The macro the students developed in Josh's assignment allows one to write Brainfuck code directly in Clojure and have it execute like it belongs there. You can just be in the middle of your Clojure program and write something like this:

```
(bf +++++++..+++.>>.<-.<.+++.------.---------.>>+.>++.)
```

I still use the assignment when teaching the class (Josh has moved on from academia), but I'll admit that sometimes I have trouble remembering the syntax for writing a Clojure macro. Writing the Brainfuck interpreter is even easier than writing the macro. That's why Brainfuck is a great tool for educators.

Real-World Applications

Each chapter in the book ends with some real-world applications, but unfortunately there are no real-world applications of Brainfuck. It's a language of curiosity, useful for learning about some fundamental ideas in computer science. Perhaps, therefore, we could say the real-world application of Brainfuck is in education.

Interpreters more broadly are critical computing infrastructure with many real-world applications. As you're probably aware, Python itself is an interpreted language. There are many ways that programming languages go from text files to machine code, but we can broadly categorize most programming language implementations as interpreted, ahead-of-time compiled, or just-in-time compiled. Some programming languages even have implementations in all three categories. For example, there are Java interpreters, ahead-of-time Java compilers, and the most popular implementations of Java are just-in-time compiled.

As a general rule, interpreted programming language implementations tend to be slower than compiled programming language implementations. You may wonder, then, why any programming languages that people use in the real world are implemented as interpreters. Take Python, for instance: Why is it implemented using an interpreter instead of a compiler? We all know Python is a relatively slow language, and surely it would be faster if it were compiled.

The answer is that many of Python's runtime dynamic features wouldn't be possible, or at least would be very difficult to implement, in anything but an interpreter. There are efforts to do so (PyPy, for instance), but they're much harder to get right.

In addition, interpreters are much easier to implement than compilers because they lack the entire backend phase of the compiler that's responsible for generating machine code. Many languages therefore start out as interpreted because it's simply the fastest way to get an implementation up and running. For instance, the first version of Java was interpreted, and it took a couple of years before a just-in-time compiled version came out.

In short, interpreters exist because they're easier to implement than compilers and because they enable certain powerful dynamic runtime features. If you're thinking of implementing a new programming language, especially a dynamic one, the easiest place to start is probably with an interpreter.

Exercises

1. Write a Brainfuck-to-Python transpiler. A *transpiler* is like a compiler, but instead of converting source code that was written in a high-level language into machine code, it converts source code from one high-level language to another high-level language. You can reuse a lot of the structure from the Brainfuck interpreter. Instead of executing each Brainfuck command, you can emit some equivalent Python code into a list of strings. The final output of your program should be the equivalent Python code saved to a file. The trickiest part will be figuring out what to do with the brackets.

2. Add a debug mode to the interpreter that lets you step through a Brainfuck program one command at a time. After each command, a table is output to the console containing all the Brainfuck interpreter's state, similar to the tables at the beginning of this chapter for walking through the "repeat" program.

3. Write a Brainfuck program that reads two numbers, compares them, and outputs the larger number. Write a test in Python that verifies the program works correctly with randomly generated numbers. Tip: You may need to modify sys.stdin similarly to how we modified sys.stdout in the run() function for the tests.

Notes

1. "Brainfuck," Esolangs.org, accessed May 22, 2024, *https://esolangs.org/wiki/Brainfuck#Hello.2C_World.21*.

2. Terrence W. Pratt and Marvin V. Zelkowitz, *Programming Languages: Design and Implementation*, 3rd ed. (Prentice Hall, 1996), 409.

3. Allen B. Tucker and Robert E. Noonan, *Programming Languages: Principles and Paradigms*, 1st ed. (McGraw-Hill, 2002), 84.

4. Urban Müller, "Brainfuck, or How I Learned to Change the Problem," lecture at Tamedia TX 2017, Zurich, Switzerland, June 13, 2017, accessed June 10, 2022, YouTube, 3:50:11, *https://youtu.be/gjm9irBs96U?t=8610*.

5. "bf core," Esolangs.org, accessed May 22, 2024, *https://esolangs.org/wiki/Bf_core*.

2

WRITING A BASIC INTERPRETER

In Chapter 1, we built a simple interpreter for Brainfuck, a minimalist, esoteric language. But Brainfuck is just a toy; while we *could* solve real problems in Brainfuck, we wouldn't actually *want* to. There are other programming languages that aren't much more complex than Brainfuck yet are "real" in the sense that regular programmers actually use(d) them for their day-to-day work. In this chapter, we'll build an interpreter for one such language, NanoBASIC, and we'll learn more about how interpreters work in the process.

While Brainfuck has just eight commands, NanoBASIC, a pared-down dialect of BASIC, has just six types of statements. To be fair, each of those statements has more functionality than a Brainfuck command, but it's still not much. It's just complex enough that it will enable us to explore several aspects of an interpreter that got mashed together in our Brainfuck implementation. In particular, we'll write a separate tokenizer, parser, and runtime, whereas our Brainfuck interpreter handled all three tasks at once. We'll use a scalable approach for each component, meaning what we do here could be expanded to work with larger languages.

Understanding NanoBASIC

With its simple syntax and ubiquitous presence, BASIC (Beginner's All-purpose Symbolic Instruction Code) democratized the computing world and became the de facto standard language of the personal computer revolution. NanoBASIC is a version of the BASIC programming language that's derived from a popular dialect for 1970s microcomputers known as Tiny BASIC. NanoBASIC is even simpler (or smaller, if you will) than Tiny BASIC, hence the Nano designation.

NanoBASIC is almost completely the same as Tiny BASIC, but I've made a few changes: it's missing a couple statements, and there are some minor differences regarding variable names and integer widths. As we discuss the language, you may wonder about some of its esoteric syntax or limitations. These quirks are intentional because NanoBASIC is meant to be largely compatible with Tiny BASIC. At the end of the chapter, you'll be able to take actual Tiny BASIC programs you find online and run them in our NanoBASIC interpreter. Therefore, you'll be implementing a language that was used in the real world.

You can learn everything you need to know about NanoBASIC in just a few minutes. Do you remember how long it took you to learn Python? By the end of this section, you'll be fully capable of writing a program in NanoBASIC.

BASIC History

BASIC was originally developed in 1964 by John Kemeny and Thomas Kurtz at Dartmouth College to make computers more accessible, including to students not pursuing science or math majors.[1] In fact, it was undergraduate students who built the first BASIC implementation alongside Kemeny and Kurtz. When the personal computer revolution got started in the mid-1970s, BASIC was a natural fit for the hobbyists and other "regular" people who bought the first machines. As a result, it became the most popular high-level programming language for personal computers from the mid-1970s to the mid-1980s. Common computers of the era, like the Commodore 64 and the Apple II, came with built-in BASIC interpreters. BASIC was therefore the way that many people interacted with early personal computers. For example, BASIC was Linus Torvalds's first programming language on the Commodore VIC-20 in 1981.[2]

Interestingly, Microsoft got its start in 1975 when Bill Gates and Paul Allen developed a BASIC interpreter for one of the first personal computers, the Altair 8800.[3] Their company flourished when they ported their interpreter to other machines of the late 1970s. Microsoft BASIC was shipped with many personal computers, and it became the de facto standard dialect of BASIC. Eventually, Microsoft entered the operating system business in 1981 with DOS on the original IBM PC, but BASIC was the company's start. Now you'll be developing a BASIC interpreter too!

Tiny BASIC, which NanoBASIC is a form of, in turn got its start because of Microsoft. Many of the people involved with the early development of Tiny BASIC were partially motivated by the high cost of Microsoft's interpreters.[4] Some of them further believed that people should be free to share software as they see fit. This was an early form of the Free Software Movement. Beyond skirting Microsoft's high fees, the developers also wanted a language that would be small enough to fit within the extreme memory constraints of the microcomputers of the time (often just 4 kilobytes [KB]) and portable enough that programs could be run on multiple kinds of machines. Ultimately, Tiny BASIC was ported to a wide variety of different personal computers across multiple different microprocessor architectures and was widely used.

NanoBASIC's Paradigm, Syntax, and Semantics

As you've read, BASIC was intended to be easy to use for nontechnical people, and many BASICs were designed to work in memory-constrained environments. Hence, BASICs tend to be stripped-down languages with relatively few features, even in comparison to other languages of the time. The dialect we're developing, NanoBASIC, is imperative, but we'd barely even call it procedural. Let's review what those terms mean.

An *imperative* language is one in which you provide detailed instructions telling the computer how you want it to complete a task. This contrasts with *declarative* languages, which concentrate on "what" you want to do instead of "how" you want to do it. Say I wanted you to draw a square in the center of a piece of graph paper. The imperative way to do it would be to tell you: "Start at point (4, 4) and draw a line up five units. Then, draw a line to the right five units. Then, draw a line down five units. Then, draw a line to the left five units." The declarative way to do it would be to say, "Draw a 5×5 square in the middle of the paper." In a declarative world, I declare what I want and let you (or the computer) figure out the specifics of how to accomplish it.

Modern imperative programming languages generally fall into two main sub-paradigms: procedural and object-oriented. *Procedural* programming languages use the subroutine/procedure/function (these terms are often, but not always, used interchangeably) as the main point of abstraction. Code is broken into multiple functions that each have a specific purpose and work in concert to form the whole program. *Object-oriented* programming uses objects as the main point of abstraction, and since you're an intermediate or advanced Python programmer, I assume you know what that means. Of course, Python can be programmed in either style.

NOTE *The most popular declarative programming sub-paradigms are* functional *and* logic *programming. Getting into the details of those is beyond the scope of this chapter.*

NanoBASIC is decidedly not a declarative programming language. It's firmly in the imperative camp. It's also definitely not object-oriented. But is it procedural? While it technically has a way of making a call to a subroutine with its GOSUB statement, which we'll discuss shortly, there's nothing resembling a modern function in the sense of having parameters and return values. That's why I wrote we would "barely even call it procedural."

Some versions of BASIC, like Tiny BASIC and NanoBASIC, not only have no sense of a function, they also have no loops or other modern control structures. Instead, all control is handled with GOTO and GOSUB, which trigger direct jumps to a specific line number of the program. These, coupled with if statements, are the only way to control a Tiny BASIC or NanoBASIC program. Early BASICs were famous for encouraging "spaghetti code" due to these explicit jumps from one part of a program to another and poor mechanisms for organization. This criticism is completely fair. Without functions or objects as organizing mechanisms, an imperative language invariably devolves into spaghetti code. Don't be surprised to see some spaghetti as we start cooking up some NanoBASIC!

Now, let's get into NanoBASIC's syntax and how its six statements work.

Comments and Line Numbers

Comments in NanoBASIC start with the REM designation and can finish with any string. Comments won't be processed at all by the interpreter.

Every non-comment line in NanoBASIC begins with a line number and is followed by a statement. The programmer can pick any arbitrary line numbers, as long as they're all in increasing order from the top of the source file to the bottom. For example, the following line numbers are valid:

```
10 PRINT "Hello"
REM This is a comment
20 PRINT "Goodbye"
30 PRINT "WOW"
```

By contrast, these line numbers aren't valid, and so the program's behavior is undefined:

```
10 PRINT "Hello"
REM This is a comment
40 PRINT "Goodbye"
30 PRINT "WOW"
```

Programs that have GOTO or GOSUB statements and out-of-order line numbers won't function correctly.

There are only six ways to start a statement in NanoBASIC: PRINT, IF, GOTO, GOSUB, RETURN, and LET. If you know these six statement types, you basically know the whole language. This is why you can learn NanoBASIC in just a few minutes if you already know another programming language.

LET, Variables, and Mathematical Expressions

A LET statement binds a value to a variable. All variables represent integers. There are no other variable types. The original Tiny BASIC was limited to just 26 single-letter variable names (A through Z). In NanoBASIC, this is expanded to include any arbitrary-length identifier composed of letters and underscores. The following statement sets the variable A to 5:

```
10 LET A = 5
```

The LET keyword must be followed by a variable name and an equal sign (=). After that, any mathematical expression can appear. NanoBASIC mathematical expressions can be composed of variables; integer literals; the operators for addition (+), subtraction (-), multiplication (*), and division (/); and parentheses ((and)). In addition, you can negate any mathematical value in NanoBASIC with a negative sign (-). All math takes place in the realm of signed integers. From this point forward, we'll just refer to mathematical expressions as *expressions*. The following are all valid uses of LET:

```
20 LET B = A
30 LET C = 23 - A
40 LET D = 5 * (24 + 25)
50 LET E = -(24 + 23 - (2 * (5 + 3)))
```

Due to machine limitations, most Tiny BASIC implementations were limited to 16-bit integers. Our variables are backed by Python integers behind the scenes, which are of arbitrary precision, so they aren't limited to 16 bits. This, and the arbitrary-length variable names, are some of the few areas where NanoBASIC is superior to Tiny BASIC instead of simply being a subset of it.

PRINT Statements

Any string literal or expression can be output to the console with PRINT. NanoBASIC string literals are any characters that lie between double quotation marks ("). Unfortunately, there's no way in NanoBASIC to include actual double quotes in your strings. In other words, there's no escape mechanism. I'll leave that as an exercise at the end of the chapter. Here are some valid PRINT statements with string literals:

```
10 PRINT "What a nice program"
20 PRINT "Who said sit down?"
30 PRINT "6734 spells HELP upside down sorta"
```

As mentioned, PRINT can also print the result of any expression:

```
REM This was the first thing Paul Allen ran on the Altair 8800
70 PRINT 2 + 2
```

You can also supply a comma-separated list of items (string literals and expressions) to PRINT. All items printed will have tab characters between them, and PRINT always finishes printing by inserting a newline character. For example:

```
30 PRINT "2 plus 2 is", 2 + 2, "and 3 times 5 is", 3 * 5
```

This will output text that looks as follows:

```
2 plus 2 is  4  and 3 times 5 is  15
```

Note that the spaces between expressions are caused by tab characters. Due to various console settings, they may not look the same in your terminal.

IF Statements and Boolean Expressions

NanoBASIC IF statements are like if statements in other languages, but they are simpler and more succinct. They can have only a single Boolean expression (there's no and or or operator, for example), and they have no else clause. Finally, they can execute only a single statement if they're true. The statement to execute on truth is always preceded by the literal THEN. For example:

```
500 IF N < 10 THEN PRINT "Small Number"
700 IF V >= 34 THEN GOTO 20
```

Boolean expressions mostly involve the comparisons you'd expect, but the operators differ slightly from standard C-style operators. For instance, *not equal* can be either <> or >< in NanoBASIC, and *equal* is =, not ==.

GOTO, GOSUB, and RETURN Statements

A GOTO directly jumps to a line number with no way to go back. A GOSUB jumps to a line number, but a matching RETURN statement will send the program back to the line just after where the GOSUB was originally called. Here's an example:

```
10 GOTO 50
20 LET A = 10
40 RETURN
50 LET A = 5
60 GOSUB 20
REM RETURN returns to here; we expect A to be 10
70 PRINT A
```

This program will ultimately output 10 to the console.

NanoBASIC Style and Minutiae

It's generally considered good style to write BASIC keywords in all capital letters. Because NanoBASIC doesn't have great organizational facilities, it's also a good idea to include comments throughout your program explaining what's going on.

Unfortunately, it's normal for BASIC code to quickly fill up with GOTO statements and become "spaghetti code." This is par for the course, and there's not much you can do about it in NanoBASIC if you want to write a program of any moderate complexity. Eventually, people unhappy with the GOTO style of programming created the *structured programming* movement. For example, Edsger Dijkstra famously wrote a letter called "Go To Statement Considered Harmful."[5]

Here are a couple other things you should know about NanoBASIC:

- NanoBASIC is case insensitive. This means that LET A = 5 is the same as let a = 5.

- Behavior not described in this chapter is undefined.

Ultimately, NanoBASIC is purposely damaged goods because I wanted to keep the interpreter simple and provide a real-world analog—Tiny BASIC—to make this chapter's work feel more "real." I also think the fact that NanoBASIC is based on a real language and is able to run real Tiny BASIC programs found on the internet makes writing the interpreter more fun. However, it would have been fairly simple for us to make the language more powerful. We'll leave that for the exercises.

An Example NanoBASIC Program

Several example NanoBASIC programs are included in the *NanoBASIC/ Examples* directory of the companion repository. One of those programs prints all the numbers in the Fibonacci sequence that are less than 100. The Fibonacci sequence is a progressive sequence of numbers where each number (except the special first two) is the sum of the previous two. It starts with the numbers 0 and 1. It then follows that $0 + 1 = 1$, so the next number in the sequence is 1. Then, $1 + 1 = 2$, so the next number is 2. It continues 3, 5, 8, 13, and so on.

Here's *fib.bas*, the NanoBASIC Fibonacci program:

NanoBASIC/ Examples/fib.bas
```
REM Printing the Fibonacci numbers less than 100
REM A is the last number
10 LET A = 0
REM B is the next number
11 LET B = 1
20 PRINT A
21 PRINT B
REM C is last + next
30 LET C = A + B
31 LET A = B
32 LET B = C
40 IF B < 100 THEN GOTO 21
```

In Tiny BASIC fashion, we only use single capital letters as variable names. This highlights the importance of plentiful comments. As previously discussed, the chosen values for the line numbers are arbitrary as long as they're in increasing order. On lines 10 and 11, we start the sequence with the hardcoded initial values 0 and 1. On line 30, we form the next number in the sequence, C, by summing the previous two numbers. Lines 21 through 40 make up a kind of loop through the use of IF and GOTO on line 40. Some later versions of Tiny BASIC had actual loop statements like FOR, but the earliest versions did all loops using syntax similar to this, much like how loops work in most assembly languages.

When you finish the chapter, you'll be able to run this program yourself with a command like the following:

```
% python3 -m NanoBASIC NanoBASIC/Examples/fib.bas
0
1
1
2
3
5
8
13
21
34
55
89
```

That looks right.

We're almost ready to write an implementation of NanoBASIC, but before we get there, it's important to more formally specify the language's syntax. We can directly use that specification to write our implementation.

Formalizing NanoBASIC's Syntax

A programming language's syntax is formally defined by a *grammar*. Backus–Naur form (BNF) is the typical way the grammar of a programming language is specified. There are many extensions and augmentations of BNF; we'll use a form of it that I think will be very clear to intermediate programmers because it includes some regular expression–like syntax.

A grammar consists of a set of production rules that define what's allowable syntax in the programming language. The term *production rule* sounds fancy, but it's just a way of substituting one thing for another. Let's say I was creating a grammar for a language that could only consist of the letters A and B and the numbers 1 and 2. Its production rules may look like this:

```
<expression> ::= (<letter> | <number>)*
<letter> ::= 'A' | 'B'
<number> ::= '1' | '2'
```

An identifier wrapped in angle brackets, like <expression>, is a *nonterminal*. This is an item in a grammar that, when expanded, is replaced by something else. What it gets replaced by is specified by the right side of its production rule. In a production rule, the ::= symbol separates a non-terminal from its replacement. The replacement can be composed of non-terminals or terminals.

A *terminal* is something that will appear in the language in its literal form. It doesn't get expanded any further. In our syntax, a terminal is wrapped in single quotes, like `'A'`. Our syntax also uses | to mean *or*. An *or* means that there's a selection of options to choose from for that part of the production. We use parentheses for grouping, and * signifies zero or more repetitions of something.

With this in mind, we can read the three production rules shown earlier as indicating:

1. An *expression* is zero or more of letters or numbers.
2. A *letter* is A or B.
3. A *number* is 1 or 2.

We can use a grammar to check whether a particular string of text is valid syntax for a language by simply following its production rules. For instance, our grammar specifies that "AAA21B" is valid syntax but "AB123" is not. More than one grammar can specify the same language. The non-terminal names are largely arbitrary and should be chosen to make the most human sense. For example, there's no reason that letters and numbers need to be separated in our grammar. We could simplify the grammar to be:

```
<expression> ::= <character>*
<character> ::= 'A' | 'B' | '1' | '2'
```

We could even eliminate the second production rule altogether:

```
<expression> ::= ('A' | 'B' | '1' | '2')*
```

We generally shouldn't use unnecessary production rules, because they overcomplicate the grammar. However, if the additional non-terminal represents multiple possible terminals and it will be used again somewhere else in the grammar, it makes sense to give it its own production rule instead of duplicating a long list of terminals. This will become clearer as we work with larger grammars with richer structures. It's analogous to programming, where it can be better style to have many small functions that we reuse rather than just a few large ones.

Let's look at another example. Say I were specifying production rules for a numbered list. It may look something like this:

```
<list> ::= <item>*
<item> ::= <number>'.' <text>'\n'
<number> ::= <digit><digit>*
<digit> :: = '0' | '1' | ... | '8' | '9'
<text> ::= .*
```

We've introduced a couple more special forms. The ... symbol indicates a list of terminals continues in the implied way (this isn't super formal, but it saves space), and . just means any user-imaginable terminal, like in a regular expression. Let's again put the five rules of this grammar into a more English-like form:

1. A *list* is composed of zero or more items.
2. An *item* is a number followed by a period, some text, and a newline.
3. A *number* is one or more digits.
4. A *digit* is one of the characters 0 through 9.
5. A *text* is any arbitrary string.

Did you notice a problem with this grammar regarding how it handles numbers? A number with leading zeros, like 0020, would be allowed, but that wouldn't make sense in a numbered list. How can it be fixed? I'll leave that as an exercise for the reader. If you can fix it, you probably have a decent understanding of terminals and non-terminals.

The grammars described with BNF are said to be *context free*, meaning that each production rule can stand alone for a non-terminal that appears within a larger string. Without any context about the rest of the string, the production rule can still be expanded for the single non-terminal in question. In other words, in a context-free grammar, each non-terminal isn't dependent on other non-terminals around it to be expanded.

NanoBASIC's grammar is based on the original Tiny BASIC grammar published by Dennis Allison, the creator of the first Tiny BASIC implementation, in 1976.[6] It looks like this:

❶ `<line> ::= <number> <statement> '\n' | 'REM' .*'\n'`

❷ `<statement> ::= 'PRINT' <expr-list> |`
`    'IF' <boolean-expr> 'THEN' <statement> |`
`    'GOTO' <expression> |`
`    'LET' <var> '=' <expression> |`
`    'GOSUB' <expression> |`
`    'RETURN'`

❸ `<expr-list> ::= (<string> | <expression>) (',' (<string> | <expression>))*`

❹ `<expression> ::= <term> (('+'|'-') <term>)*`

❺ `<term> ::= <factor> (('*'|'/') <factor>)*`

❻ `<factor> ::= ('-'|ε) <factor> | <var> | <number> | '('<expression>')'`

`<var> ::= ('_'|<letter>) ('_'|<letter>)*`

`<number> ::= <digit> <digit>*`

`<digit> ::= '0' | '1' | ... | '8' | '9'`

`<letter> ::= 'a'|'b'| ... |'y'|'z'|'A'|'B'| ... |'Y'|'Z'`

```
<relop> ::= '<' ('>'|'='|ε) | '>' ('<'|'='|ε) | '='
```

❼ `<boolean-expr> ::= <expression> <relop> <expression>`

```
<string> ::= '"' .* '"'
```

The only new syntax in the full NanoBASIC grammar is the epsilon character (ε). It means there could be nothing ("empty") in the spot where it appears. It always appears as part of an *or*, meaning there could be something, or there could be nothing.

The NanoBASIC grammar looks a lot more sophisticated than the previous two examples—it's a whole programming language, after all—but it's actually pretty easy to pick apart:

1. A *line* is either a number (the line number) followed by a statement, or a comment (REM precedes all comments) ❶.

2. A *statement* is one of the six statements we learned (PRINT, IF, GOTO, LET, GOSUB, RETURN) ❷. This is the first place we see a kind of recursion: an IF statement contains another statement in its THEN clause, so any of the six statements can appear after THEN.

3. An *expression list* (expr-list) is a comma-separated list of strings or expressions ❸. As you can see from the PRINT section in the previous production rule, expression lists are only used for PRINT statements. This is also the only rule connecting to strings. Therefore, a string can only be used as part of a PRINT statement's expression list. We call it a list, but really an expression list could have just one expression or string in it. If there are more, that's when we utilize the * part of the grammar, which is attached to the comma and the following choice of expression or string.

4. An *expression* is something to do with arithmetic. It could be adding some numbers, multiplying some numbers, or just retrieving a value from a variable. The expression production rule itself only includes the possibility of addition or subtraction ❹.

5. An expression is made up of *terms*. Whereas the expression production rule handled addition and subtraction, the term production rule handles multiplication and division ❺. The reason for this has to do with precedence: the "deeper" we go down the walk of non-terminals, the higher the precedence of our operators when we ultimately turn this grammar into a working language. That's why you find multiplication and division after addition and subtraction.

6. Precedence is also why you find parentheses in the production rule for a *factor* ❻ and not in the production rules for expressions or terms. Parentheses have the highest precedence of any arithmetic operator. The other thing we may replace a factor with is a variable (which in the runtime will pull its value), a number literal, or a negation (the option of a leading -).

7. The rules for *variables, numbers, digits, letters, relational operators* (relops), and *strings* are largely self-explanatory. Notice how easy it is to expand

what's allowed as a variable identifier: we permit one or more under-scores or letters, as opposed to the original Tiny BASIC's single letters. Those early PCs really were memory constrained if they had to limit us to just 26 single-letter variable names.

8. A *Boolean expression* is just two numeric expressions with a relational operator between them ❼. Since NanoBASIC doesn't have and or or operators, there's no need for the * special form here as we needed for arithmetic operations like addition and multiplication.

This grammar provides a blueprint for implementing our interpreter's tokenizer and parser. If you recall from Chapter 1 what those pieces are, you may now be able to see how the terminals in the grammar will become the tokens that our tokenizer reads. And here's something even more use-ful: the production rules for the non-terminals will end up each mapping to a function in our recursive descent parser. We'll return to that in a little bit. Ultimately, though, the grammar specifies the *syntax* for a programming language, but it doesn't give each element of the language *meaning*. That will be the magic of our interpreter.

The NanoBASIC Implementation

Now that we've discussed NanoBASIC and how its syntax is specified, it's finally time to start writing our implementation. You may recall from Chapter 1 that a basic interpreter has at least three parts:

- A *tokenizer* (sometimes known as a *lexer*) that takes the original source code and divides it into the smallest recognizable constructs allowed in the programming language. These are known as *tokens*. For the code a + 2, the tokens may be a, +, and 2.

- A *parser* that takes tokens that are next to each other and figures out their meaning (that is, the expressions or statements they form). Parsers typically produce a tree of nodes representing the relative relationships between expressions, statements, and literal values. This tree is called the *abstract syntax tree (AST)*. For example, if a Python interpreter saw the token a followed by the token + followed by the token 2, it may con-struct an arithmetic expression node and connect it to nodes for the a and the 2.

- A *runtime environment* that walks through the nodes of the AST and runs the appropriate operations to execute the meaning inherent in them. For our a + 2 arithmetic expression node, this would mean looking up the value represented by a and adding 2 to it.

We'll build these three parts in order, but before we can even get to the tokenizer, we need to be able to open a NanoBASIC code file:

NanoBASIC/
__main__.py
```
from argparse import ArgumentParser
from NanoBASIC.executioner import execute
```

```
if __name__ == "__main__":
    # Parse the file argument
    file_parser = ArgumentParser("NanoBASIC")
    file_parser.add_argument("basic_file",
                             help="A text file containing NanoBASIC code.")
    arguments = file_parser.parse_args()
    execute(arguments.basic_file)
```

We load a source code file based on a command line argument, much the same as we did in our Brainfuck interpreter, and pass it a function called execute(). That function lives in a separate file so that it's easier to reach for our tests. It pulls together the tokenizer, parser, and interpreter (runtime) components. The output of one is fed as the input to another (source code ▶ tokenizer ▶ parser ▶ interpreter):

NanoBASIC/
executioner.py

```
from pathlib import Path
from NanoBASIC.tokenizer import tokenize
from NanoBASIC.parser import Parser
from NanoBASIC.interpreter import Interpreter


def execute(file_name: str | Path):
    # Load the text file from the argument
    # Tokenize, parse, and execute it
    with open(file_name, "r") as text_file:
        tokens = tokenize(text_file)
        ast = Parser(tokens).parse()
        Interpreter(ast).run()
```

Each line of code in execute() passes us from one major section of the interpreter to the next. The result of the tokenizer goes to the parser, and the result of the parser goes to the runtime environment. For the rest of the chapter, we'll be building each of these components in sequence.

The Tokenizer

The tokenizer takes a string of source code (the contents of a text file) and turns it into tokens. The tokens represent all of the smallest individual chunks of a program that can be processed. The valid tokens in NanoBASIC come directly from the terminals in the NanoBASIC grammar described in the prior section.

We'll use regular expression patterns to find tokens: we'll associate a regular expression pattern with each type of token and then just search for them one at a time. The difficulty with this setup is that we need to be careful about the order in which the searches occur. If two regular expressions could match the same token, then the order will matter. For instance, in our tokenizer the regular expression for a variable name could also match the token PRINT (or any other statement name), so the search for a variable name token purposely comes last.

We'll start our tokenizer by defining all the different types of tokens as enum cases. Each case will be attached to a regular expression for finding it. Some tokens will also have user-specified values associated with them, indicated by `True` or `False` at the end of each enum case. For example, a variable token will have the actual variable name connected to it as an associated value. Here's what our `TokenType` enum looks like:

NanoBASIC/
tokenizer.py

```
from enum import Enum
from typing import TextIO
import re
from dataclasses import dataclass

class TokenType(Enum):
    COMMENT = (r'rem.*', False)
    WHITESPACE = (r'[ \t\n\r]', False)
    PRINT = (r'print', False)
    IF_T = (r'if', False)
    THEN = (r'then', False)
    LET = (r'let', False)
    GOTO = (r'goto', False)
    GOSUB = (r'gosub', False)
    RETURN_T = (r'return', False)
    COMMA = (r',', False)
    EQUAL = (r'=', False)
    NOT_EQUAL = (r'<>|><', False)
    LESS_EQUAL = (r'<=', False)
    GREATER_EQUAL = (r'>=', False)
    LESS = (r'<', False)
    GREATER = (r'>', False)
    PLUS = (r'\+', False)
    MINUS = (r'-', False)
    MULTIPLY = (r'\*', False)
    DIVIDE = (r'/', False)
    OPEN_PAREN = (r'\(', False)
    CLOSE_PAREN = (r'\)', False)
    VARIABLE = (r'[A-Za-z_]+', True)
    NUMBER = (r'-?[0-9]+', True)
    STRING = (r'".*"', True)

    def __init__(self, pattern: str, has_associated_value: bool):
        self.pattern = pattern
        self.has_associated_value = has_associated_value

    def __repr__(self) -> str:
        return self.name
```

The `TokenType` enum just describes the kind of token. Beyond a token's kind, we also want to know where it appeared in the source code file. This will be useful so that we can pinpoint the location of syntax errors and report that information back to the programmer. We'll encompass all this information using `Token`, a composite type that combines a token's kind, location, and associated value if applicable:

```
@dataclass(frozen=True)
class Token:
```

```
kind: TokenType
line_num: int
col_start: int
col_end: int
associated_value: str | int | None
```

The type of the associated_value property, str | int | None, uses enhanced type hint syntax that was introduced with Python 3.10 via PEP 604.[7] I mentioned it briefly in Chapter 1, and here we'll discuss it a little more formally. It's a way of creating a *union type*. A variable that's declared to be of a union type can refer to values that are of any of the types composing the union. In versions of Python prior to 3.10, you would need to import Union from typing and the type hint would look like Union[str, int, None]. This new syntax is obviously much less verbose. In short, it means that an associated_value can be a string, an integer, or None.

We're ready to read a source code file and break it up into its constituent tokens using a tokenize() function:

```
def tokenize(text_file: TextIO) -> list[Token]:
    tokens: list[Token] = []
    for line_num, line in enumerate(text_file.readlines(), start=1):
        col_start: int = 1
```

The function takes in a TextIO object, a type that represents an object that can act as a text stream. We initialize the tokens list, where we'll collect all the tokens in the entire file. Then, we iterate through each line of the file. Because we want to report line and column numbers back to the user as they may expect them to appear in their text editor, we have both start at 1. Next, we extract all the tokens:

```
    while len(line) > 0:
        found: re.Match | None = None
        for possibility in TokenType:
            # Try each pattern from the beginning, case-insensitive
            # If it's found, store the match in *found*
    ❶      found = re.match(possibility.pattern, line, re.IGNORECASE)
            if found:
                col_end: int = col_start + found.end() - 1
                # Store tokens other than comments and whitespace
    ❷          if (possibility is not TokenType.WHITESPACE
                        and possibility is not TokenType.COMMENT):
                    associated_value: str | int | None = None
                    if possibility.has_associated_value:
                        if possibility is TokenType.NUMBER:
                            associated_value = int(found.group(0))
                        elif possibility is TokenType.VARIABLE:
                            associated_value = found.group()
                        elif possibility is TokenType.STRING:
                            # Remove quote characters
                            associated_value = found.group(0)[1:-1]
```

```
❸ tokens.append(Token(possibility, line_num, col_start,
                      col_end, associated_value))
    # Continue search from place in line after token
    line = line[found.end():]
    col_start = col_end + 1
    break  # go around again for next token
# If we went through all the tokens and none of them were a match
# then this must be an invalid token
❹ if not found:
    print(f"Syntax error on line {line_num} column {col_start}")
    break
```

```
❺ return tokens
```

We scan through each line of the file from left to right, looking for a match of each possible token pattern in order ❶. When we find a match that isn't whitespace or a comment (those are ignored) ❷, we check if it's a token type with an associated value. If it is, we store the associated value. We create a Token containing the matched TokenType, where it was found, and any associated value, and we add it to our tokens collection ❸. It really is as simple as doing that linear process. If we find a piece of text that doesn't match any known TokenType for NanoBASIC, that's a syntax error and we alert the user ❹. Finally, tokens is returned ❺.

The tokenizer is the simplest part of our interpreter. It's responsible for turning the original source code file into a collection of valid tokens from the language. Those tokens next get passed to the parser. But before we look at the parser, let's take a look at the building blocks that the parser is going to generate for the interpreter's runtime: nodes.

Nodes

Our parser is ultimately going to generate an AST that contains nodes representing each of the meaningful pieces of the program. For example, each IF statement will be a node, and each time a variable's value is retrieved, that will be a node too. Since it's a tree, the AST links all the nodes together into a hierarchy of relationships. To illustrate this concept, let's take a look at a real potential branch (using the actual node names) of the AST from our interpreter. This branch will represent the IF statement IF A < 10 THEN GOTO 40.

The root node of the branch will be an IfStatement. That IfStatement node will be linked to a BooleanExpression node (A < 10) and a GoToStatement node (GOTO 40). The BooleanExpression node will have an internal variable to represent the TokenType of its operator (<), a link to a VarRetrieve node (A), and a link to a NumberLiteral node (10). The GoToStatement node will be linked to a single NumberLiteral node (40). Figure 2-1 illustrates this structure. Note that the labels on the arrows represent the actual names of the links between nodes in the code.

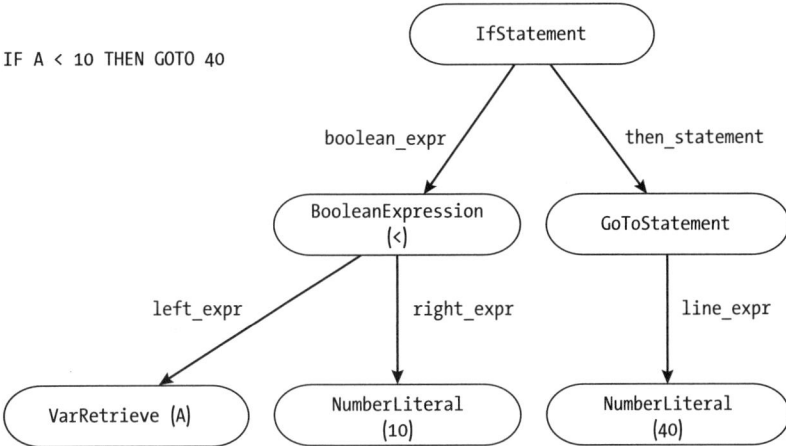

IF A < 10 THEN GOTO 40

Figure 2-1: The nodes for IF A < 10 THEN GOTO 40

The job of our parser is to turn collections of meaningfully adjacent tokens into AST nodes. In the final phase of our interpreter, the AST nodes will be *walked*, which involves completing whatever action each node is connected to, in order. Every node that can appear in our AST has its own class in *nodes.py*. All nodes inherit from the Node class. Every Node keeps track of its location in the original source code file for debugging purposes:

NanoBASIC/
nodes.py
```
from dataclasses import dataclass
from NanoBASIC.tokenizer import TokenType

# For debug purposes, we'll need to know the locations of all Nodes
@dataclass(frozen=True)
class Node:
    line_num: int
    col_start: int
    col_end: int
```

Now let's define the Statement node:

```
# All statements in NanoBASIC have a line number identifier
# that the programmer puts in before the statement (*line_id*).
# This is a little confusing because there's also the "physical"
# line number (*line_num*), that actual count of how many lines down
# in the file where the statement occurs.
@dataclass(frozen=True)
class Statement(Node):
    line_id: int
```

Every statement in NanoBASIC appears after a user-defined line number. This is for GOTO and GOSUB calls. We shouldn't confuse those line numbers with each Node object's line_num, the place where the Node appeared in the source code file. For clarity, we call the user-defined line number the line_id in the Statement class. For example, if the first line of my source code file is 23 PRINT "HELLO", then the line_id is 23, but the line_num is 1.

A NumericExpression is a type of Node that can produce a single integer when it's evaluated. It could be a binary operation, a unary operation, a number literal, or a variable lookup, so we'll declare all of those nodes as subclasses of NumericExpression:

```
# A numeric expression is something that can be computed into a number.
# This is a superclass of literals, variables & simple arithmetic operations.
@dataclass(frozen=True)
class NumericExpression(Node):
    pass

# A numeric expression with two operands like 2 + 2 or 8 / 4
@dataclass(frozen=True)
class BinaryOperation(NumericExpression):
    operator: TokenType
    left_expr: NumericExpression
    right_expr: NumericExpression

    def __repr__(self) -> str:
        return f"{self.left_expr} {self.operator} {self.right_expr}"

# A numeric expression with one operand, like -4
@dataclass(frozen=True)
class UnaryOperation(NumericExpression):
    operator: TokenType
    expr: NumericExpression

    def __repr__(self) -> str:
        return f"{self.operator}{self.expr}"

# An integer written out in NanoBASIC code
@dataclass(frozen=True)
class NumberLiteral(NumericExpression):
    number: int

# A variable *name* that will have its value retrieved
@dataclass(frozen=True)
class VarRetrieve(NumericExpression):
    name: str
```

In order to be evaluated, these different kinds of numeric expression need to hold onto some information. For example, a VarRetrieve needs to have the name of the variable that's having its value looked up. Likewise, a BinaryOperation, which can also be thought of as an arithmetic operation, needs to store the actual arithmetic operation that's being done (addition, subtraction, multiplication, or division), so we store the operator token with it.

While a NumericExpression resolves to an integer, a BooleanExpression is for producing a Boolean. It takes two NumericExpression nodes and compares them using a Boolean operator (stored as a token):

```
# A Boolean expression can be computed to a true or false value.
# It takes two numeric expressions, *left_expr* and *right_expr*, and compares
# them using a Boolean *operator*.
@dataclass(frozen=True)
class BooleanExpression(Node):
    operator: TokenType
    left_expr: NumericExpression
    right_expr: NumericExpression

    def __repr__(self) -> str:
        return f"{self.left_expr} {self.operator} {self.right_expr}"
```

The rest of the nodes are for representing the six types of NanoBASIC statements:

```
# Represents a LET statement, setting *name* to *expr*
@dataclass(frozen=True)
class LetStatement(Statement):
    name: str
    expr: NumericExpression


# Represents a GOTO statement, transferring control to *line_expr*
@dataclass(frozen=True)
class GoToStatement(Statement):
    line_expr: NumericExpression


# Represents a GOSUB statement, transferring control to *line_expr*
# Return line_id is not saved here, it will be maintained by a stack
@dataclass(frozen=True)
class GoSubStatement(Statement):
    line_expr: NumericExpression


# Represents a RETURN statement, transferring control to the line after
# the last GOSUB statement
@dataclass(frozen=True)
class ReturnStatement(Statement):
    pass


# A PRINT statement with all that it is meant to print (comma separated)
@dataclass(frozen=True)
class PrintStatement(Statement):
    printables: list[str | NumericExpression]


# An IF statement
# *then_statement* is what statement will be executed if the
# *boolean_expression* is true
@dataclass(frozen=True)
class IfStatement(Statement):
    boolean_expr: BooleanExpression
    then_statement: Statement
```

The properties of these nodes reflect the pieces of data that each type of statement requires. For example, since a LET statement assigns a value to a variable, a LetStatement node needs a string variable name and a NumericExpression representing the value.

Errors

Let's take a quick detour to discuss error handling in our interpreter. There's nothing more annoying when you're programming than poor error messages. When you make a mistake in your code, you want to know what happened and where. As the creator of a programming language, you have a responsibility to provide your user (the NanoBASIC programmer) with good error messages.

NanoBASIC is going to report two general types of errors: parser errors and interpreter errors. *Parser errors* can be thought of as syntax errors, such as when the tokens are in the wrong order. For example, there needs to be a numeric expression (representing a line number) after a GOTO, but not after an IF statement. *Interpreter errors* are semantic errors. They occur when the program tries to do something that doesn't make sense, such as trying to use a variable before it's initialized. We'll define error classes for both kinds of errors:

NanoBASIC/
errors.py
```
from NanoBASIC.tokenizer import Token
from NanoBASIC.nodes import Node

class NanoBASICError(Exception):
    def __init__(self, message: str, line_num: int, column: int):
        super().__init__(message)
        self.message = message
        self.line_num = line_num
        self.column = column

    def __str__(self):
        return (f"{self.message} Occurred at line {self.line_num} "
                f"and column {self.column}")

class ParserError(NanoBASICError):
    def __init__(self, message: str, token: Token):
        super().__init__(message, token.line_num, token.col_start)

class InterpreterError(NanoBASICError):
    def __init__(self, message: str, node: Node):
        super().__init__(message, node.line_num, node.col_start)
```

Both ParserError and InterpreterError are subclasses of NanoBASICError, which in turn is a subclass of Exception, a built-in Python class that you can override for creating custom exceptions to throw in your program. The classes report a message associated with an error and where it occurred in the original program. For example, say we have the following program:

```
10 PRINT(A)
```

This would lead to the following error being reported:

```
NanoBASIC.errors.InterpreterError: Var A used before initialized. Occurred at
line 1 and column 10
```

This error occurs because the variable A was never initialized using a LET statement. You'll see many throws of ParserError and InterpreterError in the sections that follow.

The Parser

The parser takes the tokens from the tokenizer and tries to convert them into structures that are meaningful for interpreting the program. Parsing is a heavily studied area of computer science, and there are many different parsing algorithms. There are even programs that will generate a parser for you. Not surprisingly, they're known as *parser generators*. A parser generator can take a grammar in BNF form and spit out a parser.

We certainly could have used a parser generator here, but that wouldn't be as educational as writing the parser ourselves. And while there are many parsing algorithms, it turns out that one of the simplest is also one of the most effective, customizable, and widely used. It's known as *recursive descent*, and it underlies the C/C++ parsers in the two most popular compilers in the world, GCC and Clang.[8] It was also the technique used in the original version of Tiny BASIC by Dennis Allison.[9]

In recursive descent, generally each non-terminal defined in the grammar becomes a function. That function is responsible for checking that the sequence of tokens it's analyzing follows a production rule specified in the grammar. The parser checks the tokens by looking at them sequentially. If the token being analyzed is expected to be a part of another production rule, the recursive descent parser just calls the function representing that other production rule. The recursive descent functions return respective nodes when they're successful—*success* meaning the function did indeed find the tokens it expected.

Recursive descent is a *top-down* parsing technique, meaning the parsing begins from the "start" of the grammar (<line> in our case) and "descends" until reaching the most specific point necessary. That's the *descent* part, but the *recursive* part requires a little more visualization. Imagine we're parsing an IF statement. An IF statement is a type of statement, and each non-terminal, including both "statement" and "IF statement," may get a corresponding function in our recursive descent parser. An IF statement has a THEN clause that's also a statement. Therefore, when we're parsing an IF statement, we may again call our function to parse a statement for the THEN clause—the same function to parse a statement that called our function to parse the IF statement! It's a kind of recursion. We end up calling the function that called the function we're currently within.

Both the *descent* and the *recursion* will become clearer as we dig into the code for the Parser class:

NanoBASIC/
parser.py

```python
from NanoBASIC.tokenizer import Token
from typing import cast
from NanoBASIC.nodes import *
from NanoBASIC.errors import ParserError

class Parser:
    def __init__(self, tokens: list[Token]):
        self.tokens = tokens
        self.token_index: int = 0

    @property
    def out_of_tokens(self) -> bool:
        return self.token_index >= len(self.tokens)

    @property
    def current(self) -> Token:
        if self.out_of_tokens:
            raise (ParserError(f"No tokens after "
                                f"{self.previous.kind}", self.previous))
        return self.tokens[self.token_index]

    @property
    def previous(self) -> Token:
        return self.tokens[self.token_index - 1]
```

The Parser class receives a collection of tokens from the tokenizer. As parsing proceeds, an internal token_index keeps track of which token we're currently on. We also define some convenience properties for retrieving the current or previous token.

The consume() helper method checks if the current token is the expected token, increments token_index, and returns the token that was checked. If the token is not the expected token, we raise a ParserError:

```python
def consume(self, kind: TokenType) -> Token:
    if self.current.kind is kind:
        self.token_index += 1
        return self.previous
    raise ParserError(f"Expected {kind} after {self.previous}"
                        f"but got {self.current}.", self.current)
```

A helper function like consume(), sometimes called eat() or accept() instead, is common in parsers because checking if a token is the expected token and moving on if it is, is a very common pattern. If we didn't have consume(), you'd see a lot of unnecessary duplicative code.

The goal of our parser is to produce an AST that can be walked by the runtime to execute the NanoBASIC program. The root of the AST will be a list of statements. Another way of thinking about it is that a NanoBASIC program is just a list of statements, written in order, from the top to the bottom of a source code file. Ultimately, our runtime will execute these statements one at a time. Our recursive descent parser therefore starts in parse(), which will "descend" through the other parser methods and finally return the list of statements:

```python
def parse(self) -> list[Statement]:
    statements: list[Statement] = []
    while not self.out_of_tokens:
        statement = self.parse_line()
        statements.append(statement)
    return statements
```

Each statement must be written on its own line, next to a line identifier, so the first step in the descent is parsing a line:

```python
def parse_line(self) -> Statement:
    number = self.consume(TokenType.NUMBER)
    return self.parse_statement(cast(int, number.associated_value))
```

We expect the line identifier to be at the beginning of a line. Therefore, parse_line() starts by trying to consume a NUMBER token. If that's successful, we continue parsing the statement itself. The use of cast() here is for type checking. If you recall from the tokenizer's code (go back and look, if it's helpful), a token's associated_value can be either an integer, a string, or None. We know a NUMBER will only ever have an integer as its associated_value, so it's safe to cast to int. A type checker like mypy or Pyright can make use of this cast.

Notice how the parse_line() method corresponds to the <line> non-terminal in the grammar. From this point forward, many of our methods will be direct analogs of non-terminals in the grammar or their respective production rules (go back and look at the grammar as a guide). For example, our next method, parse_statement(), corresponds to the <statement> non-terminal:

```python
def parse_statement(self, line_id: int) -> Statement:
    match self.current.kind:
        case TokenType.PRINT:
            return self.parse_print(line_id)
        case TokenType.IF_T:
            return self.parse_if(line_id)
        case TokenType.LET:
            return self.parse_let(line_id)
        case TokenType.GOTO:
            return self.parse_goto(line_id)
        case TokenType.GOSUB:
            return self.parse_gosub(line_id)
        case TokenType.RETURN_T:
            return self.parse_return(line_id)
    raise ParserError("Expected to find start of statement.",
                      self.current)
```

This method is responsible for figuring out which of the six statements in NanoBASIC appears in the next few tokens. Luckily, every statement in NanoBASIC can be identified by its single starting token (PRINT, IF, LET, GOTO, GOSUB, or RETURN), so we just need to match the current token against the six possibilities.

For organizational purposes, I've broken up each statement type into its own method, even though these don't directly correspond to non-terminals. Instead, you can think of each of the production rules of <statement> as receiving its own method. We start with the PRINT statement, which is one of the trickier statements to parse because it can have multiple different comma-separated types in its <expr-list>.

```
# PRINT "COMMA",SEPARATED,7154
def parse_print(self, line_id: int) -> PrintStatement:
    print_token = self.consume(TokenType.PRINT)
    printables: list[str | NumericExpression] = []
    last_col: int = print_token.col_end
    while True:  # keep finding things to print
        if self.current.kind is TokenType.STRING: ❶
            string = self.consume(TokenType.STRING)
            printables.append(cast(str, string.associated_value))
            last_col = string.col_end
        elif (expression := self.parse_numeric_expression()) is not None: ❷
            printables.append(expression)
            last_col = expression.col_end
        else: ❸
            raise ParserError("Only strings and numeric expressions "
                              "allowed in print list.", self.current)
        # Comma means there's more to print
        if not self.out_of_tokens and self.current.kind is TokenType.COMMA: ❹
            self.consume(TokenType.COMMA)
            continue
        break
    return PrintStatement(line_id=line_id, line_num=print_token.line_num,
                          col_start=print_token.col_start, col_end=last_col,
                          printables=printables)
```

We hold the items to be printed in the printables Python list. To gather them, we keep going forward (using a loop), token after token, checking for a string ❶ or a numeric expression ❷. As long as we find one of these, followed by a comma ❹, we keep looping. If we find something that isn't a string or a numeric expression ❸, we throw a ParserError. As we loop, we also keep track of the last item's column end for debug purposes. The ultimate PrintStatement node that's returned needs to know where it starts and where it ends; it starts where the PRINT token starts and it ends at the end of the last column of the last item in the expression list.

Next, let's look at parse_if(), which includes a nice example of the recursive aspect of recursive descent:

```
# IF BOOLEAN_EXPRESSION THEN STATEMENT
def parse_if(self, line_id: int) -> IfStatement:
```

```
if_token = self.consume(TokenType.IF_T)
boolean_expression = self.parse_boolean_expression()
self.consume(TokenType.THEN)
statement = self.parse_statement(line_id)
return IfStatement(line_id=line_id, line_num=if_token.line_num,
                col_start=if_token.col_start, col_end=statement.col_end,
                boolean_expr=boolean_expression, then_statement=statement)
```

As we've discussed, the THEN clause of an IF statement is another statement. To parse the THEN clause, we call parse_statement(), the same method that higher up in the call chain led us to parse_if() in the first place. First, though, we parse the Boolean expression at the start of the IF statement. We'll look at how to do this shortly.

In all of the parsing methods discussed so far, notice how we call other parsing methods and assume they work. It's up to the other methods to do their own error handling and continually move the token_index along, usually by calling consume(). That pattern continues in the methods for the other four kinds of statements:

```
# LET VARIABLE = VALUE
def parse_let(self, line_id: int) -> LetStatement:
    let_token = self.consume(TokenType.LET)
    variable = self.consume(TokenType.VARIABLE)
    self.consume(TokenType.EQUAL)
    expression = self.parse_numeric_expression()
    return LetStatement(line_id=line_id, line_num=let_token.line_num,
                    col_start=let_token.col_start, col_end=expression.col_end,
                    name=cast(str, variable.associated_value), expr=expression)


# GOTO NUMERIC_EXPRESSION
def parse_goto(self, line_id: int) -> GoToStatement:
    goto_token = self.consume(TokenType.GOTO)
    expression = self.parse_numeric_expression()
    return GoToStatement(line_id=line_id, line_num=goto_token.line_num,
                        col_start=goto_token.col_start, col_end=expression.col_end,
                        line_expr=expression)


# GOSUB NUMERIC_EXPRESSION
def parse_gosub(self, line_id: int) -> GoSubStatement:
    gosub_token = self.consume(TokenType.GOSUB)
    expression = self.parse_numeric_expression()
    return GoSubStatement(line_id=line_id, line_num=gosub_token.line_num,
                        col_start=gosub_token.col_start,
                        col_end=expression.col_end,
                        line_expr=expression)


# RETURN
def parse_return(self, line_id: int) -> ReturnStatement:
    return_token = self.consume(TokenType.RETURN_T)
    return ReturnStatement(line_id=line_id, line_num=return_token.line_num,
                        col_start=return_token.col_start,
                        col_end=return_token.col_end)
```

These four parse methods are fairly similar to one another. In each case, we expect a certain starting token (LET or GOTO, for example), and then we parse some information that we need to create a node for that type of statement. For instance, we need a variable and a numeric expression for a LET statement, and we need just a numeric expression (what line to go to) for a GOTO statement. The simplest statement to parse is RETURN because nothing comes after a RETURN.

As promised, here's the parse_boolean_expression() method:

```
# NUMERIC_EXPRESSION BOOLEAN_OPERATOR NUMERIC_EXPRESSION
def parse_boolean_expression(self) -> BooleanExpression:
    left = self.parse_numeric_expression()
    if self.current.kind in {TokenType.GREATER, TokenType.GREATER_EQUAL, TokenType.EQUAL,
                             TokenType.LESS, TokenType.LESS_EQUAL, TokenType.NOT_EQUAL}:
        operator = self.consume(self.current.kind)
        right = self.parse_numeric_expression()
        return BooleanExpression(line_num=left.line_num,
                                 col_start=left.col_start, col_end=right.col_end,
                                 operator=operator.kind, left_expr=left, right_expr=right)
    raise ParserError(f"Expected boolean operator but found "
                      f"{self.current.kind}.", self.current)
```

A Boolean expression must contain two numeric expressions and one of the allowed operator tokens between them. We call the numeric expression before the token left and the numeric expression after the token right. The operator token is stored in the BooleanExpression node so that we can do the appropriate comparison in the runtime.

Parsing numeric expressions closely follows the hierarchy of non-terminals in the grammar, from <expression> to <term> to <factor>, with a method for each. A <factor> can include a <var> or a <number>, but these are handled directly in parse_factor() because their needed information is already contained in their respective tokens:

```
def parse_numeric_expression(self) -> NumericExpression:
    left = self.parse_term()
    # Keep parsing +s and -s until there are no more
    while True:
        if self.out_of_tokens:  # what if expression is end of file?
            return left
        if self.current.kind is TokenType.PLUS:
            self.consume(TokenType.PLUS)
            right = self.parse_term()
            left = BinaryOperation(line_num=left.line_num, col_start=left.col_start,
                                   col_end=right.col_end, operator=TokenType.PLUS,
                                   left_expr=left, right_expr=right)
        elif self.current.kind is TokenType.MINUS:
            self.consume(TokenType.MINUS)
            right = self.parse_term()
            left = BinaryOperation(line_num=left.line_num, col_start=left.col_start,
                                   col_end=right.col_end, operator=TokenType.MINUS,
                                   left_expr=left, right_expr=right)
```

```
        else:
            break  # no more, must be end of expression
    return left

def parse_term(self) -> NumericExpression:
    left = self.parse_factor()
    # Keep parsing *s and /s until there are no more
    while True:
        if self.out_of_tokens:  # what if expression is end of file?
            return left
        if self.current.kind is TokenType.MULTIPLY:
            self.consume(TokenType.MULTIPLY)
            right = self.parse_factor()
            left = BinaryOperation(line_num=left.line_num, col_start=left.col_start,
                            col_end=right.col_end, operator=TokenType.MULTIPLY,
                            left_expr=left, right_expr=right)
        elif self.current.kind is TokenType.DIVIDE:
            self.consume(TokenType.DIVIDE)
            right = self.parse_factor()
            left = BinaryOperation(line_num=left.line_num, col_start=left.col_start,
                            col_end=right.col_end, operator=TokenType.DIVIDE,
                            left_expr=left, right_expr=right)
        else:
            break  # no more, must be end of expression
    return left

def parse_factor(self) -> NumericExpression:
    if self.current.kind is TokenType.VARIABLE:
        variable = self.consume(TokenType.VARIABLE)
        return VarRetrieve(line_num=variable.line_num,
                        col_start=variable.col_start, col_end=variable.col_end,
                        name=cast(str, variable.associated_value))
    elif self.current.kind is TokenType.NUMBER:
        number = self.consume(TokenType.NUMBER)
        return NumberLiteral(line_num=number.line_num,
                        col_start=number.col_start, col_end=number.col_end,
                        number=int(cast(str, number.associated_value)))
    elif self.current.kind is TokenType.OPEN_PAREN:
        self.consume(TokenType.OPEN_PAREN)
        expression = self.parse_numeric_expression()
        if self.current.kind is not TokenType.CLOSE_PAREN:
            raise ParserError("Expected matching close parenthesis.", self.current)
        self.consume(TokenType.CLOSE_PAREN)
        return expression
    elif self.current.kind is TokenType.MINUS:
        minus = self.consume(TokenType.MINUS)
        expression = self.parse_factor()
        return UnaryOperation(line_num=minus.line_num,
                        col_start=minus.col_start, col_end=expression.col_end,
                        operator=TokenType.MINUS, expr=expression)
    raise ParserError("Unexpected token in numeric expression.", self.current)
```

Notice the order of precedence here. In arithmetic, we expect division to have higher precedence than subtraction, and parentheses to have higher precedence than anything. As I hinted when we first discussed the NanoBASIC grammar, this can be modeled in recursive descent by the order in which non-terminals are parsed. The further you descend, the higher the precedence. In this case, anything handled in parse_term() will have higher precedence than anything in parse_numeric_expression(), and anything in parse_factor() will have higher precedence than anything in parse_numeric_expression() or parse_term(). This is also the reason that - and + appear in the same production rule while / and * appear "deeper."

Each time we need a left or right side of an expression in parse_numeric _expression() or parse_term(), we descend. For example, parse_numeric_expression() never calls parse_numeric_expression(). Instead, it calls parse_term(). This might seem counterintuitive, since you might be wondering how multiple additions in a row are handled. The key is that parse_numeric_expression() and parse_term() both use loops, much like we had in parse_print() to accommodate an arbitrary amount of arithmetic (such as many addition operations). One way of thinking about it is that we descend and handle anything of higher precedence, and then fall back up to continue looping in parse_numeric_expression() if there are any more addition or subtraction tokens.

Let's try working through an example. Say we're parsing the expression 2 + 3 * 4 + 5. The initialization of left in parse_numeric_expression() calls parse_term(), which calls parse_factor(), which returns a NumberLiteral for 2. Then, we end up returning the 2 all the way back up to parse_numeric _expression(), which stores it in left. Next, a + token is encountered and parse_term() is called. It parses 3 * 4 using multiple calls to parse_factor(). We end up back in parse_numeric_expression() with a BinaryOperation node for 3 * 4 referred to as right. Then, left and right are combined into a new BinaryOperation and associated with left (a new binding for it). Finally, the last + token is encountered, and 5 is parsed in much the same way that 2 was (descending all the way to parse_factor()) and associated with right. Once again, left and right are combined together into left for the final return value of parse_numeric_expression().

Try working through some arithmetic examples of your own to better understand how operators at a deeper level of descent have a higher precedence. You'll probably want to have the parser code open as you work. The combination of loops and the reuse of variables for different nodes can be hard to reason about, but once you work through a couple examples, it starts to make sense. You can also try adding some print() calls to the various methods to illustrate a parsing progression. You can eliminate the calls to run the AST through the runtime in *executioner.py* if you haven't yet finished entering the whole program.

NOTE   *There are more efficient ways to parse arithmetic expressions. One popular method discovered by Dijkstra is called the* shunting yard algorithm. *A more efficient algorithm like shunting yard is sometimes combined with a recursive descent parser for the arithmetic expression parts in a kind of hybrid model.*

The Runtime

The end result of our parser will be a collection of AST Statement nodes stored as a list that the runtime can step through and execute. I've named the class that walks the AST Interpreter, although I realize this can be a little confusing since this whole chapter is about building an interpreter. Yes, the tokenizer and the parser are parts of the overall interpreter, but this Interpreter class is the place where the language is actually interpreted in the sense that the tokens that became nodes are turned into something meaningful—a program that executes with some output. Regardless of whether or not it's a good name, the Interpreter class provides a runtime environment and an understanding of how to modify the environment or provide output based on the statement and expression nodes that it encounters.

The Interpreter class starts off similarly to Parser:

NanoBASIC/
interpreter.py

```
from NanoBASIC.nodes import *
from NanoBASIC.errors import InterpreterError
from collections import deque

class Interpreter:
    def __init__(self, statements: list[Statement]):
        self.statements = statements
        self.variable_table: dict[str, int] = {}
        self.statement_index: int = 0
        self.subroutine_stack: deque[int] = deque()

    @property
    def current(self) -> Statement:
        return self.statements[self.statement_index]
```

Instead of a list of tokens as we had in the Parser class, Interpreter receives a list of statements. There's also a current property for convenience, to access the current statement. The runtime environment consists of the statements, a statement_index, a variable_table to keep track of each variable's value, and a subroutine_stack that will help us get to the right place after a GOSUB and RETURN pair.

Next, we need a way to connect a line identifier to a statement index. Consider the following NanoBASIC program:

```
27 PRINT "HELLO"
38 GOTO 50
45 PRINT "NEVER"
50 PRINT "BYE"
```

When GOTO 50 is executed, the interpreter will need to find the statement associated with line identifier 50 and continue running from there. In NanoBASIC, the programmer can arbitrarily choose any line identifier for any line, as long as all of the line identifiers are integers in increasing order, so how can we find 50? We need to search the list of statements for it. Since the lines have to be in order, our find_line_index() method can perform a binary search:

```python
# Returns the index of a *line_id* using a binary search,
# or None if not found; assumes the statements list is sorted
def find_line_index(self, line_id: int) -> int | None:
    low: int = 0
    high: int = len(self.statements) - 1
    while low <= high:
        mid: int = (low + high) // 2
        if self.statements[mid].line_id < line_id:
            low = mid + 1
        elif self.statements[mid].line_id > line_id:
            high = mid - 1
        else:
            return mid
    return None
```

Next, the run() method sequentially executes the statements in statements:

```python
def run(self):
    while self.statement_index < len(self.statements):
        self.interpret(self.current)
```

Notice that we're using a while loop controlled by statement_index instead of a for...in loop. This is because we may in fact jump around and skip or repeat some statements due to GOTO and GOSUB. In other words, as we interpret various statements within the loop, statement_index may be modified.

The interpret() method is the heart of the interpreter. It interprets Statement nodes and modifies the runtime environment or creates some output depending on the meaning of each particular statement:

```python
def interpret(self, statement: Statement):
    match statement:
        case LetStatement(name=name, expr=expr):
            value = self.evaluate_numeric(expr)
            self.variable_table[name] = value
            self.statement_index += 1
        case GoToStatement(line_expr=line_expr):
            go_to_line_id = self.evaluate_numeric(line_expr)
            if (line_index := self.find_line_index(go_to_line_id)) is not None:
                self.statement_index = line_index
            else:
                raise InterpreterError("No GOTO line id.", self.current)
        case GoSubStatement(line_expr=line_expr):
            go_sub_line_id = self.evaluate_numeric(line_expr)
            if (line_index := self.find_line_index(go_sub_line_id)) is not None:
                self.subroutine_stack.append(self.statement_index + 1)  # setup for RETURN
                self.statement_index = line_index
            else:
                raise InterpreterError("No GOSUB line id.", self.current)
```

```
case ReturnStatement():
    if not self.subroutine_stack:  # check if the stack is empty
        raise InterpreterError("RETURN without GOSUB.", self.current)
    self.statement_index = self.subroutine_stack.pop()
case PrintStatement(printables=printables):
    accumulated_string: str = ""
    for index, printable in enumerate(printables):
        if index > 0:  # put tabs between items in the list
            accumulated_string += "\t"
        if isinstance(printable, NumericExpression):
            accumulated_string += str(self.evaluate_numeric(printable))
        else:  # otherwise, it's a string
            accumulated_string += str(printable)
    print(accumulated_string)
    self.statement_index += 1
case IfStatement(boolean_expr=boolean_expr, then_statement=then_statement):
    if self.evaluate_boolean(boolean_expr):
        self.interpret(then_statement)
    else:
        self.statement_index += 1
case _:
    raise InterpreterError(f"Unexpected item {self.current} "
                           f"in statement list.", self.current)
```

Walking the AST turns out to be much easier than constructing it, since we can make use of the structural pattern matching that Python's match statement provides. In each case (except ReturnStatement, which has no properties), we capture some of the properties of the Statement subclass that we are matching. For example, the line case LetStatement(name=name, expr=expr): says that, assuming statement is a LetStatement, statement.name will be stored in a local name variable and statement.expr will be stored in a local expr variable.

Three of the cases keep the interpreter moving along by incrementing statement_index after they do their business. The GoToStatement, GoSubStatement, and ReturnStatement cases don't, because they're jumping around the code by modifying statement_index directly. Every time a GoSubStatement is encountered, we need to know where to come back to when a ReturnStatement is next executed—a sort of bookmark, if you will. This is the purpose of subroutine _stack. In the GoSubStatement case, we store statement_index + 1 on the stack to avoid an infinite loop (going back to the source of the GOSUB); then, in the ReturnStatement case, we pop from the stack.

Note how, if the IfStatement node's boolean_expr evaluates to True, interpret() is called recursively and the statement_index isn't incremented. This is because the statement associated with the THEN clause will itself modify statement_index.

Evaluating numeric expressions is mostly just a matter of executing the right Python operator to coincide with a NanoBASIC arithmetic operator token, or retrieving a variable from the variable_table:

```
def evaluate_numeric(self, numeric_expression: NumericExpression) -> int:
    match numeric_expression:
        case NumberLiteral(number=number):
```

```
                return number
        case VarRetrieve(name=name):
            if name in self.variable_table:
                return self.variable_table[name]
            else:
                raise InterpreterError(f"Var {name} used "
                                       f"before initialized.", numeric_expression)
        case UnaryOperation(operator=operator, expr=expr):
            if operator is TokenType.MINUS:
                return -self.evaluate_numeric(expr)
            else:
                raise InterpreterError(f"Expected - "
                                       f"but got {operator}.", numeric_expression)
        case BinaryOperation(operator=operator, left_expr=left, right_expr=right):
            if operator is TokenType.PLUS:
                return self.evaluate_numeric(left) + self.evaluate_numeric(right)
            elif operator is TokenType.MINUS:
                return self.evaluate_numeric(left) - self.evaluate_numeric(right)
            elif operator is TokenType.MULTIPLY:
                return self.evaluate_numeric(left) * self.evaluate_numeric(right)
            elif operator is TokenType.DIVIDE:
                return self.evaluate_numeric(left) // self.evaluate_numeric(right)
            else:
                raise InterpreterError(f"Unexpected binary operator "
                                       f"{operator}.", numeric_expression)
        case _:
            raise InterpreterError("Expected numeric expression.",
                                   numeric_expression)
```

Notice all of the recursive calls in evaluate_numeric(). When you're first learning to program in an imperative language like Python, recursion may seem like an esoteric topic. As you then graduate to be an intermediate or advanced programmer, you start to see its use. This project is a good illustration. We've seen in both the Parser and Interpreter classes how useful recursion can be to express ourselves algorithmically.

Believe it or not, there are whole programming languages (mostly in the functional paradigm) that have no loops, just recursion. That may sound extreme, and using only recursion would certainly be a terrible way to program Python, since it would make your code a lot less readable to other Python programmers and incur some performance penalties. But it underscores what a powerful technique recursion can be. Anything you can do with loops, you can also do recursively, but the magic is when the recursion actually helps you express yourself better, as is the case in this project. In particular, recursion can be really helpful when working with hierarchical data structures like an AST.

Evaluating Boolean expressions is much the same as evaluating numeric ones. It's a conversion from NanoBASIC operators to Python operators:

```
def evaluate_boolean(self, boolean_expression: BooleanExpression) -> bool:
    left = self.evaluate_numeric(boolean_expression.left_expr)
    right = self.evaluate_numeric(boolean_expression.right_expr)
```

```
match boolean_expression.operator:
    case TokenType.LESS:
        return left < right
    case TokenType.LESS_EQUAL:
        return left <= right
    case TokenType.GREATER:
        return left > right
    case TokenType.GREATER_EQUAL:
        return left >= right
    case TokenType.EQUAL:
        return left == right
    case TokenType.NOT_EQUAL:
        return left != right
    case _:
        raise InterpreterError(f"Unexpected boolean operator "
                               f"{boolean_expression.operator}.", boolean_expression)
```

And that's it! Running a NanoBASIC program is much easier than parsing one.

NOTE   *If this were a simple compiler and not a simple interpreter, instead of walking the AST and running some action, we would be generating machine code as we encounter each node.*

Running a Program

Now that our NanoBASIC interpreter is complete, we can run some NanoBASIC programs. You can find Tiny BASIC programs online that can be run in NanoBASIC (or modified if they use INPUT or another feature that NanoBASIC doesn't have). You can also write your own NanoBASIC programs, and that's actually a great way to test your interpreter. As mentioned, I've also provided several simple NanoBASIC programs in the project's *Examples* folder. For instance, we saw *fib.bas* early in the chapter. Another one of the examples, *gcd.bas*, finds the greatest common divisor of two numbers specified in the source code. Here it is finding the greatest common divisor of 350 and 539:

```
% python3 -m NanoBASIC NanoBASIC/Examples/gcd.bas
7
```

Again, as in Chapter 1, the command to run the program assumes you're in the main directory of the repository. Don't forget to run the program as a module using the -m option.

Testing NanoBASIC

Like with Brainfuck, it's helpful to have some integration tests that ensure our interpreter is running correctly. The NanoBASIC tests are very similar to the Brainfuck tests. We hijack the standard output and ensure the expected output is the same as the actual output for many of the programs in the *Examples* folder:

```
import unittest
import sys
from pathlib import Path
from io import StringIO
from NanoBASIC.executioner import execute

# Tokenizes, parses, and interprets a NanoBASIC
# program; stores the output in a string and returns it
def run(file_name: str | Path) -> str:
    output_holder = StringIO()
    sys.stdout = output_holder
    execute(file_name)
    return output_holder.getvalue()

class NanoBASICTestCase(unittest.TestCase):
    def setUp(self) -> None:
        self.example_folder = (Path(__file__).resolve().parent.parent
                               / 'NanoBASIC' / 'Examples')

    def test_print1(self):
        program_output = run(self.example_folder / "print1.bas")
        expected = "Hello World\n"
        self.assertEqual(program_output, expected)

    def test_print2(self):
        program_output = run(self.example_folder / "print2.bas")
        expected = "4\n12\n30\n7\n100\t9\n"
        self.assertEqual(program_output, expected)

    def test_print3(self):
        program_output = run(self.example_folder / "print3.bas")
        expected = "E is\t-31\n"
        self.assertEqual(program_output, expected)

    def test_variables(self):
        program_output = run(self.example_folder / "variables.bas")
        expected = "15\n"
        self.assertEqual(program_output, expected)

    def test_goto(self):
        program_output = run(self.example_folder / "goto.bas")
        expected = "Josh\nDave\nNanoBASIC ROCKS\n"
        self.assertEqual(program_output, expected)

    def test_gosub(self):
        program_output = run(self.example_folder / "gosub.bas")
        expected = "10\n"
        self.assertEqual(program_output, expected)

    def test_if1(self):
        program_output = run(self.example_folder / "if1.bas")
```

```
        expected = "10\n40\n50\n60\n70\n100\n"
        self.assertEqual(program_output, expected)

    def test_if2(self):
        program_output = run(self.example_folder / "if2.bas")
        expected = "GOOD\n"
        self.assertEqual(program_output, expected)

    def test_fib(self):
        program_output = run(self.example_folder / "fib.bas")
        expected = "0\n1\n1\n2\n3\n5\n8\n13\n21\n34\n55\n89\n"
        self.assertEqual(program_output, expected)

    def test_factorial(self):
        program_output = run(self.example_folder / "factorial.bas")
        expected = "120\n"
        self.assertEqual(program_output, expected)

    def test_gcd(self):
        program_output = run(self.example_folder / "gcd.bas")
        expected = "7\n"
        self.assertEqual(program_output, expected)

if __name__ == "__main__":
    unittest.main()
```

One additional feature of the NanoBASIC tests is that many of them isolate a single statement type. For example, *print2.bas* only uses PRINT statements and numeric expressions, so if GOTO isn't working correctly, test_print2() can still pass (but hopefully GOTO errors will be caught by another test). This isolationist methodology provides more granular testing results, but we still need more comprehensive integration tests like *fib.bas* to ensure the statements work correctly in concert. A more robust set of unit tests would also include tests that check the tokenizer, parser, and interpreter independently.

You should find that all of the tests pass. You can also try adding a BASIC program of your own creation as an additional test.

CODE MEETS LIFE

My dad, Danny Kopec,[10] who was a computer science professor, learned programming at Dartmouth College, where he took a course in BASIC with Dartmouth president John Kemeny,[11] one of the language's creators. When I was first learning to program at about eight years old in the mid-1990s, he bought me a copy of True BASIC,[12] the "official" BASIC released by a company started by Kemeny and BASIC co-creator Thomas Kurtz.[13] BASIC was kind of anachronistic by 1995, but I didn't know it. I spent a lot of time making games with True BASIC, though I don't think I ever quite learned subroutines. I guess I was writing spaghetti code.

(continued)

Like my dad, I ended up going to Dartmouth for my undergraduate studies (as an economics major), and after briefly working in a job on Wall Street that I hated, I applied to graduate programs in computer science. The programming thread that started with BASIC was still in me. How can somebody without a computer science degree go to graduate school in computer science? I took five computer science courses as an undergrad, most of which I did well in, and published some projects on my own time, and that was enough to get into a few programs. I ended up back at Dartmouth for a master's degree. For anyone considering this route, let me say that not having a full undergraduate degree in computer science made the transition to the master's program quite difficult. I wouldn't recommend going into a very different field for a graduate degree without a lot of self-study.

To keep doubling down on my mistakes, during the first semester of my master's program, I decided to take a class in the thorny subject of compilers. It ended up being the lowest grade of my graduate career. The class involved a big project building a C compiler in C (with some missing features). I had a partner for the project, and we broke the work up into phases of the compiler, similar to the phases we went over in this chapter (tokenizer, parser, code generator, and so on). The compiler would work only if all the phases worked. By the time the last week of the semester rolled around, I had written a couple thousand lines of code for my phases, while my partner had written fewer than 100 for his part, despite my consistent prodding. I think about that experience a lot today when I assign group projects to students: sometimes when they blame their partner, they're telling the truth. No doubt my code wasn't great either, but at least I wrote it.

We worked in a mad dash with several all-nighters to get something working, putting my partner's pittance of code together with mine and writing a lot more to fill in all of the blanks. In the end, our compiler did some basic things correctly, but it failed the majority of the professor's automated tests.

How did someone who nearly flunked a compilers course end up writing this chapter on interpreters? Eight years later, and a couple years into my career in computer science education, I remembered my experience with BASIC. I had also used a children's programming language called Logo[14] when I was growing up, and together the two languages were a really good way to learn to program as a kid. As a challenge to myself, I decided to build my own children's programming language that's a cross between BASIC and Logo. It's not a novel idea—many people have done similar projects—but I wanted to make something polished and prove to myself that the compilers class didn't have to be the end of programming language development for me.

The result was a product called SeaTurtle[15] that sold hundreds of copies. Hundreds, not thousands. It's not going to make me rich, but it proved to me that I could write a programming language that people would actually want to buy. A real programming language. Okay, a real "kid" programming language.

That experience with SeaTurtle led me to create NanoBASIC as a Swift project for my Emerging Languages class (mentioned in the "Code Meets Life" box in Chapter 1). And that experience led me to this chapter. NanoBASIC is very simple, but it's real, and once you've built something real, you're not that far from building something interesting. In the end, the perspective I gained from all of these experiences, including the painful compilers class, made me the right person to write this chapter. Now that you've read it, hopefully you don't have to struggle the same way I did in that class.

Real-World Applications

As previously discussed in "BASIC History" on page 22, BASIC was the standard language of the personal computing revolution. Millions of programmers got their start writing BASIC, and Tiny BASIC was a real and widely used dialect of BASIC. Some of the progenitors of Tiny BASIC pioneered the Free Software movement. Thanks to their open licensing, Tiny BASIC was ported to a wide variety of platforms where its simplicity was actually an advantage. It ran on machines with so little memory that they couldn't run languages much more sophisticated than Tiny BASIC.

It may not seem like much, but for an early personal computer user with no other alternatives (due to cost or availability) and limited memory, Tiny BASIC was a huge improvement over having to write machine code. Because it was freely licensed and ported to so many platforms, it also offered a kind of portability for programs written in it. If a machine could run Tiny BASIC, then it could run your program.

Tiny BASIC is still in use today. Like Brainfuck, it serves as an educational tool, but it's also being used for more than that. As of this writing, a German company ships microcontrollers running a version of Tiny BASIC.[16]

The interpreters you'll find running modern popular programming languages are much more sophisticated than the one we built in this chapter, yet they have the same essential building blocks—a tokenizer, a parser, an intermediate representation like an AST, and a runtime environment. The added sophistication is generally there to support additional features or performance, but the relatively simple techniques from this chapter are sufficient to build a working prototype of a new language or even a production-ready domain-specific language (DSL) for your work. Generally, DSLs don't require high performance.

Many successful real-world programming languages start out with quite simple implementations and evolve over time. For example, Ruby was originally an AST-walking interpreter like NanoBASIC. Ruby later compiled to bytecode that executes on a virtual machine (more about virtual machines in Chapter 5), and more recent versions of Ruby have incorporated a just-in-time (JIT) compiler.

Whether a language implementation walks an AST, uses bytecode, or has a JIT compiler, it needs the principles we covered in this chapter.

Exercises

1. Make it possible for escaped double-quote characters to appear in NanoBASIC strings. This will require learning a bit about regular expressions.

2. Turn NanoBASIC into Tiny BASIC by implementing INPUT statements, which allow the user to type a numeric value that gets stored in a variable. This is enough to implement the "baseline" Tiny BASIC (and to be able to run Tiny BASIC programs you find online with your interpreter), but many real-world versions also had extensions, such as a way of generating random numbers called RND().

3. Tiny BASIC runs in an interactive mode that supports the commands (seen as statements in the original grammar) CLEAR, LIST, RUN, and END. Lines that start with a line number are stored. That storage can be cleared, listed, or run. The program can also be terminated. Create an interactive mode (basically a REPL) for NanoBASIC with these same four commands. I said Exercise 2 would turn NanoBASIC into Tiny BASIC, but with this interactive mode, you'll have truly implemented Tiny BASIC.

4. Add support for string interpolation to NanoBASIC. When a string contains a dollar sign before an identifier, check if that identifier is defined in the variable table and output its value in place of it. For example, "The value of X is $X" would print The value of X is 24 if the variable X has the value 24. This will require modifying the tokenizer, the parser, and the runtime.

5. Write a NanoBASIC program that does something interesting and tests every statement in the interpreter. Think of this as the final integration test.

Notes

1. "BASIC Begins at Dartmouth," BASIC at 50, 2014, accessed May 22, 2024, *https://www.dartmouth.edu/basicfifty/basic.html*.

2. Linus Torvalds and David Diamond, *Just for Fun* (HarperCollins, 2001), 7–8.

3. James Wallace and Jim Erickson, *Hard Drive: Bill Gates and the Making of the Microsoft Empire* (HarperBusiness, 1993).

4. Tom Pittman, "Itty Bitty Computers & Tiny Basic," Itty Bitty Computers, 2004, last modified July 10, 2017, accessed May 22, 2024, *http://www.itty bittycomputers.com/IttyBitty/TinyBasic*.

5. Edsger Dijkstra, "Letters to the Editor: Go To Statement Considered Harmful," *Communications of the ACM* 11, no. 3 (1968): 147–148, *https://dl .acm.org/doi/10.1145/362929.362947*.

6. Dennis Allison, "Design Notes for Tiny BASIC," *Dr. Dobb's Journal of Computer Calisthenics and Orthodontia* 1 (1976): 9, *https://archive.org/details/ dr_dobbs_journal_vol_01/page/n9/mode/2up*.

7. See *https://peps.python.org/pep-0604*.

8. Joseph Sibony, "GCC vs. Clang: Battle of the Behemoths," Incredibuild, May 27, 2021, *https://www.incredibuild.com/blog/gcc-vs-clang-battle-of-the-behemoths*.

9. Tom Pittman, "Tiny Basic Experimenter's Kit," 1977, accessed December 4, 2024, *http://www.ittybittycomputers.com/IttyBitty/TinyBasic/TBEK.txt*.

10. See *https://en.wikipedia.org/wiki/Danny_Kopec*.

11. See *https://en.wikipedia.org/wiki/John_G._Kemeny*.

12. See *https://en.wikipedia.org/wiki/True_BASIC*.

13. See *https://en.wikipedia.org/wiki/Thomas_E._Kurtz*.

14. See *https://en.wikipedia.org/wiki/Logo_(programming_language)*.

15. See *https://oaksnow.com/seaturtle*.

16. See *https://www.tinybasic.de*.

PART II

COMPUTATIONAL ART

3

RETRO IMAGE PROCESSING

What do you do when you need to show an image on a display with fewer colors than are in the image itself? Solving that problem is the realm of dithering algorithms, which strategically use a limited color palette to create the illusion of more colors. In this chapter, we'll write a program that can take any modern photo and display it on a classic monochrome Macintosh. It will convert the photo to a dithered 1-bit black-and-white version of itself and export it to a format that an early Macintosh can read: MacPaint. Along the way, we'll learn a dithering algorithm, a compression algorithm, and a bit about file formats.

What Is Dithering?

Dithering algorithms purposely introduce noise into an image in a specific way that makes the image appear to have more color depth than it actually does. This trick on the human eye has both practical and artistic applications. If you've ever seen full-motion graphics on an early 1990s game console or computer, then you probably have a sense of what dithering looks like. The technique is also prevalent in animated GIFs, since GIFs can only support 256 colors. (There's a hacky way to get more than 256 colors in a GIF, but most export programs don't support it.)

If you look at Figure 3-1, you'll see the same image in JPEG and GIF formats. The JPEG has 45,807 colors, while the GIF has just 256. Thanks to dithering, it's not as easy to see the difference as you might expect. (If you're reading this book in print, see the *figures* directory of the book's GitHub repository for color versions of the images.)

Figure 3-1: A 45,807-color JPEG reduced to a 256-color GIF with dithering

Another common use of dithering and techniques like it is to make a black-and-white image appear to be grayscale. Newspapers have done something similar to dithering (a technique called *halftone*) for a long time to make their purely black-and-white printers reproduce photographs. On computing devices, dithering allows for images that have depth, even on a 1-bit screen that can only show two colors (typically black and white). It's a technique that's still relevant today. For example, the Panic Playdate, a game console released in 2022, has a 1-bit black-and-white screen. Most Amazon Kindle devices support 16 levels of grayscale, so many book covers and photographs displayed on the Kindle must be approximated via dithering (albeit not 1-bit dithering).

The original 1984 Apple Macintosh had a 1-bit black-and-white screen, as did several subsequent models. In fact, Apple continued to sell 1-bit Macintoshes right up until the Classic II was discontinued in 1993, and the company only stopped providing user support for the Classic II in 2001. During those 17 years of supported life, third-party developers created plenty of cool graphics for monochrome Macintoshes, and they did this using dithering algorithms.

We'll target those classic monochrome Macintoshes in our project, along with a beloved graphics editor that they ran, MacPaint. Figure 3-2 shows the end result: the image from Figure 3-1 displayed on MacPaint running on a Mac Plus emulator. (The 1986 Mac Plus was a slight evolution of the original 1984 Macintosh but had the same screen constraints.) The figure was created using the program built in this chapter.

Figure 3-2: The beach scene from Figure 3-1, converted by our program to display in MacPaint

You may notice the beach scene is more "zoomed in" in Figure 3-2 than it is in Figure 3-1. For Figure 3-1, I first scaled the scene to a lower resolution so that both versions could fit next to each other in the same figure (I used software to count the colors of the lower-resolution versions). I ran the original full-resolution image through our program to convert it to MacPaint for Figure 3-2. MacPaint is limited to documents that are 576 pixels wide by 720 pixels tall, so as we'll see, our program will always first resize images to fit within that constraint. However, MacPaint's display window on a Mac Plus is even smaller because a Mac Plus display is only 512 pixels across and some of those pixels are taken up by the toolbar. Therefore, we're only seeing roughly 400 of the 576 pixels across in Figure 3-2. The full height of the image is also obscured.

Getting Started

The pipeline our project will follow is pretty straightforward:

1. Read an image from disk.
2. Resize it and convert it to grayscale.

3. Dither it to black and white.

4. Write it to disk in MacPaint format.

The unique and interesting parts of the project are steps 3 and 4, so we'll use a library to complete steps 1 and 2. Probably the most popular imaging library in the Python world is Pillow. Installing it should be as easy as pip install pillow.

Pillow can read an image in any popular format in a single line of code, and it's just a few more lines to resize an image and convert it to grayscale. We'll complete this simple preparatory work right in our *__main__.py* file, along with handling command line arguments as we've done in the prior two projects. Let's start with the code for resizing and converting to grayscale, which appears in a function aptly called prepare():

```
# RetroDither/__main__.py
from PIL import Image
from argparse import ArgumentParser
from RetroDither.dither import dither
from RetroDither.macpaint import MAX_WIDTH, MAX_HEIGHT, write_macpaint_file


def prepare(file_name: str) -> Image.Image:
    with open(file_name, "rb") as fp:
        image = Image.open(fp)
        # Size to within the bounds of the maximum for MacPaint
        if image.width > MAX_WIDTH or image.height > MAX_HEIGHT:
            desired_ratio = MAX_WIDTH / MAX_HEIGHT
            ratio = image.width / image.height
            if ratio >= desired_ratio:
                new_size = (MAX_WIDTH, int(image.height * (MAX_WIDTH / image.width)))
            else:
                new_size = (int(image.width * (MAX_HEIGHT / image.height)), MAX_HEIGHT)
            image.thumbnail(new_size, Image.Resampling.LANCZOS)
        # Convert to grayscale
        return image.convert("L")
```

As noted earlier, MacPaint images are limited to a resolution of 576 pixels wide by 720 pixels tall. We define those values as constants in *macpaint.py*. In prepare(), if the image is too large, we scale it proportionally. For that, we figure out the ratio of the image's width to its height and compare it to the ratio of MacPaint's maximum dimensions. By scaling one dimension to the maximum size allowed in MacPaint and the other dimension according to the appropriate ratio, we get a final image that's as large as possible in MacPaint without any part of it getting cut off. To figure out the resizing formula, I did some very simple cross-multiplication algebra on pen and paper. I recommend you do the same if you're curious about how this works.

Like reading an image file, doing a resize in Pillow is an easy one-liner with the image.thumbnail() method. It offers multiple built-in algorithms for actually calculating what colors each of the resized pixels will be; LANCZOS is perhaps the highest quality (at some performance cost). Finally, image .convert("L") converts the image to grayscale. The "L" for grayscale mode is short for *luminance*, which in computer graphics is also sometimes known as *luma*.

Now let's handle the command line arguments:

```
if __name__ == "__main__":
    argument_parser = ArgumentParser("RetroDither")
    argument_parser.add_argument("image_file", help="Input image file.")
    argument_parser.add_argument("output_file", help="Resulting MacPaint file.")
    argument_parser.add_argument('-g', '--gif', default=False, action='store_true',
                                 help='Create an output gif as well.')
    arguments = argument_parser.parse_args()
    original = prepare(arguments.image_file)
    dithered_data = dither(original)
    if arguments.gif:
        out_image = Image.frombytes('L', original.size, dithered_data.tobytes())
        out_image.save(arguments.output_file + ".gif")
    write_macpaint_file(dithered_data, arguments.output_file, original.width, original.height)
```

At this point, on our third project, we've seen ArgumentParser quite a bit. For Retro Dither, we have a couple more command line options compared to the earlier projects. One, output_file, is for the user to specify an output filename and path for the results. The optional -g or --gif parameter is for the user to specify if they want GIF output in addition to MacPaint output. If the user requests GIF output, we use Pillow to write a GIF version of the dithered image.

Pillow is a very full-featured and powerful library. We won't use many of its features in this chapter, but if you need to do image manipulation in Python, it's well worth the invested time to learn it. We'll also see it again in the next chapter. For more information, check out the Pillow documentation at *https://pillow.readthedocs.io*.

The Dithering Algorithm

There are many different dithering algorithms, the most popular class of which are known as *error-diffusion* algorithms. This type of algorithm takes some of the difference between where a pixel ends up and where it began (the *error*) and spreads (*diffuses*) it among nearby pixels. The most popular error-diffusion dithering algorithm is known as Floyd-Steinberg dithering (invented by Robert Floyd and Louis Steinberg in 1976). In fact, Pillow has built-in support for Floyd-Steinberg dithering.

Just using Pillow to do the dithering wouldn't be any fun, and we wouldn't learn anything in the process. Instead, we'll implement an algorithm that Pillow doesn't have: the Atkinson dithering algorithm. It was created by Bill Atkinson in 1984 specifically for use with software on the original Macintosh, like MacPaint, which Atkinson was the author of. It's therefore not a surprise that Atkinson dithering was a popular technique on monochrome Macs. It will make our results look more authentic. Like Floyd-Steinberg, Atkinson dithering is an error-diffusion algorithm. As we'll see, it only takes a few changes to go from one error-diffusion algorithm to another.

Before we dive into the specifics of Atkinson dithering, let's talk about error-diffusion dithering algorithms more generally. Most of these algorithms look at an image's pixels one at a time from the top left through to the bottom right. The movement is from left to right across each row, and then down one row after each row is complete. For every pixel processed, the following steps occur:

1. Find which of the output colors it's closest to. (In dithering, the output colors are specified in advance, for example, black and white.)

2. Find the difference between the output color and the original color of the pixel.

3. Add part of the difference to some of the pixels to the right and below the current pixel.

Let's take those general steps and apply them to our specific scenario, where the pixels are being converted from grayscale to black and white via Atkinson dithering:

1. Find whether black or white is closer to the gray in the pixel. This will be based on some kind of threshold. For instance, if the grays are stored as 8-bit unsigned integers, there may be 256 shades of gray numbered 0 through 255, and our threshold could be 127. Any pixel greater than 127 may be marked as white (255 in this scheme), and any pixel less than or equal to 127 may be marked as black (0).

2. Subtract the difference between the new pixel color and its original color. Imagine the original gray was 204. The difference would be $255 - 204 = 51$. This is our error.

3. Add one-eighth of the error to six specific pixels close to the original pixel. This is the diffusion step. In this case, $51 // 8 = 6$ (we need to do integer division). The pixels adjusted are: one to the right, two to the right, one diagonally down and left, one diagonally down and right, one straight below, and one two below.

Only step 3 is different between Floyd-Steinberg dithering and Atkinson dithering. You'll note that since we're distributing one-eighth of the error among six pixels, we're only distributing a total of six-eighths or three-quarters of the total error. In Floyd-Steinberg dithering, *all* of the error is distributed among four nearby pixels. This difference in how the error is distributed gives Atkinson dithering a look that seems to emphasize changes in contrast, whereas Floyd-Steinberg dithering can have a smoother appearance. Figure 3-3 shows an original image (first panel), Atkinson dithering (second panel), and Floyd-Steinberg dithering (third panel).

Figure 3-3: The author's grandmother in a portrait that shows good contrast between various colors illustrating how edges appear in dithering

Tables 3-1 and 3-2 contain matrices representing the error diffusion in Atkinson dithering and Floyd-Steinberg dithering, respectively. The X indicates the original pixel location, and the column and row headers indicate movement in columns or rows away from the original pixel.

Table 3-1: Error Diffusion in Atkinson Dithering

Δ	−1	0	+1	+2
0		X	1/8	1/8
+1	1/8	1/8	1/8	
+2		1/8		

Table 3-2: Error Diffusion in Floyd-Steinberg Dithering

Δ	−1	0	+1
0		X	7/16
+1	3/16	5/16	1/16

Although we'll be implementing Atkinson dithering, we'll keep the matrix separated in such a way that it will be easy for you to plug in a different matrix. For example, you can easily change the code to Floyd-Steinberg dithering or another error-diffusion variant, or you can try out your own method. In fact, doing so is one of the exercises at the end of the chapter.

Our dithering code begins by defining some constants:

RetroDither/
dither.py

```
from PIL import Image
from array import array
from typing import NamedTuple

THRESHOLD = 127

class PatternPart(NamedTuple):
    dc: int  # change in column
    dr: int  # change in row
    numerator: int
    denominator: int

ATKINSON = [PatternPart(1, 0, 1, 8), PatternPart(2, 0, 1, 8),
            PatternPart(-1, 1, 1, 8), PatternPart(0, 1, 1, 8),
            PatternPart(1, 1, 1, 8), PatternPart(0, 2, 1, 8)]
```

We set THRESHOLD to 127 (about the middle point between 0 and 255) as described in our algorithm. In ATKINSON, we flatten the Atkinson dithering matrix into six PatternPart named tuples, each of which specifies where one of the pixels being changed is located relative to the original pixel and what fraction of the error should be added to it.

Next, we'll start defining a dither() function, where the dithering takes place:

```
# Assumes we are working with a grayscale image (Mode "L" in Pillow)
# Returns an array of dithered pixels (255 for white, 0 for black)
def dither(image: Image.Image) -> array:
    # Distribute error among nearby pixels
    def diffuse(c: int, r: int, error: int, pattern: list[PatternPart]):
        for part in pattern:
            col = c + part.dc
            row = r + part.dr
            if col < 0 or col >= image.width or row >= image.height:
                continue
            current_pixel: float = image.getpixel((col, row))  # type: ignore
            # Add *error_part* to the pixel at (*col*, *row*) in *image*
            error_part = (error * part.numerator) // part.denominator
            image.putpixel((col, row), current_pixel + error_part)
```

The dither() function begins with a diffuse() helper function that takes the error and distributes it among nearby pixels in portions specified by a pattern, which is just a list of PatternPart tuples. We iterate through each PatternPart in the pattern, find the pixel associated with that part, and add its fraction of the error to it. As discussed, the pattern is at the heart of what makes one error-diffusion algorithm differ from another. Note that all the arithmetic here is integer arithmetic. This is because pixel values are stored as integers.

In the rest of dither(), we go through every pixel in the image, change it to black or white depending on THRESHOLD, calculate the difference from the original gray, and diffuse the error among nearby pixels using the diffuse() helper function:

```
result = array('B', [0] * (image.width * image.height))
for y in range(image.height):
    for x in range(image.width):
        old_pixel: float = image.getpixel((x, y))  # type: ignore
        # Every new pixel is either solid white or solid black
        # since this is all that the original Macintosh supported
        new_pixel = 255 if old_pixel > THRESHOLD else 0
        result[y * image.width + x] = new_pixel
        difference = int(old_pixel - new_pixel)
        # Disperse error among nearby upcoming pixels
        diffuse(x, y, difference, ATKINSON)

return result
```

The ATKINSON pattern is currently hardcoded, but there's an easy hook here to change to a different pattern. Note that the result variable is actually an array of pixels, not another Pillow Image. This is because we'll need to further process the raw pixel data of the dithered image in order to save it in MacPaint format. In Python's array type from the standard library, an array defined using type code 'B' holds unsigned bytes. Since we'll be manipulating a lot of raw bytes, we'll see this array type repeatedly both in this chapter and in the later chapters on emulators.

Confusingly, Python provides at least three different types for working with raw bytes: bytes, bytearray, and array("B"). You could ultimately write your code using any of them. The array type is particularly geared toward compact representation and working with files.

The MacPaint File Format

There were painting programs before it, but for everything that would come after it, MacPaint set the standard. It was written by Bill Atkinson and released in 1984 by Apple alongside the original Macintosh. Although preceded by the Xerox Star and the Apple Lisa, the Macintosh was the first widely available personal computer with a mouse and a graphical user interface (GUI). MacPaint was one of the showcase pieces of software that demonstrated how powerful a mouse and GUI could be. A reviewer in the *New York Times* said, "It is better than anything else of its kind offered on personal computers by a factor of 10."[1] Many of the tools and graphical manipulation techniques that first appeared in MacPaint are still with us today in modern graphics software.

I encourage you to play around with MacPaint to get a sense of it. There's a live demo of it on the Internet Archive,[2] but you may get the maximum level of fulfillment from this chapter by taking the time to download an emulator so that you can load the actual images our program will be outputting directly in MacPaint. You could even go find an old Mac on eBay! I've collected far too many myself.

Despite being revolutionary, MacPaint was limited by the hardware of its pioneering platform. Like the original Macintosh, MacPaint only supported black and white. As mentioned earlier, its documents were also limited to a fixed size of 576 pixels wide by 720 pixels tall. The original Macintosh didn't even have a hard drive; disk space was limited because everything had to run off of a floppy disk. To accommodate this space constraint, MacPaint used a simple compression scheme known as *run-length encoding*. We'll come back to some of these quirks shortly.

The next step in our project will be to write code that translates the dithered pixels of an image into the MacPaint format. My experience has been that programming against binary file formats is just a matter of very carefully following a specification document. Unfortunately, the MacPaint format is somewhat obscure today, so finding a specification document requires a little bit of digging. Apple itself documented the format in Technical Note PT24.[3] However, the most accessible and comprehensive description I've found was on a site called FileFormat.info.[4]

On the surface, a MacPaint file is pretty simple. It consists of a 512-byte header followed by pixel data that's compressed using run-length encoding. Before being run-length encoded, each pixel is stored as a bit, either a 1 for black or a 0 for white. That all sounds straightforward enough. However, there's a peculiarity: unlike almost any other operating system, the classic Mac operating system stored files in two "forks." We'll dive into that more in a bit, but in short, MacPaint files that get transported or created on operating systems other than the classic Mac OS should be encoded in a special format called *MacBinary* in order to have their metadata survive transfer. We'll therefore need to turn our output file into a MacBinary file too, by adding a special additional header.

We'll tackle this esoteric file format step by step. First, we'll handle the pixel data. Then, we'll implement run-length encoding. And last, we'll create the MacPaint and MacBinary headers. As we work, we'll need to use various bitwise operations including shifts, ORs, and ANDs. If this kind of low-level bit manipulation is new to you, or if you're just a bit rusty, see the book's appendix for an overview of bitwise operations in Python.

Translating Bytes to Bits

In "L" mode, our Pillow Image is encoded using 1 byte per pixel. However, in a MacPaint bitmap, pixels are encoded with 1 bit per pixel, meaning each byte represents eight pixels. This is a big savings for black and white, and it makes total sense since we only need two values (1 and 0) to represent two colors. After we define some constants, our first function in *macpaint.py* is a converter that takes the byte array we got from dither() and converts it into a "bit array":

RetroDither/
macpaint.py

```
from array import array
from pathlib import Path
from datetime import datetime

MAX_WIDTH = 576
MAX_HEIGHT = 720
MACBINARY_LENGTH = 128
HEADER_LENGTH = 512

# Convert an array of bytes where each byte is 0 or 255
# to an array of bits where each byte that is 0 becomes a 1
# and each byte that is 255 becomes a 0
def bytes_to_bits(original: array) -> array:
    bits_array = array('B')

    for byte_index in range(0, len(original), 8):
        next_byte = 0
        for bit_index in range(8):
            next_bit = 1 - (original[byte_index + bit_index] & 1)
            next_byte = next_byte | (next_bit << (7 - bit_index))
            if (byte_index + bit_index + 1) >= len(original):
                break
        bits_array.append(next_byte)
    return bits_array
```

The loops here iterate through 8 bytes at a time from the original array, checking whether each is a white (255) or black (0) pixel. MacPaint's bitmap format inverts this, making a white pixel 0 and a black pixel 1. The line next_bit = 1 - (original[byte_index + bit_index] & 1) does the inversion. Note that we don't actually check values against 255, instead preferring to only check the first bit (& 1) because it makes the code more compact and more performant. We know we only stored 255s and 0s in the array before bytes_to_bits() was called, so there's no reason to fear we're accidentally capturing intermediate values; if there's a 1 anywhere in the byte, it must be 255. The 8 bits are encoded in next_byte by putting each bit into the appropriate place with an OR operation: next_byte = next_byte | (next_bit << (7 - bit_index)). We then append next_byte to bits_array.

We don't call bytes_to_bits() on all of the pixel data at once, because MacPaint bitmaps need to be padded with white pixels (0s) on every row of the bitmap where the pixel data doesn't extend the full length. We handle the padding with the prepare() function:

```
# Convert the array of bytes into bits using the helper function.
# Pad any missing spots with white bits due to the original
# image having a smaller size than 576x720.
def prepare(data: array, width: int, height: int) -> array:
    bits_array = array('B')
    for row in range(height):
        image_location = row * width
        image_bits = bytes_to_bits(data[image_location:(image_location + width)])
        bits_array += image_bits
        remaining_width = MAX_WIDTH - width
        white_width_bits = array('B', [0] * (remaining_width // 8))
        bits_array += white_width_bits
    remaining_height = MAX_HEIGHT - height
    white_height_bits = array('B', [0] * ((remaining_height * MAX_WIDTH) // 8))
    bits_array += white_height_bits
    return bits_array
```

We look through the raw pixel data coming from dither() one row at a time and convert the row to bits using bytes_to_bits(). If the row doesn't extend the full width of a MacPaint document, we add white pixels to the row. We do the same for any full-length rows beneath the pixel data.

Implementing Run-Length Encoding

Storing pixels as individual bits rather than bytes saves a significant amount of space, but it's not enough. When MacPaint launched in 1984, the original Macintosh had floppy disks that supported just 400KB of data. There was no hard drive, and a standard configuration had just one floppy drive. Think about how big a MacPaint file would be if it weren't compressed. The 576 pixels in a row take up 576 bits, which is 72 bytes. There are 720 rows, so 720 multiplied by 72 bytes is 51,840 bytes. Adding in the 512-byte header, a MacPaint file would be 52,352 bytes with no compression. That would mean a floppy disk couldn't even store eight MacPaint files!

To relieve this disk space problem, the MacPaint file format incorporates a simple compression scheme called run-length encoding. In this scheme, instead of repeating the same thing, you say how many times it should repeat. For example, suppose we want to store the string *AAAAAABCCCCCABBBB*. If each character uses 1 byte, it would be 17 bytes. Would it not be more efficient to say seven *A*s instead of repeating *A* seven times? Or saying five *C*s?

Suppose we use up to 1 byte before a character to store its number of repetitions. The string could then be encoded as *6AB5CA4B*, which is 8 bytes. However, there's a problem with this scheme. Remember, in computer memory these would be raw bytes. How do we know that *B* is a character and not a byte indicating a certain number of repetitions of the next character? In other words, *B* would likely be stored in memory using its ASCII/Unicode code, 66. Our program would likely interpret it as indicating 66 of the next character, not a single letter *B*.

We could instead have a scheme where every character is preceded by a number, even single characters. This would change the encoded string to *6A1B5C1A4B*. That's 10 bytes, a 7-byte savings over the original, which is significant.

This encoding scheme is a form of run-length encoding, but it breaks down pretty quickly: for many strings, it's actually less efficient than just storing the raw characters. For example, the string *ABC* would be *1A1B1C*. That's double the size.

There's a compromise. You can have an encoding scheme where each number indicates either a repetition or a certain number of literal characters. Then, *ABC* becomes *3ABC*. That's still longer, but this new scheme may be a good compromise for more complex cases. For instance, the string *AAAAABCBCAAAAAA* would be *5A4BCBC6A*.

This version is close to the encoding scheme the MacPaint file format uses, but there's still a problem: How would you know that the 5 means five *A*s, but the 4 means a literal sequence of four characters (*BCBC*) rather than four *B*s? You may say, "Well, you could read ahead two characters and see that *C* isn't a number, so the 4 couldn't mean four *B*s," but even that doesn't work, because (again) in computer memory, the *C* is stored as a number. We need another improvement.

MacPaint eliminates the ambiguity between numbers that indicate literal runs and numbers that indicate repetition runs by representing both using signed 1-byte integers. A number n between 0 and 127 indicates $n + 1$ literal bytes follow. A number n between -1 and -127 indicates $1 - n$ repetitions of the following byte. The number -128 isn't used. This compression scheme is known as *PackBits*,[5] and it was used beyond just MacPaint in several other popular file formats.

A PackBits function was actually built into classic versions of Mac OS. According to Apple's own technical note on the subject, "typical MacPaint documents compress to about 10K" with PackBits.[6] Table 3-3 summarizes the PackBits encoding scheme.

Table 3-3: The PackBits Encoding Scheme (Signed)

Value of n	Meaning
0 to 127	$n + 1$ literal bytes follow.
-1 to -127	The next byte is repeated $1 - n$ times.
-128	Skip.

We'll be working with unsigned integers, so it's convenient to rewrite the table instead of doing conversions on every byte from signed to unsigned (or thinking about two's complements). Table 3-4 is the encoding scheme with the bytes converted to unsigned integers.

Table 3-4: The PackBits Encoding Scheme (Unsigned)

Value of n	Meaning
0 to 127	n + 1 literal bytes follow.
129 to 255	The next byte is repeated 257 – n times.
128	Skip.

Have you thought of a limitation of this scheme? What if there are more than 128 bytes in a run? Thankfully, we won't run into this problem when encoding MacPaint files, because they're encoded one row at a time. A row in MacPaint can only be 576 pixels, stored as 72 bytes. Since 72 is less than 128, we don't need to worry about the limit.

To check your understanding, try working with an example that Apple provides in Technical Note TN1023. I've converted it from hexadecimal to decimal for your convenience in Table 3-5. One row is the unpacked data, and the other row is the packed data. Try to reformulate the packed data from the unpacked data using Table 3-4 as a reference. Then, check your work against the packed data in Table 3-5.

Table 3-5: A PackBits Example

Type	Bytes
Unpacked	170, 170, 170, 128, 0, 42, 170, 170, 170, 170, 128, 0, 42, 34, 170, 170, 170, 170, 170, 170, 170, 170, 170
Packed	254, 170, 2, 128, 0, 42, 253, 170, 3, 128, 0, 42, 34, 247, 170

Let's implement a PackBits encoder. The function run_length_encode() takes an array of bytes and returns a run length–encoded array of bytes using the PackBits scheme. It starts with an inner helper function, take_same(), that can find runs of repeated values and return their length:

```
# MacPaint expects RLE to happen on a per-line basis (MAX_WIDTH).
# In other words there are line boundaries.
def run_length_encode(original_data: array) -> array:
    # Find how many of the same bytes are in a row from *start*
    def take_same(source: array, start: int) -> int:
        count = 0
        while (start + count + 1 < len(source)
                and source[start + count] == source[start + count + 1]):
            count += 1
        return count + 1 if count > 0 else 0
```

To find a run, take_same() just repeatedly looks at whether the byte after the current byte is the same as it. It's also careful to not run off the end of the source array. We increment count every time a match is found, but because the first byte examined (the byte at start) isn't itself a match of a previous byte, count will always be one less than the number of items in a run. Hence, count + 1 is returned if any matches are found, or 0 otherwise. This makes it impossible to have a repeated run with just one of the same character: that would just be a lone character, which would be part of a literal since in PackBits there's no way to "repeat once." In other words, the domain of take_same() is 0 and all integers greater than or equal to 2.

The run_length_encode() function continues with a little setup:

```
rle_data = array('B')
# Divide data into MAX_WIDTH size boundaries by line
for line_start in range(0, len(original_data), MAX_WIDTH // 8):
    data = original_data[line_start:(line_start + (MAX_WIDTH // 8))]
```

Output will be stored in rle_data. We iterate through the original_data array one row at a time. The MacPaint file format specifies that each row is individually run-length encoded, instead of all the pixels being run-length encoded at once. The data variable represents a single row of pixel data ready for run-length encoding. The next step is to look for repetitions and literal runs:

```
index = 0
while index < len(data):
    not_same = 0
    while (((same := take_same(data, index + not_same)) == 0)
            and (index + not_same < len(data))):
        not_same += 1
```

We iterate through each row's data 1 byte at a time, with index keeping track of the current byte that's being examined. Two counts are gathered: same (initialized on the fly using the so-called walrus := operator) is the number of items in a row that are the same, and not_same is the length of a literal run. Here's how they're calculated in the while loop:

1. We attempt to find a repeated run using take_same().
2. If the attempt fails (same is 0), then this must be a literal run, so not_same is incremented.
3. Steps 1 and 2 repeat until a repeated run is found (same is not equal to 0) or the byte being looked at (index + not_same) is beyond the end of the row.

There are three possibilities after this loop:

1. A repeated run is immediately found (same is then not equal to 0) and not_same is never incremented, meaning it equals 0.
2. A literal run is initially found and not_same is incremented until a repeated run is found, filling in same.
3. A literal run is initially found that goes all the way to the end of the row, and the loop exits because index + not_same < len(data) doesn't hold.

Due to the second possibility, there can be a scenario where both same and not_same are greater than 0. Keep that in mind as we examine the remaining code for this function:

```
if not_same > 0:
    rle_data.append(not_same - 1)
    rle_data += data[index:index + not_same]
    index += not_same
if same > 0:
    rle_data.append(257 - same)
    rle_data.append(data[index])
    index += same
return rle_data
```

This is the part that writes the PackBits-encoded data to the array. These patterns are directly from Table 3-4. Because of the possibility of finding both a not_same and a same run in a single iteration of the loop, there are two if statements here instead of an else clause. Further, because of the way that the inner while loop is structured, not_same runs will always be found prior to same runs. This is why the if statement for not_same appears first. If there's one of each run, then index gets incremented the right amount by not_same to be in the right place for the encoding of the same run.

AN ALTERNATIVE IMPLEMENTATION

Do you find the run_length_encode() function elegant or too clever? I made several attempts to rewrite my original version in a more compact and readable form, and the end result is what you see here. I found centering the code on take_same() and just counting when it fails to be more readable than simultaneously trying to establish same and not_same runs. Yet it's less efficient than my original version, which uses a lot more conditionals; is a bit longer; and has no inner function. If you don't like this version, I left my original version as a comment at the bottom of the source file on GitHub. You can find that file at *https:// github.com/davecom/ComputerScienceFromScratch/blob/main/RetroDither/ macpaint.py*.

Testing Run-Length Encoding

As I tried rewriting run_length_encoding() a few different ways to make it more readable, I realized I needed a quick way of making sure my new implementations were correct, so I wrote some unit tests. Like all tests for the book, the file for these appears in the *tests* directory in the root of the source code repository.

```
# tests/test_retrodither.py
import unittest
from array import array
from RetroDither.macpaint import run_length_encode

class RetroDitherTestCase(unittest.TestCase):
    # Example from
    # web.archive.org/web/20080705155158/http://developer.apple.com/technotes/tn/tn1023.html
    def test_apple_rle_example(self):
        unpacked = array("B", [0xAA, 0xAA, 0xAA, 0x80, 0x00, 0x2A, 0xAA, 0xAA, 0xAA, 0xAA,
                               0x80, 0x00, 0x2A, 0x22, 0xAA, 0xAA, 0xAA, 0xAA, 0xAA, 0xAA,
                               0xAA, 0xAA, 0xAA, 0xAA])
        packed = run_length_encode(unpacked)
        expected = array("B", [0xFE, 0xAA, 0x02, 0x80, 0x00, 0x2A, 0xFD, 0xAA, 0x03, 0x80,
                               0x00, 0x2A, 0x22, 0xF7, 0xAA])
        self.assertEqual(expected, packed)

    # Example where packed data is longer than unpacked data
    def test_longer_rle(self):
        unpacked = array("B", [0x55, 0x55, 0xBB, 0xBB, 0x55, 0xBB, 0xBB, 0x55])
        packed = run_length_encode(unpacked)
        expected = array("B", [0xFF, 0x55, 0xFF, 0xBB, 0x00, 0x55, 0xFF, 0xBB, 0x00, 0x55])
        self.assertEqual(expected, packed)

    def test_simple_literal(self):
        unpacked = array("B", [0x00, 0x01, 0x02, 0x03, 0x04])
        packed = run_length_encode(unpacked)
        expected = array("B", [0x04, 0x00, 0x01, 0x02, 0x03, 0x04])
        self.assertEqual(expected, packed)

    def test_simple_literal2(self):
        unpacked = array("B", [0x00])
        packed = run_length_encode(unpacked)
        expected = array("B", [0x00, 0x00])
        self.assertEqual(expected, packed)

    def test_simple_same(self):
        unpacked = array("B", [0x11, 0x11, 0x11, 0x11])
        packed = run_length_encode(unpacked)
        expected = array("B", [0xFD, 0x11])
        self.assertEqual(expected, packed)

    def test_simple_same2(self):
        unpacked = array("B", [0x11, 0x11, 0x11, 0x11, 0x22, 0x22, 0x22, 0x22])
        packed = run_length_encode(unpacked)
        expected = array("B", [0xFD, 0x11, 0xFD, 0x22])
        self.assertEqual(expected, packed)

if __name__ == "__main__":
    unittest.main()
```

These tests ensure run-length encoding is working correctly and conclude our implementation of the MacPaint file format. There's just one
more step to get our dithered pictures ready to be usable on a retro Mac.

Converting to MacBinary

On most operating systems, a file is just a single blob of data. The filesystem or the operating system may hold onto some metadata about each file, but the file itself stands alone. That wasn't the case on the classic Mac OS, where many files had two forks. The *data fork* would hold the primary data of the file, while a *resource fork* may hold ancillary data like bitmaps, sounds, or even executable code. The resource fork could hold many different kinds of data in one place, so it was kind of like a resource database. This is one of the features of the operating system that allowed many applications to be completely self-contained—a single executable that could be dragged and dropped as a single icon, with no additional files.

Unfortunately, since resource forks don't exist on other operating systems, classic Mac files often get messed up when transferred to or from them. Care needs to be taken. This was a problem from the beginning, so "bundling" file formats were quickly developed. One of the most popular and well standardized is known as MacBinary. In a MacBinary file, a special header is followed by the data fork and resource fork together.

We need to bundle our MacPaint files as MacBinary files in order for them to work properly on the classic Mac OS and open by default in MacPaint. Ironically, a MacPaint file doesn't actually have a resource fork, it just has a data fork. But MacBinary files also bundle metadata that was stored in the filesystem (MFS/HFS/HFS+) of the classic Mac OS. The important bits are *type* and *creator codes*. The classic Mac OS doesn't use file extensions to associate a file with the program that should open it. Instead, it uses type and creator codes, which are largely transparent to the user. This allows the user to name their files anything they want and still have the files be "double-clickable." After the MacBinary file our program creates is unbundled by MacBinary (or another program like Stuffit) on the classic Mac OS, the resulting MacPaint file should open MacPaint when it's double-clicked.

Luckily, the MacBinary file format is fairly simple. To comply with the MacBinary specification, our program needs to:

1. Add the 128-byte MacBinary header before the rest of the file (which is just the data fork since we have no resource fork).
2. Fill in the MacBinary header with the right values in several indicated places.
3. Ensure the file ends in a multiple of 128 bytes by padding the end of it if necessary.

MacBinary has an official specification that was approved by a committee of interested parties.[7] However, we only need to fill out a few fields for our MacBinary file to be properly recognized. (The rest of the header should be 0s.) Table 3-6 lists these values, their lengths, and their respective offsets within the 128-byte header.

Table 3-6: Required MacBinary Header Fields

Offset	Length	Type	Value
1	1	Integer	Filename length (up to 63)
2	1 to 63	MacRoman	Filename
65	4	MacRoman	File type (should be "PNTG")
69	4	MacRoman	File creator (should be "MPNT")
83	4	Integer	Data fork length
91	4	Integer	Creation time as seconds since 1/1/1904
95	4	Integer	Modification time as seconds since 1/1/1904

Note that values are stored big-endian, since the classic Mac OS ran on big-endian microprocessors. (If that doesn't mean anything to you, see the "Big-Endian vs. Little-Endian" box.) MacRoman is a character encoding used on the classic Mac OS.[8]

The macbinary_header() function is a codification of Table 3-6:

```
def macbinary_header(outfile: str, data_size: int) -> array:
    macbinary = array('B', [0] * MACBINARY_LENGTH)
    filename = Path(outfile).stem
    filename = filename[:63] if len(filename) > 63 else filename  # limit to 63 characters max
    macbinary[1] = len(filename)  # filename length
    macbinary[2:(2 + len(filename))] = array("B", filename.encode("mac_roman"))  # filename
    macbinary[65:69] = array("B", "PNTG".encode("mac_roman"))  # file type
    macbinary[69:73] = array("B", "MPNT".encode("mac_roman"))  # file creator
    macbinary[83:87] = array("B", data_size.to_bytes(4, byteorder='big'))  # size of data fork
    timestamp = int((datetime.now() - datetime(1904, 1, 1)).total_seconds())  # Mac timestamp
    macbinary[91:95] = array("B", timestamp.to_bytes(4, byteorder='big'))  # creation stamp
    macbinary[95:99] = array("B", timestamp.to_bytes(4, byteorder='big'))  # modification stamp
    return macbinary
```

Any filenames that are more than 63 characters simply have their ends chopped off.

BIG-ENDIAN VS. LITTLE-ENDIAN

What order should the bytes representing a piece of data, such as a number, be stored in? This is a much-debated question, with the computer science world split between two camps: big-endian and little-endian.

Think for a moment about how we represent numbers in everyday life. If you come from a culture that uses the Arabic numeral system, like the English-speaking world, you're probably used to writing numbers from left to right starting with the digit representing the largest part of the number

(continued)

---

and decreasing from there. For example, the number 450 starts with the 4 representing the hundreds place, then the 5 representing the tens place, and then the 0 representing the ones place. The 4 represents the largest part of the number (400) and comes first. The decision to put the 4 first was made a long time ago and is largely arbitrary. In theory, we could have a numeral system that writes 450 from smallest to largest as 054, but obviously we don't.

The number 450 requires 2 bytes to represent in binary: 00000001 and 11000010. If you know binary, you know that each 1 represents a single power of 2 that, added with the other "on" powers of 2, gives us the final number. The first byte, 00000001, puts its lone 1 in the 2^8 place and represents 256. The second byte, 11000010, represents the number 194 because the 1s for 2^1 (2), 2^6 (64), and 2^7 (128) are turned on, and $128 + 64 + 2 = 194$. We have bytes for 256 and 194, and $256 + 194 = 450$.

Since we write 450 from largest to smallest, you might assume that your computer would similarly store the byte representing the larger portion of 450 first, yielding 0000000111000010 when the bytes are put together. This is known as *big-endian* order, but it's not how most computers actually work nowadays. The typical modern computer is built with a microprocessor that uses one of two architectures: x86-64 (Intel, AMD) or ARM64 (Apple, Qualcomm, and so on). For technical and historical reasons, those architectures store numbers in *little-endian* order, where the byte representing the smallest end of the number comes first. In a little-endian system, the 2-byte number 450 is stored as 1100001000000001. It's important to know which system is at play, since interpreting the little-endian 1100001000000001 as if it were in big-endian order would result in a completely different value.

While little-endian order dominates today's computer architectures, certain systems, such as those that run on the 68K microprocessor architecture (originally by Motorola)—including the original Macintosh—store their numbers in big-endian order. Yes, on the original Macintosh, 450 was stored "the right way" as 0000000111000010, but on the computer in front of you it's probably stored as 1100001000000001. Further complicating matters, most data transmitted over the internet is sent in big-endian order. When you're browsing the web on your x86-64 or ARM64 microprocessor, there's endian conversion going on in the background.

Putting It All Together

To write our MacPaint file bundled as a MacBinary file, we need to take our pixel array from dither() and:

1. Call prepare() to convert it from bytes to bits and pad it with 0s.
2. Call run_length_encode() to run-length encode the bit array.

3. Call `macbinary_header()` to combine the result with a MacBinary header.

4. Add a 512-byte MacPaint header as well.

5. Pad the end result with 0s up to a multiple of 128 bytes to follow the MacBinary specification requiring this.

This is mostly just a matter of calling functions we already have:

```
# Writes array *data* to *out_file*
def write_macpaint_file(data: array, out_file: str, width: int, height: int):
    bits_array = prepare(data, width, height)
    rle = run_length_encode(bits_array)
    data_size = len(rle) + HEADER_LENGTH  # header requires this
    output = macbinary_header(out_file, data_size) + array('B', [0] * HEADER_LENGTH) + rle
    output[MACBINARY_LENGTH + 3] = 2  # Data Fork Header Signature ❶
    # MacBinary format requires that there be padding of 0s up to a
    # multiple of 128 bytes for the data fork
    padding = 128 - (data_size % 128)
    if padding > 0:
        output += array('B', [0] * padding)
    with open(out_file + ".bin", "wb") as fp:
        output.tofile(fp)
```

The only part of this code we haven't yet discussed is the 512-byte MacPaint header. MacPaint mostly used this header to store user-defined pattern data. Programs that export to MacPaint don't generally have any user-defined patterns since they're artifacts created by a user in MacPaint. We can therefore leave the vast majority of the MacPaint header as 0s. The only thing we must do is put a little signature into the MacPaint header at byte 3, which is always set to 2 ❶.

The Results

To run the program, you need to specify both an input file and an output file. For example:

```
% python3 -m RetroDither -g /Users/dave/Downloads/IMG_0892.jpeg
/Users/dave/Downloads/AmericanFlag
```

The program adds the *.bin* extension for the output file automatically.

Figure 3-4 shows an image created using our program that I think has a nice artistic quality to it.

Figure 3-4: The space shuttle taking off

But how can you view your own results? On a vintage Mac, of course! MacPaint runs on machines with System 1 all the way through Mac OS 9. You should be able to find a real-life classic Mac running one of these OSes to display your photos on. You'll also need a program for unbundling the MacBinary file. There's a program aptly called MacBinary that you can download. Stuffit Expander, a very popular decompression app for the classic Mac OS, can also open MacBinary files. Both are distributed as freeware. Most Macs you find out in the wild from the 1990s will have Stuffit Expander already installed.

I realize that not everybody is going to be committed enough to this project to go out and find an actual retro computer. No problem—you can still experience the fruits of your labor through emulation. Apple started freely distributing early versions of the Mac OS as well as MacPaint (by releasing the full MacPaint source code) many years ago. It's possible to obtain all of the software you need, legally and at no charge, to create a true retro Macintosh experience in an emulator.

There are several emulators available, but probably the most retro of all is Mini vMac,[9] which I used to create some of the screenshots in this chapter. Setting up Mini vMac or one of the several other popular classic Mac emulators (Basilisk II, SheepShaver, and the like) is beyond the scope of this book, but I think that, as a programmer, you'll find it pretty easy to do. Each emulator has a different mechanism for transferring files from your machine to the emulated environment. Regardless of the specifics, it will probably be less of a hassle than getting an old Mac and getting that Mac online or finding a floppy disk drive for your modern machine. That said, old Macs are fun! Or maybe that fun is just my nostalgia from growing up with them.

CODE MEETS LIFE

I've been using MacPaint since my dad brought home a Macintosh LC in 1990. I was just three years old, but apparently I became adept enough at using it that he brought me in to give a demonstration at a class he was teaching at the University of Maine. It was probably partially for the novelty factor, or maybe the idea was, "This is so easy, a three-year-old can do it!" Whatever the case, he always believed in me.

I still have some of my childhood drawings saved to disk, which is what got me interested in the file format more recently. Amazingly, I couldn't find any programs on my modern Mac that could open the classic MacPaint format. I had to turn to LibreOffice or transfer the files to old Macs to view them.

Then, I found some mysterious MacPaint files that further piqued my interest on a floppy disk that had belonged to my brother 30 years ago. They contained strange artwork, quite sophisticated for the late 1980s or early 1990s, mixing digitized (a 1980s word for scanned and dithered) real-world objects with purely digital drawings. I eventually concluded that they were likely either the work of a well-known American artist named Robert W. Fichter[10] or the work of someone who admired him. They had some of the same motifs and the same exact words as some of Fichter's published pieces.

Was I in possession of a valuable digital art relict lost to time? How did my brother get ahold of these MacPaint files? I called him up. He hadn't thought about them in decades, but he said he got them from some student at the University of Maine while he was still in high school. He didn't know their exact provenance, but the student had told him they were very important and had a hidden meaning to them. It made sense that the disk came from a university. Perhaps Fichter had lectured there, or perhaps they were copied around the sneakernet (this was in an era before networking was widespread). I tried contacting Fichter himself, but to no avail. Unfortunately, he died in 2023. I still, at the time of writing, don't know if those files are the original digital artwork of Robert W. Fichter. If you're an expert on his work or knew him, please get in touch with me!

Around the same time, I was thinking about doing a dithering project for this book after coming across an article by John Earnest on Atkinson dithering on Hacker News.[11] I decided that the dithering algorithm on its own was too simple for a book chapter, but then I had an idea: the MacPaint format that I had recently become so interested in was also a product of Bill Atkinson, and it includes another interesting algorithm, run-length encoding. Why don't I combine the two into a single project?

I didn't stop there. After writing the code for this chapter, I decided I should make MacPaint more accessible to modern Mac users. I ported the code, plus some additional dithering algorithms, to Swift and created a nice AppKit-based user interface around it. I sell the software as Retro Dither on the Mac App Store.[12] As a technical author, usually things you do as professional or hobby projects turn into material for a book; it's not that usual that things go the other way.

Real-World Applications

Atkinson dithering and MacPaint were just a couple of the technologies that Bill Atkinson used to make graphics on the original Macintosh come alive. He was also the creator of QuickDraw, which provided the graphics primitives on all Lisa and classic Macintosh computers. His immense contributions go far beyond graphics too. He made several refinements to elements that we now consider as standard widgets in a GUI. Atkinson was also the creator of HyperCard, one of the first widely distributed hypertext platforms. You can think about it as a non-networked version of the web from the late 1980s. It was very influential.

You might be curious to know what Bill Atkinson originally developed Atkinson dithering for. I was too, so I obtained a copy of a rare book called *Inside MacPaint* by Jeffrey S. Young and published by Microsoft Press in 1985. I didn't exactly find my answer, but I found a probable answer. It turns out Atkinson had worked on a digitizer for the early Macintosh. It's basically a kind of scanner that allowed you to work with real-world images in MacPaint. While the book doesn't explicitly say it used Atkinson dithering, I can't imagine that it's a coincidence. It's likely that the first real-world application of Atkinson dithering was a digitizer.

Dithering was a widely used technique on 1980s and 1990s game consoles and computers, which were powerful enough to support digital images but often had a limited color palette. And limited-palette devices like the Amazon Kindle and the Panic Playdate continue to be dithering strongholds. As mentioned earlier, dithering is also how animated GIFs appear to show many more colors than they naturally support. Without hacks, a GIF is limited to 256 colors.

Run-length encoding isn't limited to MacPaint, of course. It's a widely used compression technique. Any kind of data format that has a lot of repeated characters is a candidate for run-length encoding. Beyond MacPaint, it was used as the main compression technique in several other bitmap image formats of the 1980s. It's also sometimes combined with other compression techniques to formulate more sophisticated meta-algorithms. For example, one component of DEFLATE, the algorithm used in ZIP files, utilizes run-length encoding.

I'll leave you with a quote from Bill Atkinson, from an interview he did in *Inside MacPaint*. He was asked by Jeffrey Young, "What do you consider essential for creating a great program?"

> The whole trick to designing a good program is deciding what things to kick out. I had some powerful features that I kicked out to make MacPaint cleaner, simpler, more approachable, and less frightening. I probably threw away more code than I left in. My goal was a lean, mean, and clean design. The typical programming process is 95 percent debugging and only 5 percent real creation. A lot of the bugs are simple typos, or just things that a compiler program can really help you with. I like to keep my sights focused more on the overall algorithm, because that's where I get the big wins.

I compare programming to modeling with clay. When you're throwing a pot on the wheel, you want to keep it soft and flexible as long as you can before you fire it. Because after you fire it, the pot is a lot harder to scrape into shape.[13]

Exercises

1. Add a command line option that changes our program to use Floyd-Steinberg dithering.
2. Try creating an error-diffusion dithering pattern of your own.
3. Write a program that can go the other way, converting a MacPaint file into a GIF or PNG.
4. If you completed Exercise 3, write integration tests that check that a MacPaint file converted to a GIF or PNG retains the same pixel data as the original.

Notes

1. Erik Sandberg-Diment, "Software for the Macintosh: Plenty on the Way," *New York Times*, January 31, 1984.
2. See *https://archive.org/details/mac_Paint_2*.
3. "Technical Note PT24: MacPaint Document Format," Apple, October 1, 1988, accessed August 5, 2022, *https://web.archive.org/web/20040626093131/http://developer.apple.com/technotes/pt/pt_24.html*.
4. See *https://www.fileformat.info/format/macpaint/egff.htm*.
5. See *https://en.wikipedia.org/wiki/PackBits*.
6. "Technical Note TN1023: Understanding PackBits," Apple, November 1, 1987, accessed August 4, 2022, *https://web.archive.org/web/20030218001420/http://developer.apple.com/technotes/tn/tn1023.html*.
7. "MacBinary II Standard," Stairways.com, July 24, 1987, accessed May 27, 2024, *https://files.stairways.com/other/macbinaryii-standard-info.txt*.
8. See *https://en.wikipedia.org/wiki/Mac_OS_Roman*.
9. See *https://www.gryphel.com/c/minivmac/index.html*.
10. See *https://en.wikipedia.org/wiki/Robert_W._Fichter*.
11. John Earnest, "Atkinson Dithering," *Beyond Loom*, March 29, 2020, *https://beyondloom.com/blog/dither.html*.
12. See *https://oaksnow.com/retrodither/*.
13. Jeffrey S. Young, *Inside MacPaint: Sailing Through the Sea of FatBits on a Single-Pixel Raft* (Microsoft Press, 1985), 320.

4

A STOCHASTIC PAINTING ALGORITHM

All the other chapters in this book follow a specification such as a programming language grammar, a file format, or a machine architecture. This chapter is different. In this chapter, we're going to create art. And it's going to be subjective. Can a simple stochastic algorithm use randomly generated shapes to create drawings that resemble human works of art? I think the answer is yes, but you'll have to judge for yourself after you see some of the program's output.

How It Works

This chapter's program works by trying to redraw a photograph from scratch. We begin with a blank canvas. We try drawing a single randomly sized and placed colored shape. If the shape brings the canvas to look more similar to the photograph, then we keep it. Otherwise, we try a different shape. We repeat this process for some specified number of iterations. That's the whole algorithm.

If it sounds simple, that's because it is. Of course, there are many more complex details to fill in, but they don't change the overarching thrust of the program. How is "looking similar" measured? Should a shape be modified to try to improve its fit? How is the color of the shape selected? What kinds of shapes should be used?

That last question will lead to many different abstract looks for our "paintings." For example, Figure 4-1 utilizes ellipses to approximate a photograph of a hot air balloon. (For print readers, see the *figures* directory of the companion repository for color versions of the chapter's images.)

Figure 4-1: A hot air balloon with 540 ellipses

The figure shows both the original photograph and an "impression" created by our program using 540 ellipses over 100,000 iterations, which took 104 seconds to complete on my laptop. I think it looks pretty good. Almost impressionistic.

In my opinion, ellipses give a kind of stained-glass look. It helps if the shape used somewhat resembles the contours of the subject in the original photograph, like ellipses for the hot air balloon. Figure 4-2 shows the same photograph painted using 307 triangles over 100,000 iterations, taking 109 seconds on my laptop. In my subjective opinion, it doesn't look as good.

Figure 4-2: A hot air balloon with 307 triangles

While the hot air balloon's curvaceous exterior doesn't get filled well by triangles, a butterfly does much better. Figure 4-3 is an impression of a photo of a butterfly, using 573 triangles generated with 1 million iterations over 4,512 seconds.

Figure 4-3: A butterfly with 573 triangles

The butterfly image took a bit longer to generate than the average million-iteration image because I used the "most common color" method instead of the "average color" method—more on that in a bit. The result is that the colors in each shape are sharper and blend together less.

The output can often be improved by utilizing more shapes placed over more iterations, and hence more time. However, since this is based on a stochastic (randomly determined) process, the results will vary greatly—even with the same settings for the same picture. The examples I'm presenting here are cherry-picked.

Photographs with a lot of detail take the most time to paint with a reasonable degree of accuracy. With a tool like this, you have to strike a balance between abstraction and recognizability. If an image is too abstract, it won't be recognizable. But if an image has so much detail that it's almost a perfect replica of the original, then it will lose its appeal as a "work of art." This balance is particularly hard to achieve with images of people. For example, Figure 4-4 is an image of two of my friends on a beach in Santa Monica, California. It's composed of 4,212 ellipses generated with 10 million iterations over 8,262 seconds. My friends look only okay as abstract impressions, but the beach looks great!

Figure 4-4: A Santa Monica scene with 4,212 ellipses

I've found that using a line shape works really well for creating paintings of people. Because lines are so thin, many more of them are needed to draw an image. Figure 4-5 shows a tiny public domain image of John F. Kennedy giving his famous speech in Berlin, along with a painted version using 16,633 lines generated with 10 million iterations over 6,957 seconds.

Figure 4-5: JFK's Berlin speech with 16,633 lines

An interesting aspect of the JFK example is that the program-produced abstract version actually has a higher resolution than the original. This is possible because the program is working in the world of vector graphics, where math determines the output, not pixels. The algorithm isn't assiduously copying every pixel—it's providing an "impression" of the original with vector shapes.

Lines produce some of the most stunning abstract results. Figure 4-6 is a New York City skyline with the Manhattan Bridge in front via 12,303 lines generated with 1 million iterations over 909 seconds.

Figure 4-6: The New York City skyline with 12,303 lines

The program developed in this chapter will take a long time to run if you want it to utilize a high number of shapes. For example, the JFK image took almost two hours to run for me on my Apple M1–based laptop. Your mileage will vary depending on your machine's particular microprocessor. You can generally leave the program running in the background while you do your other work.

Command Line Options

This is a very configurable program with many different features and tweakable parameters. In addition to input and output filepaths, our `ArgumentParser` needs to handle all the command line options in Table 4-1.

Table 4-1: Command Line Options for Impressionist

Option	Extended	Possibilities	Default	Description
-t	--trials	Integer	10000	The number of trials to run
-m	--method	'random', 'average', 'common'	'average'	The method for determining shape colors
-s	--shape	'ellipse', 'triangle', 'quadrilateral', 'line'	'ellipse'	The shape type to use
-l	--length	Integer	256	The length (height) of the final image in pixels

(continued)

Table 4-1: Command Line Options for Impressionist *(continued)*

Option	Extended	Possibilities	Default	Description
-v	--vector	Boolean	False	Create vector output?
-a	--animate	Integer	0	If a number greater than 0 is provided, will create an animated GIF with the provided number of milliseconds per frame, showing the image being built up one shape at a time

Our main file is just a codification of Table 4-1. All the options are passed to the constructor of the Impressionist class, which we'll come back to in a bit.

```python
# Impressionist/__main__.py
from argparse import ArgumentParser
from Impressionist.impressionist import Impressionist, ColorMethod, ShapeType


if __name__ == "__main__":
    # Parse the file argument
    argument_parser = ArgumentParser("Impressionist")
    argument_parser.add_argument("image_file", help="The input image")
    argument_parser.add_argument("output_file", help="The resulting abstract art")
    argument_parser.add_argument('-t', '--trials', type=int, default=10000,
                                 help='The number of trials to run (default 10000).')
    argument_parser.add_argument('-m', '--method',
                                 choices=['random', 'average', 'common'], default='average',
                                 help='Shape color determination method (default average).')
    argument_parser.add_argument('-s', '--shape', choices=['ellipse', 'triangle',
                                                           'quadrilateral', 'line'],
                                 default='ellipse', help='The shape type (default ellipse).')
    argument_parser.add_argument('-l', '--length', type=int, default=256,
                                 help='The length of the final image in pixels (default 256).')
    argument_parser.add_argument('-v', '--vector', default=False, action='store_true',
                                 help='Create vector output. A SVG file will also be output.')
    argument_parser.add_argument('-a', '--animate', type=int, default=0,
                                 help='If greater than 0, will create an animated GIF '
                                      'with the number of milliseconds per frame provided.')
    arguments = argument_parser.parse_args()
    method = ColorMethod[arguments.method.upper()]
    shape_type = ShapeType[arguments.shape.upper()]
    Impressionist(arguments.image_file, arguments.output_file, arguments.trials, method,
                  shape_type, arguments.length, arguments.vector, arguments.animate)
```

The -v option instructs the program to output the result in a vector format. In our implementation, we'll target an SVG file. Before we get into the main algorithm of the application, let's take a little detour to see how we can support this feature.

The SVG Format

SVG stands for Scalable Vector Graphics. It's an XML-based format for specifying vector images. All modern mainstream web browsers and vector drawing programs support it. Instead of using a third-party library to write to SVG, we'll write our own short class to do it. The SVG specification is large, but we only need a small subset of it to support the shapes that our program will output, so the task will be relatively easy.

XML is a text-based format, and since we're outputting it, not parsing it, we don't even need our program to really understand XML's structure. We just need to amalgamate a string out of other strings representing the constituent XML elements. While this approach limits the testability and modularity of our SVG writer, the amount of the SVG standard we're implementing is so small that it's almost trivial to hand check for correctness. That said, this approach isn't production suitable.

Before we get into the code, here's an example of a simple SVG file that our program can output. This one has just one triangle built using the polygon element, plus the background rectangle (I've slightly improved the formatting with a couple of indentations for readability):

```
<?xml version="1.0" encoding="utf-8"?>
<svg version="1.1" baseProfile="full" width="342" height="256"
xmlns="http://www.w3.org/2000/svg">
    <rect width="100%" height="100%" fill="rgb(108, 98, 91)" />
    <polygon points="201,3 24,9 162,182 " fill="rgb(128, 120, 112)" />
</svg>
```

If you save this code in a text file with the *.svg* extension, you can open it using a web browser or vector image editor to see the resulting triangle. As we walk through creating our SVG class, keep this example in mind to visualize how the different elements come together to form a complete SVG file.

An SVG file starts with a declaration that it's an XML file, and then the first element is an svg element that describes the version of the SVG specification and the width and height of the image. In addition, every image our program generates is backed by a big rectangle containing the average color of the image. This helps the algorithm blend better. Our SVG file therefore also starts with a big rect element:

```python
# Impressionist/svg.py
class SVG:
    def __init__(self, width: int, height: int, background_color: tuple[int, int, int]):
        self.content = '<?xml version="1.0" encoding="utf-8"?>\n' \
                       f'<svg version="1.1" baseProfile="full" width="{width}" ' \
                       f'height="{height}" xmlns="http://www.w3.org/2000/svg">\n' \
                       f'<rect width="100%" height="100%" fill="rgb{background_color}" />'
```

As the `background_color` property in the constructor indicates, colors are being represented using a tuple of three integers. These are RGB color codes. Each element is an integer between 0 and 255 representing the amount of the respective primary color (red, green, or blue) in the output. For example, a "pure" red color would be (255, 0, 0), and a purple would be something like (128, 0, 128), being a blend of red and blue.

Drawing the three types of shapes that our program supports (ellipses, lines, and polygons) is just a matter of putting the respective ellipse, line, or polygon SVG elements into the output text file:

```python
def draw_ellipse(self, x1: int, y1: int, x2: int, y2: int, color: tuple[int, int, int]):
    self.content += f'<ellipse cx="{(x1 + x2) // 2}" cy="{(y1 + y2) // 2}" ' \
                    f'rx="{abs(x1 - x2) // 2}" ry="{abs(y1 - y2) // 2}" ' \
                    f'fill="rgb{color}" />\n'

def draw_line(self, x1: int, y1: int, x2: int, y2: int, color: tuple[int, int, int]):
    self.content += f'<line x1="{x1}" y1="{y1}" x2="{x2}" y2="{y2}" stroke="rgb{color}" ' \
                    'stroke-width="1px" shape-rendering="crispEdges" />\n'

def draw_polygon(self, coordinates: list[int], color: tuple[int, int, int]):
    points = ""
    for index in range(0, len(coordinates), 2):
        points += f"{coordinates[index]},{coordinates[index + 1]} "
    self.content += f'<polygon points="{points}" fill="rgb{color}" />\n'
```

Finally, to output the SVG file, we close the svg element begun in the constructor and write the amalgamated string to disk:

```python
def write(self, path: str):
    self.content += '</svg>\n'
    with open(path, 'w') as f:
        f.write(self.content)
```

If you take a look at the official SVG specification, you may find it overwhelming, but there's no need to be intimidated. As this section hopefully shows, it doesn't necessarily take much to get value out of a big standard like SVG. In just 20 lines of code, we've written a very limited, but useful, SVG creator.

The Algorithm

The algorithm that produces these (sometimes) beautiful abstract impressions of photographs is remarkably simple. In short, it tries drawing randomly sized and placed shapes, one shape at a time. If an added shape makes the abstract image look more like the original photo, it's kept. The improvement is potentially further refined by resizing the shape, which is a matter of moving each of its points. If the added shape makes the image look less like the original photo, then it's thrown away and a new shape is tried.

Here's a more detailed explanation of the algorithm in steps:

1. Create a blank canvas with the same size as the original photograph and a background color that's the same as the original photograph's average color.

2. Try drawing a shape on the canvas in a random location and of a random size. Color the shape using the average color of the corresponding region of the original photograph, the most common color of that region, or randomly.

3. Compare the colors of the pixels of the canvas (with the added shape) to the original photograph. If the added shape has made the whole canvas's pixels more similar to the original photograph's pixels, then keep the added shape.

4. Try modifying the shape at each point (expanding or contracting) one pixel at a time. Keep moving the points in directions that further reduce the difference between the whole canvas's pixels and the original photograph's pixels. Stop when the movement no longer improves the difference.

5. Repeat steps 2, 3, and 4 trials number of times.

6. Output the final image created on the canvas after trials number of experiments.

There are many configurable parameters of this algorithm. What kind of shape should be used? How many trials should be run? How should the color for each shape be picked? And there are several subproblems to solve. How is the difference between two images calculated? How do you find the pixels in a region that encompasses a shape?

The Main Implementation

Excluding comments, the main implementation of our painting algorithm is less than 150 lines of Python. A lot of that succinctness is thanks to the powerful Pillow library, which was already discussed in Chapter 3. Pillow handles reading and writing various bitmap image formats. It also has facilities for drawing simple primitives like the shapes we need. Finally, Pillow has functions for computing differences between images and computing the average color in a region of an image. These will be critical helper functions for our program, allowing us to concentrate on the core algorithm while leaving the busywork to Pillow. That's what a great library enables.

Setup

We begin with some basic imports, the definition of some needed types, a constant, and a helper function:

Impressionist/
impressionist.py

```
from enum import Enum
from PIL import Image, ImageDraw
```

```
from PIL import ImageChops, ImageStat
import random
from math import trunc
from timeit import default_timer as timer
from Impressionist.svg import SVG

ColorMethod = Enum("ColorMethod", "RANDOM AVERAGE COMMON")
ShapeType = Enum("ShapeType", "ELLIPSE TRIANGLE QUADRILATERAL LINE")
CoordList = list[int]
MAX_HEIGHT = 256

def get_most_common_color(image: Image.Image) -> tuple[int, int, int]:
    colors = image.getcolors(image.width * image.height)
    return max(colors, key=lambda item: item[0])[1]
```

The ColorMethod enum controls how we'll calculate the color in a region—that is, what color a shape will be filled with. The ShapeType enum sets the shape we'll be drawing. The current version of the program only draws one type of shape in each painting, but it would be easy to modify the code to enable more than one type of shape. I've left that for an exercise. The CoordList type applies to the coordinates that define one shape.

When running the algorithm, for performance, we need to work with a limited number of total pixels. The easiest way to accomplish this is to scale the input image if it's taller than MAX_HEIGHT. In other words, MAX_HEIGHT is the maximum height of the scaled image. Note that, technically, we should also define a maximum width, but in practice, it's very rare for an image's aspect ratio to be such that only capping one dimension will be insufficient (there aren't many images that are super wide but have very little height). For simplicity, we just defined the one maximum dimension.

The get_most_common_color() method figures out the most frequently occurring color in an image. It uses a Pillow method, getcolors(), which returns all of the colors in an image along with their counts. Then, it uses Python's built-in max() function to extract the most frequent.

The Impressionist class's constructor is responsible for setting up the unique parameters of a particular run of the algorithm, opening the input image file, scaling it, creating the initial background of the output image, calling methods to run the actual iterations of the algorithm, and calling a method to output the final file. That may sound like a lot, but the heart of the algorithm is in other methods. The constructor is just a launching point that calls methods from the Pillow library and other methods we'll get to shortly to do the actual work. Here's the start of the constructor:

```
class Impressionist:
    def __init__(self, file_name: str, output_file: str, trials: int, method: ColorMethod,
                 shape_type: ShapeType, length: int, vector: bool, animation_length: int):
        self.method = method
        self.shape_type = shape_type
        self.shapes = []
        # Open image file and store in instance variable, execute algorithm
        with open(file_name, "rb") as fp:
```

```
self.original = Image.open(fp).convert('RGB')
# Scale down image so processing is faster, 256 max height pixel dimension
width, height = self.original.size
aspect_ratio = width / height
new_size = (int(MAX_HEIGHT * aspect_ratio), MAX_HEIGHT)
self.original.thumbnail(new_size, Image.Resampling.LANCZOS)
```

The constructor starts by setting up some parameters and scaling the input image. The resulting painting should have the same aspect ratio as the original image, so the aspect ratio is preserved. Pillow's thumbnail() method is a convenient way to do scaling.

Here's the next part of the constructor:

```
# Start the generated image with a background that is the
# average of all the original's pixels in color
average_color = tuple((round(n) for n in ImageStat.Stat(self.original).mean))
self.glass = Image.new("RGB", new_size, average_color)
```

The Pillow ImageStat module can be used for finding the average color in an image. It looks at the RGB values of every pixel in the image and averages the red, green, and blue components separately. We take the resulting average color and set it as the background of our algorithm's working image (self.glass). In other words, the average color of the original image will be the starting color of every pixel in the working image.

NOTE *The variable for the working image is named glass because I originally called this program Stained Glass. After retitling it, I still feel that the name glass for the variable explains that this is a surface that's providing a filtered impression of the original.*

The constructor continues:

```
# Keep track of how far along we are, our best result so far, and
# how much time elapses as the processing takes place
self.best_difference = self.difference(self.glass)
last_percent = 0
start = timer()
for test in range(trials):
    self.trial()
    percent = trunc(test / trials * 100)
    if percent > last_percent:
        last_percent = percent
        print(f"{percent}% Done, Best Difference {self.best_difference}")
end = timer()
print(f"{end-start} seconds elapsed. {len(self.shapes)} shapes created.")
self.create_output(output_file, length, vector, animation_length)
```

The heart of the algorithm is in the trial() method, which tries drawing a shape to see if the shape improves on the similarity score between the working image and the original image. Here, trial() is called trials number of times. As the trials are executed, we keep track of how close to done we are and how much time the program is taking. Finally, the completed working image is output with the help of create_output().

Utility Methods

Before we get to trial(), we need some helper methods. A key part of the painting algorithm is verifying that each additional shape is bringing the working image closer to the original image. The difference() method calculates a similarity score for two images, measuring how similar they are to each other:

```
def difference(self, other_image: Image.Image) -> float:
    diff = ImageChops.difference(self.original, other_image)
    stat = ImageStat.Stat(diff)
    diff_ratio = sum(stat.mean) / (len(stat.mean) * 255)
    return diff_ratio
```

The ImageChops module from Pillow has a built-in difference() method. It finds the difference on a pixel-by-pixel level between two images. In other words, how are two pixels in the same locations in the two images different from each other? The difference is just the absolute values of the subtraction of each of the color channels in each pixel. For example, the difference between an RGB pixel that's colored (10, 100, 50) and another that's (10, 40, 20) would be (0, 60, 30). However, this isn't enough for our algorithm. We need a single number, a score, that expresses how similar two images are. After finding the difference pixel by pixel, we can compress this into a single number by averaging across all of the differences. We do this using the same ImageStat module that did the averaging for us to find the average color in the constructor. Finally, although not strictly necessary (pixel averages would work as scores), we divide by the maximum difference possible to get the score as a ratio.

Each time we generate a new shape it's placed in a random location on the screen. We calculate these random coordinates using random_coordinates():

```
def random_coordinates(self) -> CoordList:
    num_coordinates = 4  # ellipse or line
    if self.shape_type == ShapeType.TRIANGLE:
        num_coordinates = 6
    elif self.shape_type == ShapeType.QUADRILATERAL:
        num_coordinates = 8
    coordinates = []
    for d in range(num_coordinates):
        if d % 2 == 0:  # x coordinates
            coordinates.append(random.randint(0, self.original.width))
        else:  # y coordinates
            coordinates.append(random.randint(0, self.original.height))
    return coordinates
```

Different kinds of shapes need different numbers of coordinates. For example, a triangle has six coordinates because it has three points, and each point has one x-coordinate and one y-coordinate. The coordinates must be valid—that is, they must be somewhere on the surface of the image. The method enforces this by ensuring that the random coordinates can't be below 0 or above the width or height of the image.

We also need a way to look at a "region" of the original photograph corresponding to a shape in the working image, so we can analyze the color of that region. It would be computationally expensive to find the exact pixels below an arbitrary shape. Instead, we'll use a bounding_box() static method to identify a rectangular region that encompasses the shape:

```
@staticmethod
def bounding_box(coordinates: CoordList) -> tuple[int, int, int, int]:
    xcoords = coordinates[::2]
    ycoords = coordinates[1::2]
    x1 = min(xcoords)
    y1 = min(ycoords)
    x2 = max(xcoords)
    y2 = max(ycoords)
    return x1, y1, x2, y2
```

A *bounding box* is an axis-aligned rectangle (meaning its edges are parallel to the edges of the image) around a given shape, determined based on that shape's minimum and maximum x- and y-coordinates. We'll pass that rectangle to Pillow's built-in crop() method to crop the original image down to just the desired region. We'll leave alternative techniques for extracting a more narrowly defined region of the original image for the exercises.

Trials

The heart of the algorithm is the trial() method. Each trial is an attempt to place one shape in the working image. If the new shape brings the working image closer to the original, it's kept. If the difference score can be further improved by nudging its coordinates, the coordinates of the shape are nudged. The method begins by finding a place for the new shape using random_coordinates() and finding the backing region of those coordinates:

```
def trial(self):
    while True:
        coordinates = self.random_coordinates()
        region = self.original.crop(self.bounding_box(coordinates))
        if region.width > 0 and region.height > 0:
            break
```

There's an ugly while loop here to account for the unlikely scenario where the random coordinates are all aligned along either axis. In that case, we need to regenerate the coordinates. There's an exercise at the end of the chapter to excise this loop. The next part of the method chooses a color for the shape:

```
if self.method == ColorMethod.AVERAGE:
    color = tuple((round(n) for n in ImageStat.Stat(region).mean))
elif self.method == ColorMethod.COMMON:
    color = get_most_common_color(region)
else:  # must be random
    color = tuple(random.choices(range(256), k=3))
original = self.glass
```

Depending on the ColorMethod, we select the average color in the backing region (once again using ImageStat), select the most common color in the backing region, or simply choose a random color. Then, we preserve the current state of the working image (self.glass) in a local variable, original, to be reused in the case that coordinate nudges are tried (we try redrawing the shape a little bigger or a little smaller in various directions, so we need the original canvas it was drawn on). Now we're ready to try drawing a shape:

```
def experiment() -> bool:
    new_image = original.copy()
    glass_draw = ImageDraw.Draw(new_image)
    if self.shape_type == ShapeType.ELLIPSE:
        glass_draw.ellipse(self.bounding_box(coordinates), fill=color)
    else:  # must be triangle or quadrilateral or line
        glass_draw.polygon(coordinates, fill=color)
    new_difference = self.difference(new_image)
    if new_difference < self.best_difference:
        self.best_difference = new_difference
        self.glass = new_image
        return True
    return False
```

An inner function, experiment(), returns True if an attempt to draw a new shape is successful in terms of lowering the difference between the working image and the original image. The ImageDraw module in Pillow takes care of the actual drawing. The difference is calculated using the previously defined difference() method and compared against the best difference found so far. If the shape has improved the image, the working image is replaced with the image including the new shape.

The last part of trial() tries to make incremental improvements to each shape by nudging its coordinates. If a nudge improves the difference score compared to the version of the working image with the shape's original coordinates, then the nudge is kept and another nudge is attempted in the same direction:

```
if experiment():
    # Try expanding every direction, keep going in better directions
    for index in range(len(coordinates)):
        for amount in (-1, 1):
            while True:
```

```
            old_coordinates = coordinates.copy()
            coordinates[index] = coordinates[index] + amount
            if not experiment():
                coordinates = old_coordinates
                break
    self.shapes.append((coordinates, color))
```

This code is a kind of *hill climbing algorithm*, where we keep going in the same direction to solve a problem (in this case, optimizing for difference) as long as the solution continues to improve. We stop when it stops improving. This may lead to a local maximum, but it's a simple and effective way to improve on an existing solution. In this instance, we have an existing solution because we only keep shapes that improved on the difference to begin with (indicated by experiment() returning True). See the "Hill Climbing" box for more on how this type of algorithm works.

The overall algorithm would work without the nudging process, but the nudging improves the fit of each shape. This, in turn, improves the overall look of the final painting and reduces the number of shapes necessary to get to a reasonable result.

Once the final shape is set after any nudging, we add its coordinates and color to the shapes list. Maintaining this list, separate from drawing the shapes in the working image, is necessary for generating the final output.

HILL CLIMBING

Hill climbing is a simple optimization technique that aims to find the maximum or minimum of a function by continually going in the same direction while the search seems to be "improving." In the classic explanation of this technique, you're asked to imagine that you're wearing a blindfold and standing at the bottom of a hill that you want to climb. You can feel with your feet the gradient of the ground around you. With each step, whatever direction seems to yield the steepest upward slope will feel like the way that you should go if you want to get up the hill the fastest. You can keep choosing to go up in this direction as long as you can feel with your feet that you're climbing. Eventually you'll reach a point where you're no longer climbing no matter the direction of your next step, and then you can stop.

Will you have reached the top of the hill? It's certainly possible, especially if the hill has a single peak. But it's also possible the hill has multiple peaks and you just reached one of the smaller ones. That's called getting caught in a *local maximum*. Hill climbing will always find a local maximum, but it may not find a global maximum.

Hill climbing is a popular technique in artificial intelligence because it is so simple. It's a good starting point for many problems. In our program, we keep nudging coordinates in the same direction until the difference with the starting image is no longer improving. This is a type of hill climbing: we just keep going

(continued)

in the same direction until things aren't getting better. Of course, it's possible the placement of the shape was a mistake to begin with compared to some other alternative placement, and our nudging is just leading us down a rabbit hole toward a local maximum. With such a simple algorithm, there's no way to know for sure.

Output

The working image was scaled to MAX_HEIGHT, but the final output image should have the user-specified height (again, for simplification, we let the user just set the height and not the width). We can't simply "stretch" a bitmap without pixelation. Instead, we redraw the working image using the data in the shapes list, with each shape scaled appropriately. The method for outputting the image also incorporates options for outputting a vector file (making use of the SVG class from earlier) and outputting an animated GIF via Pillow. This adds significantly to its length. Here's the start of create_output():

```
def create_output(self, out_file: str, height: int, vector: bool, animation_length: int):
    average_color = tuple((round(n) for n in ImageStat.Stat(self.original).mean))
    original_width, original_height = self.original.size
    ratio = height / original_height
    output_size = (int(original_width * ratio), int(original_height * ratio))
    output_image = Image.new("RGB", output_size, average_color)
    output_draw = ImageDraw.Draw(output_image)
```

We begin by creating a new image of the appropriate size based on the user-specified height parameter. We fill the initial output image with the average color of the original image as was done for the working image. The method continues:

```
    svg = SVG(*output_size, average_color) if vector else None
    animation_frames = [] if animation_length > 0 else None
    for coordinate_list, color in self.shapes:
❶       coordinates = [int(x * ratio) for x in coordinate_list]
```

The output image will be generated by iteratively reproducing each shape in the shapes list at the right scale ❶. To also create SVG or animated GIF output, as the output image is generated, each step will be repeated on the svg object or copied as a picture to a list of animation_frames that make up the animated GIF "movie":

```
        if self.shape_type == ShapeType.ELLIPSE:
            output_draw.ellipse(self.bounding_box(coordinates), fill=color)
            if svg:
                svg.draw_ellipse(*coordinates, color)  # type: ignore
        else:  # must be triangle or quadrilateral or line
            output_draw.polygon(coordinates, fill=color)
            if svg:
                if self.shape_type == ShapeType.LINE:
                    svg.draw_line(*coordinates, color)  # type: ignore
                else:
                    svg.draw_polygon(coordinates, color)
        if animation_frames is not None:
            animation_frames.append(output_image.copy())
    output_image.save(out_file)
    if svg:
        svg.write(out_file + ".svg")
    if animation_frames is not None:
        animation_frames[0].save(out_file + ".gif", save_all=True,
                                 append_images=animation_frames[1:], optimize=False,
                                 duration=animation_length, loop=0,
                                 transparency=0, disposal=2)
```

The rest of the method is just drawing the shapes on the output image(s) and writing the file(s) to disk.

The Results

There's a lot packed into those 150 lines of code. The program features stochastic trials, a couple insights into how to make an educated guess about the color of each shape, a little bit of hill climbing, and the use of a good library. Cool results in computer science are so much more about the algorithm and the technique than the number of lines of code. But this algorithm is also surprisingly simple—yet extremely effective. No, the output isn't quite as impressive as the latest neural network, but it's amazing how far a simple technique can take a program.

The main downside of this algorithm is that it's slow and random. You can try the same image multiple times with the same parameters and get different results. And you might wait a long time to get those varying, sometimes bad results.

However, I have some impressive, although admittedly cherry-picked, results to share with you. The first are a couple scenes from Touro Park in Newport, Rhode Island. I like how the line shape gives almost an oil painting–like feel to each of them. Figure 4-7 is a broad view of the park with the famous Newport Tower on the right.

Figure 4-7: Touro Park with 19,578 lines

Figure 4-8 is a closer view of Newport Tower.

Figure 4-8: Newport Tower with 11,409 lines

Figure 4-9 shows a cat that I found rolling on the pavement. The ellipse shape gives the cat a nice abstract look. Could this be the work of an impressionist painter?

Figure 4-9: A cat rolling on pavement with ellipses

Finally, I present a scene from Halloween in Figure 4-10.

Figure 4-10: A Halloween scene with ellipses

My son and I were running through a public display of pumpkins. I like how the gourds and people in the background came out using ellipses.

when I was coming up with the projects for this book, I remembered it. I think it's a great illustration of the power of random algorithms and hill climbing.

After I ported my Swift code to Python for this book, I decided to test it out on my friends by posting on Facebook a picture of my one-year-old son, Daniel, on a swing.

My aunt, who has quite a trained artistic eye, thought I had taken up painting. That was when I knew the program was pretty good.

Real-World Applications

Beyond looking kind of cool, the output of this program doesn't have a lot of practical applications. However, the techniques that were used to build it certainly do. They fall under an umbrella term known as *stochastic optimization*. Suppose you have an optimization problem you want to solve, but you don't know of a deterministic algorithm (an algorithm that gives the same result every time by following the same steps every time) to solve it. In that case, a technique that involves random (stochastic) trials may be warranted.

It may not be abundantly clear, but the challenge in this chapter is an example of an optimization problem. Our program tries to optimize for a drawing that's as close to the original photograph as possible. The objective function (the thing that checks if we're going in the right direction) is the difference() method. The lower the difference, the more optimal the potential solution to the problem that a particular image represents.

One famous practical area where stochastic optimization algorithms are useful is the classic traveling salesperson problem. The problem calls for a traveler to visit every specified location on a map exactly once and return to their starting point using the shortest route possible. It's what delivery trucks (think FedEx or UPS) do every day, so it has a very practical application. Unfortunately, there's no known deterministic algorithm for solving the traveling salesperson problem optimally for a large number of locations in a reasonable amount of time. Instead, stochastic optimization techniques such as genetic algorithms provide a useful way to solve the problem, but their solutions may be suboptimal. A genetic algorithm may not always yield a perfect solution to the traveling salesperson problem, but it will almost always yield a solution that's good enough.

Our program also utilized hill climbing. Although this is one of the simplest local search procedures (just keep going in the same direction if that direction is working), it's a very common technique, and it performs as well as more advanced techniques in many scenarios. Hill climbing also forms the basis for other, more sophisticated algorithms. For example, the simplex algorithm for solving linear programming problems utilizes hill climbing.[2]

Exercises

1. Modify the program to draw more than one type of shape in the same painting. For example, it could create a drawing with both ellipses and triangles in the final output.

2. Since the pixels used to calculate the color for a new shape are based on a bounding box and not the exact area underneath the shape, the results are inaccurate. Modify trial() to experiment with not only coordinate nudges but also color nudges. This may lead to a better-matching color.

3. Modify trial() to use the exact pixels underneath a shape to determine that shape's color. This is challenging. One way to do it would be to use some geometric calculations to determine the right pixels for each type of shape. This will likely be much less computationally efficient than simply cropping the bounding box as the original program does. Consider instead using the mask facilities in Pillow.

4. The while True loop at the beginning of trial() feels like a code smell. Rewrite the beginning of trial() without it.

Notes

1. Michael Fogleman, "Primitive," accessed January 9, 2023, *https://www.michaelfogleman.com/#primitive.*

2. Steven S. Skiena, "Combinatorial Search and Heuristic Methods," in *Algorithm Design Manual,* 2nd ed. (Springer, 2008), 252–253.

PART III

EMULATORS

5

BUILDING A CHIP-8 VIRTUAL MACHINE

In this chapter, we're going to develop a version of a virtual machine known as CHIP-8, a platform from the early days of personal computing that was primarily used for playing games. Although our program will be able to play CHIP-8 games, it's not the games themselves that interest us—it's what building a CHIP-8 virtual machine can teach us about low-level programming and how a computer works at the register and instruction levels. These insights make building a CHIP-8 virtual machine a popular first step into the world of programming emulators.

Virtual Machines

Think of a *virtual machine (VM)* as a computer that's defined wholly in software. Programs that are designed to run in a VM can run on any platform that has an implementation of that VM. In this way, VMs enable truly portable software.

VMs are closely related to emulators. An *emulator* is a piece of software that's pretending to be a piece of hardware. This enables programs that were written for that hardware to run on other machines that lack the hardware. An emulator must follow the specification for the original hardware carefully so that it re-creates all the functionality that the unknowing programs running on the emulator expect. I say *unknowing* because the software running on an emulator has no idea it isn't running on the real hardware; the emulator had better work exactly like the original hardware if the program is going to function correctly.

A VM is also a piece of software that closely follows a specification of an environment that software runs on top of. The difference is that while an emulator follows a hardware specification, a VM follows a specification that may be wholly defined as an abstraction in software terms.

Although one is a hardware specification and one is a software specification, implementing a simple emulator is quite similar to implementing a simple VM. In fact, they're so similar that while the project completed in this chapter is technically a VM project, it's very commonly suggested as a first emulation project. If you're a newcomer to the emulator development community asking where you should start, CHIP-8 is almost always the answer.

Perhaps the most famous VM is the Java Virtual Machine (JVM). When Java first came out in the mid-1990s, its "write once, run anywhere" philosophy was touted. JVMs were developed for all major operating systems (Windows, Linux, Mac OS, and so on), and the same Java program could be compiled into the JVM's native bytecode format and run on any computer with a JVM unchanged, regardless of the underlying platform. That's still true today, but Java's original write-once-run-anywhere niche has largely been supplanted by web applications.

The CHIP-8 VM comes from a much earlier era. In the 1970s, Joseph Weisbecker was a pioneering engineer who developed one of the first 8-bit microprocessors, the RCA 1802. He and RCA built an early personal computer using his invention.[1] He wanted to have a way to program games for the machine in a higher-level language than machine code, so he developed CHIP-8 (and its accompanying opcode language). His daughter, Joyce Weisbecker, would go on to use CHIP-8 to become the first published female video game developer.[2] In the 1980s, CHIP-8 was ported to many other platforms, including many graphing calculators. It therefore became a truly portable VM, analogous to an early form of how we think about VMs today.

The CHIP-8 Virtual Machine

The CHIP-8 VM was originally designed for the incredibly resource-constrained personal computers of the late 1970s, like the COSMAC VIP. Released in 1977, the COSMAC VIP had an RCA 1802 8-bit microprocessor running at less than 2 megahertz (MHz), 2KB of RAM (expandable to 4KB), and a 512-byte ROM. It also had specialized chips for displaying 1-bit graphics at a resolution of up to 64×128, reading and writing cassette tapes, and playing a beep.[3]

It's amazing by today's standards that anything of value could have been programmed on a machine like the COSMAC VIP, yet it was designed for video games. In fact, those games even ran through another layer of abstraction, the CHIP-8 VM. The most popular video game console of the era, the Atari 2600, was also released in 1977 and had specifications that were in the same ballpark. These limitations were simply par for the course.

When programming a VM or an emulator, the performance of the tools you're using is a paramount concern. The VM or emulator adds another layer of abstraction between the program and the hardware, and each layer of abstraction generally comes with some performance cost. To achieve the intended speed of the original system, overhead has to be kept to a minimum, and some programming languages (or rather, some programming languages' primary runtime implementations) get in the way. This is why it's common to see VMs and emulators programmed in low-level languages like C, C++, and Rust. That said, considering how limited CHIP-8's original target hardware was, it's not difficult to create a performant CHIP-8 VM today on any modern system. Even a relatively slow programming language runtime like CPython is sufficient. You wouldn't want to program a cutting-edge game console emulator in Python, or a JVM. But CHIP-8? Python is more than fine for that.

To understand CHIP-8, let's start by discussing its registers and memory layout. Then, I'll provide a general overview of the instructions that the VM can execute, before getting into the nitty-gritty details of an implementation.

Registers and Memory

On a physical microprocessor, *registers* are the absolute fastest memory available. They sit directly within the microprocessor and don't require the latency of accessing another chip. Putting data in registers is often the only way to manipulate it, since most data manipulation instructions (for example, arithmetic) that a microprocessor supports operate on data within the registers. Separate load/store instructions transfer data between the registers and external RAM.

When it comes to registers, there's a classic time-versus-space trade-off: the registers are the fastest storage locations to hold data, but they're extremely limited in size. For example, a typical 8-bit microprocessor of the late 1970s may only have had a few 8-bit registers (yes, each can only hold a single byte), but it could address dozens of kilobytes of external RAM.

Most VMs, like the CHIP-8, also have registers, but those registers don't always map directly to physical hardware registers on the microprocessor. As such, they're not necessarily any faster than RAM. That may seem odd, but the registers provide a substrate that the instructions can operate on. There's also nothing stopping a particular implementation of the VM from mapping the virtual registers to real hardware registers for a performance gain—as long as the number of virtual registers doesn't exceed the number of physical registers.

NOTE *In the following discussion, the same names are used to refer to the CHIP-8 registers as will be used in the Python code for the implementation.*

The CHIP-8 VM has 16 general-purpose 8-bit registers, referred to as v[0] through v[15]. They can be used for any kind of data, and all the main arithmetic and logic instructions operate on these registers. Of these general-purpose registers, v[15] (or v[0xF] in hexadecimal) is special in that it's used for holding a flag. The index register, i, is for manipulations across multiple memory locations at once and for indicating where data that needs to be drawn to the screen exists in memory. The program counter, pc, is a special register that keeps track of the memory address of the next instruction to be executed.

The vs, i, and pc constitute the main registers, but they're backed up by a couple pseudo-registers for timing. These two bytes, delay_timer and sound_timer, are used for implementing a pause in the game or indicating how long the sound of a beep should be played. There are specialized instructions for modifying these timers. All the registers are listed in Table 5-1. The registers were originally described in the RCA COSMAC VIP CDP18S711 Instruction Manual.[4]

Table 5-1: CHIP-8 Registers and Pseudo-Registers

Register	Name	Description
v[0] to v[14]	General-purpose registers	Each can hold any kind of 8-bit data.
v[15]	Flag register	Stores a flag (1 or 0) after certain operations, like a carry flag after addition.
pc	Program counter	Keeps track of the 16-bit address in memory of the current instruction being executed.
i	Memory index register	Stores a 16-bit address used for completing instructions that span multiple contiguous places in memory.
delay_timer	Delay timer	Stores an 8-bit value that's decremented 60 times per second until it reaches 0.
sound_timer	Sound timer	Stores an 8-bit value that's decremented 60 times per second until it reaches 0; while it's above 0, a beep is played by the computer speaker.

A typical CHIP-8 VM has 4KB of general-purpose RAM. This is in line with the COSMAC VIP when loaded with expansion memory. However, there's a catch: on the VIP, the first 512 bytes of memory had to contain the code for the actual CHIP-8 VM itself (yes, the whole VM fit into just 512 bytes of machine code—think about that as we write our version). That left only 3.5KB of usable RAM. To be backward compatible today, our VM must also reserve the first 512 bytes of RAM.

Instructions

The CHIP-8 VM was largely used to program games, so it includes specialized instructions for actions like moving sprites and playing a beep. Those sit alongside all the mundane, utilitarian instructions you'd find in any microprocessor instruction set or low-level programming language—instructions for manipulating memory, doing arithmetic, overseeing control flow, handling timers, and managing the display. In total, there are 35 instructions that we'll be implementing. All the instructions are specified in hexadecimal—see the "Hexadecimal" box for more on that numbering system.

HEXADECIMAL

Hexadecimal, or *base-16*, is the number system typically used for working with low-level bytes on computing systems (RAM addresses, CPU instructions, and the like). It can more compactly and consistently refer to values in bytes than binary or standard decimal (base-10, the number system we're used to). For instance, you can represent any 8-bit number using two hexadecimal digits, and helpfully, each of those two digits corresponds to exactly half of the byte when written out in binary (half of a byte is known as a *nibble*). If you were a programmer in the 1970s or 1980s, you would work with hexadecimal often, but today the average Python developer seldom uses it outside of low-level programming.

In hexadecimal, in addition to the 10 symbols 0–9, six further symbols are provided, A–F, corresponding to the decimal values 10–15. In Python, hexadecimal literals start with the 0x prefix. For example, 0xFF is the same as the decimal number 255, or the binary number 0b11111111. One F in the hexadecimal version refers to the first half of the ones in the binary version (1111), and the other F refers to the second set of ones (1111). This is the maximum value of 1 byte. To illustrate the conversion more clearly, the hexadecimal number 0xF0 can be written in binary as 0b11110000, with the F for the 1111 and the 0 for the 0000.

To convert from hexadecimal to decimal, multiply each hex digit from right to left by a power of 16, starting with 16^0. For example, 0xFF can be rewritten as $(15 \times 16^0) + (15 \times 16^1)$. The right digit (F) becomes $15 \times 1 = 15$, the left digit becomes $15 \times 16 = 240$, and $240 + 15 = 255$. Here's another example: 0xA5B is $(11 \times 16^0) + (5 \times 16^1) + (10 \times 16^2)$. This is equivalent to 2,651 in decimal.

The instructions are here as a quick reference and to give you a sense of the "lay of the land." We'll get into the details of how each instruction works in the code, but the reality is that most of the code is pretty self-explanatory based on the instruction descriptions. The vast majority of instructions can be implemented in just a couple lines of Python.

I spent a lot of time thinking about how to group the instructions for this discussion. Ultimately, I decided to order them numerically so that they appear in the same order here as they do in the code. Every instruction in CHIP-8 is 16 bits, or in other words, 2 bytes or 4 nibbles, so it translates to four hexadecimal digits. Any uppercase hexadecimal digit 0–F in an instruction is a literal. Any lowercase letter indicates a value that will be used as part of the implementation of the instruction. An underscore (_) indicates the nibble is arbitrary. The instructions were originally described in the RCA COSMAC VIP CDP18S711 Instruction Manual.[5]

NOTE *A few instructions listed here weren't present in the original CHIP-8 specification (for example, 8x_6 and 8x_E). Their functionality sometimes differs across varying CHIP-8 implementations.*

Screen Clearing and Basic Jumps

The first set of instructions are used for cleaning up the entire screen all at once and for moving from one part of the program to another part of the program.

00E0   Clear the screen.

00EE   Return from a subroutine.

0nnn   Call the program at nnn, reset the timers and registers, and clear the screen.

1nnn   Jump to address nnn without resetting.

2nnn   Call the subroutine at nnn.

Conditional Skips

The next set of instructions are for jumps to another part of the program if a particular condition is true.

3xnn   Skip the next instruction if v[x] equals nn.

4xnn   Skip the next instruction if v[x] doesn't equal nn.

5xy_   Skip the next instruction if v[x] equals v[y].

General-Purpose Register Adjustments, Arithmetic, and Bit Manipulation

Next come standard instructions that you would find in any CPU or VM for actions like doing math, setting registers, and shifting bits.

6xnn   Set v[x] to nn.

7xnn   Add nn to v[x].

8xy0   Set v[x] to v[y].

8xy1   Set v[x] to v[x] | v[y] (bitwise OR).

8xy2   Set v[x] to v[x] & v[y] (bitwise AND).

8xy3   Set v[x] to v[x] ^ v[y] (bitwise XOR).

8xy4   Add v[y] to v[x] and set the carry flag.

8xy5   Subtract v[y] from v[x] and set the borrow flag.

8x_6   Shift v[x] right one bit and set the flag to the least-significant bit.

8xy7   Subtract v[x] from v[y] and store the result in v[x]; set the borrow flag.

8x_E   Shift v[x] left one bit and set the flag to the most-significant bit.

Miscellaneous Instructions

These instructions don't quite have a unified subject area, but their opcodes are close to one another numerically.

9xy0   Skip the next instruction if v[x] doesn't equal v[y].

Annn   Set i to nnn.

Bnn   Jump to nnn + v[0].

Cxnn   Set v[x] to a random integer (0–255) & nn (bitwise AND).

Dxyn   Draw a sprite that's n high at (v[x], v[y]); set the flag on a collision.

Key and Timer Instructions

The next batch of instructions are for manipulating the VM's timers and checking on the status of various keys or waiting for a particular key to be pressed.

Ex9E   Skip the next instruction if key v[x] is set (pressed).

ExA1   Skip the next instruction if key v[x] is not set (not pressed).

Fx07   Set v[x] to the delay timer.

Fx0A   Wait until the next key press, then store the key in v[x].

Fx15   Set the delay timer to v[x].

Fx18   Set the sound timer to v[x].

Register i Instructions

All the instructions in this last set are related to the memory index register (i).

Fx1E   Add v[x] to i.

Fx29   Set i to the location of character v[x] in the font set.

Fx33   Store the binary-coded decimal (BCD) value in v[x] at memory locations i, i + 1, and i + 2. (See the "Binary-Coded Decimal" box on page 122 for more on this.)

Fx55   Dump registers v[0] through v[x] in memory, starting at i.

Fx65   Store memory from i through i + x in registers v[0] through v[x].

Consider for a moment how mundane these instructions sound. You really don't need any sophisticated mechanisms to have a working "computer." Contrast the 35 CHIP-8 instructions described here with the 8 instructions in our implementation of Brainfuck from Chapter 1. Both are memory-constrained Turing machines, and they aren't as different from each other as their superficial instruction syntax may make it appear.

BINARY-CODED DECIMAL

Binary-coded decimal (BCD) is a way of storing decimal numbers in binary. It's not widely used today, but it was common in early computers. For example, several microprocessors from the 1970s included explicit instructions for BCD arithmetic, which offered more precision when dealing with decimal rounding and to some extent made machine code more readable. For the average modern programmer, there isn't much value in learning BCD except as a curiosity. There were multiple different BCD schemes, and frankly I don't think that learning the particular scheme used in the CHIP-8 VM is a valuable use of our space in this book.

The Implementation

Now that we know the CHIP-8 architecture, we're ready to implement our VM. The file *__main__.py* will contain the main run loop that handles user input, updates the display, manages timers, and most importantly, tells the VM to step through the next instruction. This file is also where the command line argument that specifies the ROM file is parsed. Meanwhile, *vm.py* is the actual VM.

ROMS

Did you ever wonder why the files that hold games used in emulators are called ROMs? *ROM* stands for *read-only memory*. Most early video game systems used plastic cartridges that were glorified holders for ROM chips that directly plugged into the consoles. When the games were converted into files for emulators, someone would have to go and plug the ROM chip into a specialized device connected to their computer and "rip" the data from the ROM chip to store it in a file. The file would have an exact copy of the data on the ROM chip, perhaps with some extra header information depending on the emulation ecosystem.

> While the original ROM chips couldn't have their data modified, these "ROM files" are just like any other files and can be modified to change the games. Hence, the subculture of *ROM hacking*, in which developers change the graphics or gameplay of games meant to be run in emulators.

We'll utilize two external libraries in our implementation. Pygame, a Python library designed for game development, provides an easy way to get a window on the screen, fill that window with the pixels from our VM's display, and handle keyboard input. NumPy, a numerical computing library, can help create the two-dimensional array used as the backing buffer for the Pygame window's pixels. This array will serve as the "graphics RAM" of our VM. Pygame natively works with NumPy arrays, and NumPy arrays are more performant than anything in the Python standard library for representing this buffer. Make sure you've installed Pygame and NumPy before running the program.

Like replicating a file format in Chapter 3, implementing a VM or emulator requires a fair amount of low-level bit manipulation. See the appendix to read up on Python's bitwise operators.

The Run Loop

The run loop is responsible for advancing the VM by one instruction, redrawing the screen, handling any events (key presses to be passed to the VM), playing the beep sound, and updating CHIP-8's two timers. Pygame makes drawing, playing sounds, and reading keyboard input almost trivial; it's a very easy-to-use library. Let's start with some initialization code and continue through to the beginning of the run loop:

Chip8/
__main__.py
```
import sys
from argparse import ArgumentParser
from Chip8.vm import VM, SCREEN_WIDTH, SCREEN_HEIGHT
from Chip8.vm import TIMER_DELAY, FRAME_TIME_EXPECTED, ALLOWED_KEYS
import pygame
from timeit import default_timer as timer
import os

def run(program_data: bytes, name: str):
    # Startup Pygame, create the window, and load the sound
    pygame.init()
    screen = pygame.display.set_mode((SCREEN_WIDTH, SCREEN_HEIGHT),
                                     pygame.SCALED)
    pygame.display.set_caption(f"Chip8 - {os.path.basename(name)}")
    bee_sound = pygame.mixer.Sound(os.path.dirname(os.path.realpath(__file__))
                                   + "/bee.wav")
    currently_playing_sound = False
    vm = VM(program_data) # load the virtual machine with the program data
```

```
timer_accumulator = 0.0 # used to limit the timer to 60 Hz
# Main virtual machine loop
while True:
    frame_start = timer()
    vm.step()
    if vm.needs_redraw:
        pygame.surfarray.blit_array(screen, vm.display_buffer)
        pygame.display.flip()
```

At the beginning of the run loop, the time is recorded with frame_start = timer() to measure the duration of each iteration of the loop. This is because CHIP-8's timers need to be decremented 60 times per second (if they're above zero). The VM is then told to execute an instruction (and therefore to move to the next instruction) via vm.step(). If indicated by vm.needs_redraw, the display is then redrawn via two simple calls to Pygame. One copies the VM's display buffer to the screen, and the other shows it.

Note that the code uses the term *frame* a little differently than is typical. In most programs, a frame is one full refresh of the entirety of the program's graphical output, but in this context, our run loop won't necessarily redraw the graphics every iteration, since vm.needs_redraw may not always be True.

What definitely *will* happen every "frame" is that one instruction will be executed as a result of the call to vm.step(). As such, I thought about using the word *instruction* rather than *frame* in this section of the code, for example, instruction_start rather than frame_start. However, more than just the execution of an instruction is happening in the run loop—there's also graphical output, keyboard handling, and sound output—so *instruction* sounded too limited. But again, *frame* isn't quite accurate either. It's true what they say: one of the hardest problems in computer science is naming.

The run loop finishes by handling keyboard events, playing a sound when the VM's Boolean vm.play_sound indicates, and handling timing:

```
# Handle keyboard events
for event in pygame.event.get():
    if event.type == pygame.KEYDOWN:
        key_name = pygame.key.name(event.key)
        if key_name in ALLOWED_KEYS:
            vm.keys[ALLOWED_KEYS.index(key_name)] = True
    elif event.type == pygame.KEYUP:
        key_name = pygame.key.name(event.key)
        if key_name in ALLOWED_KEYS:
            vm.keys[ALLOWED_KEYS.index(key_name)] = False
    elif event.type == pygame.QUIT:
        sys.exit()

# Sound
if vm.play_sound:
    if not currently_playing_sound:
        bee_sound.play(-1)
        currently_playing_sound = True
```

```
    else:
        currently_playing_sound = False
        bee_sound.stop()

    # Handle timing
    frame_end = timer()
    frame_time = frame_end - frame_start # time it took in seconds
    timer_accumulator += frame_time
    # Every 1/60 of a second decrement the timers
    if timer_accumulator > TIMER_DELAY:
    ❶ vm.decrement_timers()
        timer_accumulator = 0
    # Limit the speed of the entire machine to 500 "frames" per second
    if frame_time < FRAME_TIME_EXPECTED:
        difference = FRAME_TIME_EXPECTED - frame_time
    ❷ pygame.time.delay(int(difference * 1000))
        timer_accumulator += difference
```

Even though we aren't using frames to measure traditional frames per second (FPS), as you may be familiar with from gaming, the timing of each iteration is still important. We need to keep track of timing to ensure the VM's countdown timers are ticked every 1/60 of a second as required by the CHIP-8 specification ❶, and to limit the overall speed of the VM ❷. If the VM runs too fast, games will be unplayable since they were designed for the slow computers of the 1970s. You can adjust the speed of the VM, and therefore any software running on it, by changing the FRAME_TIME_EXPECTED constant in *vm.py*. In testing, I found that 500 "frames" per second, or in other words, each "frame" being approximately 1/500 of a second, to be a solid speed for most games.

Command Line Arguments

As in previous programs, we use ArgumentParser to handle command line arguments:

```
if __name__ == "__main__":
    # Parse the file argument
    file_parser = ArgumentParser("Chip8")
    file_parser.add_argument("rom_file",
                             help="A file containing a Chip-8 game.")
    arguments = file_parser.parse_args()
    with open(arguments.rom_file, "rb") as fp:
        file_data = fp.read()
        run(file_data, arguments.rom_file)
```

In this case, we have just a single command line argument—the name of the file containing the program data for the CHIP-8 VM. The file's raw bytes are read and passed to run(), where they in turn are passed to the constructor of the VM.

VM Setup and Helper Functions

We're ready for the actual VM implementation. We start, as we so often do, with some constants:

Chip8/vm.py

```python
from array import array
from random import randint
import numpy as np
import pygame
import sys

RAM_SIZE = 4096  # in bytes, aka 4 kilobytes
SCREEN_WIDTH = 64
SCREEN_HEIGHT = 32
SPRITE_WIDTH = 8
WHITE = 0xFFFFFFFF
BLACK = 0
TIMER_DELAY = 1/60  # in seconds... about 60 Hz
FRAME_TIME_EXPECTED = 1/500  # for limiting VM speed
ALLOWED_KEYS = ["0", "1", "2", "3", "4", "5", "6", "7", "8", "9",
                "a", "b", "c", "d", "e", "f"]

# The font set, hardcoded
FONT_SET = [
    0xF0, 0x90, 0x90, 0x90, 0xF0,  # 0
    0x20, 0x60, 0x20, 0x20, 0x70,  # 1
    0xF0, 0x10, 0xF0, 0x80, 0xF0,  # 2
    0xF0, 0x10, 0xF0, 0x10, 0xF0,  # 3
    0x90, 0x90, 0xF0, 0x10, 0x10,  # 4
    0xF0, 0x80, 0xF0, 0x10, 0xF0,  # 5
    0xF0, 0x80, 0xF0, 0x90, 0xF0,  # 6
    0xF0, 0x10, 0x20, 0x40, 0x40,  # 7
    0xF0, 0x90, 0xF0, 0x90, 0xF0,  # 8
    0xF0, 0x90, 0xF0, 0x10, 0xF0,  # 9
    0xF0, 0x90, 0xF0, 0x90, 0x90,  # A
    0xE0, 0x90, 0xE0, 0x90, 0xE0,  # B
    0xF0, 0x80, 0x80, 0x80, 0xF0,  # C
    0xE0, 0x90, 0x90, 0x90, 0xE0,  # D
    0xF0, 0x80, 0xF0, 0x80, 0xF0,  # E
    0xF0, 0x80, 0xF0, 0x80, 0x80   # F
]
```

Most of these constants are self-explanatory and in line with the original CHIP-8 specifications. The VM has 4KB of main memory. It specifies graphics in the form of a black-and-white output picture with a 64×32 resolution. The timers update 60 times per second. The original CHIP-8 systems had 16 keys you could press on the controller. We could probably arrange them in a more ergonomic way for gaming by mapping them to other keys, but in our implementation, we'll just leave the keys where they lie on the keyboard.

Probably the most unusual constant here is FONT_SET. This is 80 bytes of graphical data for displaying the digits 0–9 and the letters A–F. Each character is specified by bits representing the pixels of the character should it be shown on the screen. Think of it as a primitive font that only has 16 characters. Several games expect this data to live in the first 80 bytes of memory so that they can write messages on the screen to the user.

Next, we have a helper function unrelated to the state of the VM:

```
def concat_nibbles(*args: int) -> int:
    result = 0
    for arg in args:
        result = (result << 4) | arg
    return result
```

The concat_nibbles() function takes an arbitrary number of integers and concatenates one after another by shifting each 4 bits to the left and bitwise OR-ing it with the next one. This will only be useful if the integers themselves are 4 bits. Suppose we have the integer 0111. Shifting it 4 bits to the left will cause four zeros to follow the original 4 bits, as in 01110000. Now suppose we have another 4-bit integer, 1010. If we OR it with 01110000, we obtain the result 01111010, the concatenation of the original two 4-bit integers. We can keep doing this for an arbitrary number of 4-bit integers to concatenate them together.

Recall that a 4-bit integer is known as a *nibble*. The 16-bit instructions in CHIP-8 are divided into four nibbles, and each nibble often has a separate meaning. By default, we'll divide each instruction into its four constituent nibbles, but for a few instructions, we'll need to use the value of a few combined nibbles. Hence, the utility of the concat_nibbles() helper function.

The VM class starts with a constructor that initializes all of its mutable state including registers, RAM, the stack, the display buffer (what today we would call VRAM or video RAM), the timers, and a couple other helper variables:

```
class VM:
    def __init__(self, program_data: bytes):
        # Initialized registers and memory constructs
        # General Purpose Registers - CHIP-8 has 16 of these registers
        self.v = array('B', [0] * 16)
        # Index Register
        self.i = 0
        # Program Counter
        # Starts at 0x200 because addresses below that were
        # used for the VM itself in the original CHIP-8 machines
        self.pc = 0x200
        # Memory - the standard 4k on the original CHIP-8 machines
        self.ram = array('B', [0] * RAM_SIZE)
        # Load the font set into the first 80 bytes
        self.ram[0:len(FONT_SET)] = array('B', FONT_SET)
        # Copy program into RAM starting at byte 512 by convention
        self.ram[512:(512 + len(program_data))] = array('B', program_data)
        # Stack - in real hardware this is typically limited to
        # 12 or 16 PC addresses for jumps, but since we're on modern hardware,
        # ours can just be unlimited and expand/contract as needed
        self.stack = []
```

```
# Graphics buffer for the screen - 64 x 32 pixels
self.display_buffer = np.zeros((SCREEN_WIDTH, SCREEN_HEIGHT),
                               dtype=np.uint32)
self.needs_redraw = False
# Timers - really simple registers that count down to 0 at 60 hertz
self.delay_timer = 0
self.sound_timer = 0
# These hold the status of whether the keys are down
# CHIP-8 has 16 keys
self.keys = [False] * 16
```

A few of these state variables have important default values. For example, the program counter (pc) should always be set to location 0x200 (512 in decimal) since the first 512 bytes of memory in CHIP-8 machines were originally used for storing the CHIP-8 VM itself. This means CHIP-8 programs couldn't use that memory and had to start at byte 512. I've extensively commented the constructor to explain each variable as it's declared. Notice that the vast majority of our VM just uses the Python standard library for its implementation, except for display_buffer, which is a NumPy array. This is the format that Pygame expects.

Next, we have a trivial helper method, decrement_timers(), and a simple dynamic property, play_sound:

```
def decrement_timers(self):
    if self.delay_timer > 0:
        self.delay_timer -= 1
    if self.sound_timer > 0:
        self.sound_timer -= 1


@property
def play_sound(self) -> bool:
    return self.sound_timer > 0
```

Both decrement_timers() and play_sound were used in the run loop we looked at earlier in __main__.py.

Graphics

CHIP-8 sees the screen as a 64×32 pixel plane with a cartesian coordinate system having the origin, location (0,0), in the top left, and the y-axis oriented downward. In other words, the x-coordinate increases as we travel from left to right and the y-coordinate increases as we travel from top to bottom. The bottom-right pixel is therefore at location (63,31). There are no negative coordinates, and it isn't possible to access pixel locations beyond the screen.

Each pixel is represented in memory as a single bit. In our implementation, a 1 represents a white pixel and a 0 represents a black pixel. The graphics memory (or "buffer") is separate from the main program memory and can only be manipulated indirectly using CHIP-8 instructions. Pygame uses 32-bit integers to represent pixels on the screen in RGBA format (the *A* is for *alpha*, or transparency), so each of our 1-bit pixel values must become a 32-bit integer when we store it in the display_buffer.

CHIP-8 draws using *sprites*, which are little bitmaps (or images, if you like) that can move around the screen. Every sprite in CHIP-8 is 8 pixels wide and can be anywhere between 1 and 15 pixels high. Figure 5-1 illustrates an 8×3 sprite representing the word *HI* being drawn on the screen at location (28,15).

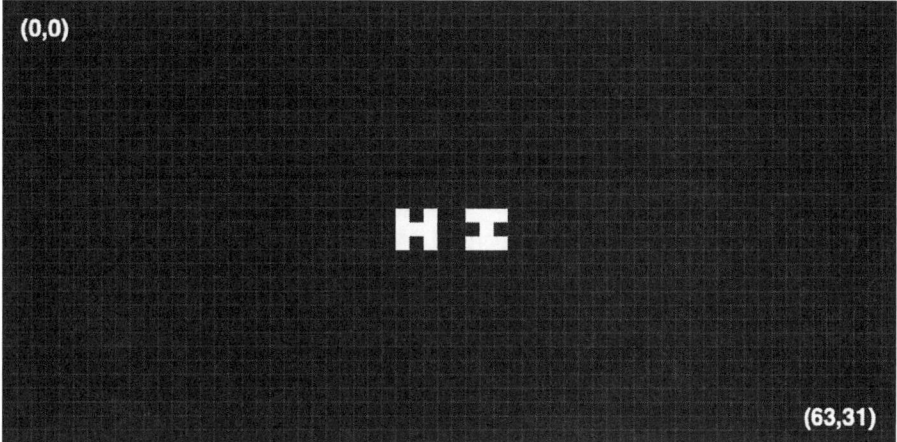

Figure 5-1: The word HI *as an 8×3 sprite*

Since each row in a CHIP-8 sprite is exactly 8 pixels, it's represented using 8 bits. Since 8 bits is 1 byte, each row of a sprite can therefore be represented by a single byte. Since the *HI* sprite is three rows high, it can be represented by 3 bytes. In binary, those 3 bytes would look like this:

```
10100111
11100010
10100111
```

Notice how each 1 maps to a white pixel and each 0 maps to a black pixel. With this information, hopefully the font set we defined earlier also makes more sense now: each character in the font set is just an 8×5 sprite.

Drawing sprites is the only way to modify the display buffer, other than clearing it, so the CHIP-8 VM has a single draw instruction, Dxyn. It draws a sprite of a specified height residing at the memory location specified by the i register. The D in the instruction is a constant nibble, and the x and y nibbles represent the indices into the v registers where the x- and y-coordinates for the top left of the sprite should be located. In other words, the x-coordinate is retrieved from register v[x] and the y-coordinate from register v[y]. The n nibble represents the height of the sprite. This is why sprites can't be taller than 15 pixels: a nibble is 4 bits, and 4 bits can maximally represent the number 15.

The nibbles of Dxyn correspond to the parameters of the draw_sprite() helper method:

```
# Draw a sprite at *x*, *y* using data at *i* with a height of *height*
def draw_sprite(self, x: int, y: int, height: int):
    flipped_black = False  # did drawing this flip any pixels?
    for row in range(0, height):
        row_bits = self.ram[self.i + row]
        for col in range(0, SPRITE_WIDTH):
            px = x + col
            py = y + row
            if px >= SCREEN_WIDTH or py >= SCREEN_HEIGHT:
                continue  # ignore off-screen pixels
            new_bit = (row_bits >> (7 - col)) & 1
            old_bit = self.display_buffer[px, py] & 1
            if new_bit & old_bit:  # if both set, flip white -> black
                flipped_black = True
            # CHIP-8 draws by XORing
            new_pixel = new_bit ^ old_bit
            self.display_buffer[px, py] = WHITE if new_pixel else BLACK
    # Set flipped flag for collision detection
    self.v[0xF] = 1 if flipped_black else 0
```

CHIP-8 draws sprites using XOR operations. *XOR*, or *exclusive or*, is a bitwise operation that returns a 1 if two bits are different and a 0 if they're the same. Python uses the ^ operator for XOR. Table 5-2 shows a truth table for XOR.

Table 5-2: XOR Truth Table

0 ^ 0	0 ^ 1	1 ^ 0	1 ^ 1
0	1	1	0

The CHIP-8 draw instruction takes a sprite and XORs its pixels with the pixels already on the screen at the location specified. If this screen location is all black pixels, this will effectively just draw the sprite. However, if the screen location contains some white pixels (1s), black pixels will be drawn where the white pixels of the sprite overlap with the white pixels of the screen. This is because 1 XOR 1 is 0. The CHIP-8 draw instruction tracks whether any of these overlaps occur (a screen white pixel was turned to a black pixel by drawing the sprite). If they do, it sets the flag register (v[0xF]).

The draw_sprite() method is a codification of this process. We iterate through all of the rows and columns of a sprite that begins at the memory location specified by register i, pulling out each pixel of the sprite using a right shift operation and storing it in new_bit. The & operation on the data going into new_bit ensures that only the single last bit of the shift operation is stored in new_bit. We compare each new_bit to the bit already on the screen, old_bit, and if an old_bit will be flipped from white to black, we set the flag register. We change the display buffer by taking the XOR of new_bit and old_bit.

Why do we need a flag to track whether drawing a sprite causes a previously lit screen pixel to be turned off? It's effectively a form of collision detection. If a sprite hits something that was already on the screen, that's particularly helpful to know in a game. For example, if you are programming a tennis game, you would want to know when the ball moves and hits a racket already on the screen.

Instruction Execution

Now it's time for the heart of the VM. We have one method left, but it's a big one: we need to implement all of the VM's instructions. This isn't dissimilar to executing the statements in our interpreters in Chapters 1 and 2. Whether executing interpreter statements, VM instructions, or microprocessor opcodes in an emulator, we need to do something pretty simple: recognize what the next instruction is and then execute a different few lines of code that manipulate the state of the VM based on its intended operation.

For example, if we see an add instruction, we should add the two specified numbers together and store the result in a specified location. If we see a jump instruction, we should move execution to a specified location in memory. It's literally about recognizing what instruction is being executed and changing a few state variables representing memory, registers, and the like based on that instruction. The simplest way to do this would be with a large number of if statements. The pseudocode may look like this:

```
if instruction == ADD:
    add some numbers together and store the sum
elif instruction == JUMP:
    jump to a location by changing the program counter
elif instruction == DRAW:
    draw the sprite where specified by changing the display buffer
etc.
```

Beyond using a bunch of if statements, there are three common patterns for writing the code that executes the instructions. The first is a giant switch statement, a construct present in many languages but not quite in Python in the same form. I assume most readers have seen a switch statement before in a language like C or Java. If you haven't, you can think of it as a primitive form of Python's match statement like we used in Chapters 1 and 2. The case of the switch statement that executes is dependent on the instruction. This is somewhat similar to the pseudocode just shown. In fact, prior to the introduction of the match statement in Python 3.10, the way you would implement this pattern in Python was indeed with a ton of if and elif clauses. This is the simplest way to implement instruction execution, but it can become unwieldy for a large instruction set.

The next pattern is to use a *jump table*, which consists of an array of function pointers. We index into the array depending on the instruction and then execute the appropriate function that's returned. Instructions are just integers, which is why they can be used as array indices. If the instructions were strings for some reason, we could instead use a dictionary where the keys are instructions and the values are function pointers, although this is a bit less efficient. Because this pattern divides the work across many helper functions, it generally results in cleaner code than a giant switch statement and may be preferred for a larger instruction set.

The third pattern is to use *dynamic recompilation*, where we translate each instruction into an instruction that the underlying hardware understands (or something that can further be translated into such). For example, if we have an addition instruction in the VM running on an x86 microprocessor, we may translate the VM's addition instruction into the machine code for an equivalent x86 addition instruction. This is the most complicated pattern to implement because it requires intimate knowledge of not just the original instruction set but also the instruction set being translated into. It will, however, result in the fastest performance.

In this program, we'll use a giant match statement since CHIP-8's instruction set is relatively small. When we create an NES emulator in the next chapter, we'll use a jump table because the 6502 microprocessor has an instruction set that's roughly double the size (although still much smaller than almost any other microprocessor). Dynamic recompilation is a significantly more complicated technique and beyond the scope of this book.

The step() method is responsible for executing instructions, but first the method needs to retrieve the next instruction to execute:

```
def step(self):
    # We look at the opcode in terms of its nibbles (4 bit pieces)
    # Opcode is 16 bits made up of next two bytes in memory
    first2 = self.ram[self.pc]
    last2 = self.ram[self.pc + 1]
    first = (first2 & 0xF0) >> 4
    second = first2 & 0xF
    third = (last2 & 0xF0) >> 4
    fourth = last2 & 0xF

    self.needs_redraw = False
    jumped = False
```

The next instruction is located at the memory address stored in the program counter (pc). Since instructions consist of 16 bits, we retrieve the next 2 bytes at pc and store them in first2 and last2. As discussed earlier, it's convenient to think about each CHIP-8 instruction as a combination of four nibbles, since each individual nibble is meaningful for many of the instructions. We store the nibbles in first, second, third, and fourth. All of the pattern-matching around our instructions will be in terms of nibbles.

As we execute the instruction, we'll also be keeping track of whether it requires any redrawing through needs_redraw and whether it modified pc through jumped. The run loop uses needs_redraw as an optimization. Why do any drawing when nothing changed? Keeping track of jumped allows for some common code to be at the bottom of step(), reducing a little bit of code duplication.

Now we arrive at the actual instructions. The giant match statement is upon us. Our implementation utilizes Python's elegant match syntax to capture the nibbles that are necessary for the execution of an instruction in temporary variables. The details of each instruction's execution follow directly from its description earlier in the chapter. Many of the instructions are able to be implemented in just a single line of code. It would be exceedingly dry to write about each of them in turn. Instead, what follows is a reproduction of the rest of step(), with comments providing a bit of additional context.

Before you look at the code, though, this is a good place to stop and try to implement the instructions yourself. You don't have to use a match statement. You could use a series of if...elif statements as I did in Python 3.9 before the match statement existed. (I tested and there was virtually no performance difference between the two.) You already have all the setup you need to be able to concentrate only on what each instruction is supposed to do instead of configuring the system's memory or register representation. You don't need to think about loading the ROM file or what some constants should be. Just think about logic and how each operation would modify the VM's state.

Some of the descriptions of the instructions earlier in this chapter were fairly brief, but you can find more detailed instructions in any of a myriad of CHIP-8 references online. Don't spend too much time on a single instruction, though. You can always look at the implementation here if you get stuck. After you try writing your own instruction implementations, you can return to this book's code to double-check your work. Doing this work yourself first will give you a good idea of what goes into writing a simple VM or emulator. Don't be afraid: you'll be amazed at how simple it is to implement many of the instructions. Remember, the original CHIP-8 VM fit in just 512 bytes of memory!

```python
match (first, second, third, fourth):
    case (0x0, 0x0, 0xE, 0x0):  # display clear
        self.display_buffer.fill(0)
        self.needs_redraw = True
    case (0x0, 0x0, 0xE, 0xE):  # return from subroutine
        self.pc = self.stack.pop()
        jumped = True
    case (0x0, n1, n2, n3):  # call program
        self.pc = concat_nibbles(n1, n2, n3)  # go to start
        # Clear registers
        self.delay_timer = 0
        self.sound_timer = 0
        self.v = array('B', [0] * 16)
        self.i = 0
        # Clear screen
        self.display_buffer.fill(0)
        self.needs_redraw = True
        jumped = True
    case (0x1, n1, n2, n3):  # jump to address
        self.pc = concat_nibbles(n1, n2, n3)
        jumped = True
    case (0x2, n1, n2, n3):  # call subroutine
        self.stack.append(self.pc + 2)  # put return place on stack
        self.pc = concat_nibbles(n1, n2, n3)  # goto subroutine
        jumped = True
```

```python
        case (0x3, x, _, _):  # conditional skip v[x] equal last2
            if self.v[x] == last2:
                self.pc += 4
                jumped = True
        case (0x4, x, _, _):  # conditional skip v[x] not equal last2
            if self.v[x] != last2:
                self.pc += 4
                jumped = True
        case (0x5, x, y, _):  # conditional skip v[x] equal v[y]
            if self.v[x] == self.v[y]:
                self.pc += 4
                jumped = True
        case (0x6, x, _, _):  # set v[x] to last2
            self.v[x] = last2
        case (0x7, x, _, _):  # add last2 to v[x]
            self.v[x] = (self.v[x] + last2) % 256
        case (0x8, x, y, 0x0):  # set v[x] to v[y]
            self.v[x] = self.v[y]
        case (0x8, x, y, 0x1):  # set v[x] to v[x] | v[y]
            self.v[x] |= self.v[y]
        case (0x8, x, y, 0x2):  # set v[x] to v[x] & v[y]
            self.v[x] &= self.v[y]
        case (0x8, x, y, 0x3):  # set v[x] to v[x] ^ v[y]
            self.v[x] ^= self.v[y]
        case (0x8, x, y, 0x4):  # add with carry flag
            try:
                self.v[x] += self.v[y]
                self.v[0xF] = 0  # indicate no carry flag
            except OverflowError:
                self.v[x] = (self.v[x] + self.v[y]) % 256
                self.v[0xF] = 1  # set carry flag
        case (0x8, x, y, 0x5):  # subtract with borrow flag
            try:
                self.v[x] -= self.v[y]
                self.v[0xF] = 1  # indicate no borrow (yes, weird it's 1)
            except OverflowError:
                self.v[x] = (self.v[x] - self.v[y]) % 256
                self.v[0xF] = 0  # indicates there was a borrow
        case (0x8, x, _, 0x6):  # v[x] >> 1 v[f] = least significant bit
            self.v[0xF] = self.v[x] & 0x1
            self.v[x] >>= 1
        case (0x8, x, y, 0x7):  # subtract with borrow flag (y - x in x)
            try:
                self.v[x] = self.v[y] - self.v[x]
                self.v[0xF] = 1  # indicate no borrow (yes, weird it's 1)
            except OverflowError:
                self.v[x] = (self.v[y] - self.v[x]) % 256
                self.v[0xF] = 0  # indicates there was a borrow
        case (0x8, x, _, 0xE):  # v[x] << 1 v[f] = most significant bit
            self.v[0xF] = (self.v[x] & 0b10000000) >> 7
            self.v[x] = (self.v[x] << 1) & 0xFF
        case (0x9, x, y, 0x0):  # conditional skip if v[x] != v[y]
            if self.v[x] != self.v[y]:
                self.pc += 4
                jumped = True
```

```python
        case (0xA, n1, n2, n3):  # set i to address n1n2n3
            self.i = concat_nibbles(n1, n2, n3)
        case (0xB, n1, n2, n3):  # jump to n1n2n3 + v[0]
            self.pc = concat_nibbles(n1, n2, n3) + self.v[0]
            jumped = True
        case (0xC, x, _, _):  # v[x] = random number (0-255) & last2
            self.v[x] = last2 & randint(0, 255)
        case (0xD, x, y, n):  # draw sprite at (vx, vy) that's n high
            self.draw_sprite(self.v[x], self.v[y], n)
            self.needs_redraw = True
        case (0xE, x, 0x9, 0xE):  # conditional skip if keys(v[x])
            if self.keys[self.v[x]]:
                self.pc += 4
                jumped = True
        case (0xE, x, 0xA, 0x1):  # conditional skip if not keys(v[x])
            if not self.keys[self.v[x]]:
                self.pc += 4
                jumped = True
        case (0xF, x, 0x0, 0x7):  # set v[x] to delay_timer
            self.v[x] = self.delay_timer
        case (0xF, x, 0x0, 0xA):  # wait until next key then store in v[x]
            # Wait here for the next key then continue
            while True:
                event = pygame.event.wait()
                if event.type == pygame.QUIT:
                    sys.exit()
                if event.type == pygame.KEYDOWN:
                    key_name = pygame.key.name(event.key)
                    if key_name in ALLOWED_KEYS:
                        self.v[x] = ALLOWED_KEYS.index(key_name)
                        break
        case (0xF, x, 0x1, 0x5):  # set delay_timer to v[x]
            self.delay_timer = self.v[x]
        case (0xF, x, 0x1, 0x8):  # set sound_timer to v[x]
            self.sound_timer = self.v[x]
        case (0xF, x, 0x1, 0xE):  # add vx to i
            self.i += self.v[x]
        case (0xF, x, 0x2, 0x9):  # set i to location of character v[x]
            self.i = self.v[x] * 5  # built-in font set is 5 bytes apart
        case (0xF, x, 0x3, 0x3):  # store BCD at v[x] in i, i+1, i+2
            self.ram[self.i] = self.v[x] // 100  # 100s digit
            self.ram[self.i + 1] = (self.v[x] % 100) // 10  # 10s digit
            self.ram[self.i + 2] = (self.v[x] % 100) % 10  # 1s digit
        case (0xF, x, 0x5, 0x5):  # reg dump v0 to vx starting at i
            for r in range(0, x + 1):
                self.ram[self.i + r] = self.v[r]
        case (0xF, x, 0x6, 0x5):  # store i through i+r in v0 through vr
            for r in range(0, x + 1):
                self.v[r] = self.ram[self.i + r]
        case _:
            print(f"Unknown opcode {(hex(first), hex(second),
                                    hex(third), hex(fourth))}!")

    if not jumped:
        self.pc += 2  # increment program counter
```

At the end of step(), we increment the program counter if we didn't jump. This ensures that we'll have moved on to the next instruction the next time step() is called. Since each CHIP-8 instruction is 2 bytes long, the program counter is incremented by 2. If there was a jump, then execution was directly moved to a specific different instruction somewhere else in memory.

Testing the VM

The most granular way to test the VM would be to write our own unit tests for each of the instructions. For each test, we would try running an instruction and then verify that the subsequent internal state of the VM was correct. While this would be ideal, in the interests of time and space we'll instead do something more akin to integration tests: we'll see how our VM performs running real CHIP-8 programs. Do they run correctly?

As it happens, there are even test ROMs that offer a kind of one-stop shop for testing a CHIP-8 VM. Two such test ROMs are included in the *Chip8/Tests* subdirectory of the book's source code repository. Both test ROMs were released under open licenses by their developers, and those licenses are included in the subdirectories. Let's run the first test ROM from the repository's home directory:

```
% python3 -m Chip8 Chip8/Tests/chip8-test-rom/test_opcode.ch8
```

If the VM is working correctly, you should see a screen of OKs, as shown in Figure 5-2.

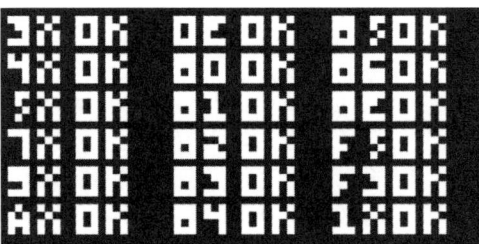

Figure 5-2: Running the first test ROM

Now let's check our work with the second test ROM:

```
% python3 -m Chip8 Chip8/Tests/chip8-test-rom-2/chip8-test-rom.ch8
```

This one just displays OK a single time in the upper-left corner (see Figure 5-3).

Figure 5-3: Running the second test ROM

These tests aren't comprehensive, but they're a good starting point. Now it's time for the ultimate integration tests: Can our VM accurately play games?

Playing Games

The *Chip8/Games* subdirectory of the book's repository contains a selection of CHIP-8 ROMs that have been placed into the public domain. If you find the control schemes of some of them a bit unwieldy, consider changing the default key bindings. Right now, ALLOWED_KEYS are read directly from their respective keys, so an *A* in the VM is the *A* key on the keyboard. The systems these were played on could have quite different key layouts, though, so a different scheme might be better for some of the games.

Most of the games are quite simple, which makes sense given the constraints of the hardware the VM was originally meant to run on. There are clones of popular games for more capable systems. First we have *BLINKY*, a kind of *Pac-Man* clone (Figure 5-4).

Figure 5-4: The BLINKY game running on the VM

INVADERS is a clone of *Space Invaders* (Figure 5-5).

Figure 5-5: The INVADERS *game running on the VM*

VBRIX is a vertical form of *Breakout* (Figure 5-6).

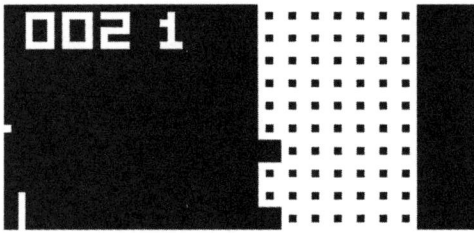

Figure 5-6: The VBRIX *game running on the VM*

And then there's *PONG* (Figure 5-7).

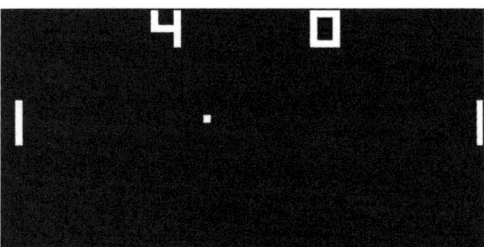

Figure 5-7: The PONG *game running on the VM*

There are several more games for you to check out bundled with the source code repository. Note the file sizes: most of these games are 500 bytes or less! The largest, *BLINKY*, is just 2KB.

Real-World Applications

VMs are ubiquitous in both historical and modern software development. Their chief advantage is portability. A program written for a VM will run on any platform that has an implementation of that VM. VMs also provide infrastructure that reduces the burden on a language author by eliminating the need to implement common language runtime features like garbage collection.

An early example was the compilation of Pascal by some compilers in the 1970s and 1980s to so-called *p-code* (a type of bytecode) that would run on a p-code VM. Two prominent modern VM environments are the JVM, mentioned earlier in this chapter, and Microsoft's competing Common Language Runtime (CLR), which is part of its .NET platform. Both the JVM and CLR are targeted by multiple popular programming languages. For example, C#, F#, and Visual Basic are languages that commonly target the CLR, but there are also implementations of popular languages like Python and Swift for the CLR.

Why do these language implementations compile into bytecode for the CLR instead of machine code? Once compiled, that bytecode can run on any platform that has an installed CLR. That's a kind of instant portability post-compilation. In addition, a sophisticated VM like the CLR will provide language services like garbage collection, multithreading, and security mechanisms. Finally, when a VM like the CLR just-in-time (JIT) compiles intermediate code into machine code, it will apply optimizations that the language author doesn't need to think about.

Beyond abstract machines utilized as language runtimes, the term *virtual machine* is also confusingly used to refer to a whole hardware implementation in software—in other words, an emulator. Building an emulator is the subject of the next chapter.

Exercises

1. Try measuring the performance of the main opcode interpreter code using three different methodologies: the already implemented `match` statement, a series of `if...elif` statements, and a jump table. Determine which method is fastest using either a profiler or a simple timer. You may need to turn off the timing code in the main run loop in order to do this, or you may do this using a set of unit tests.

2. There's a slightly extended version of CHIP-8, known as SCHIP (Super-Chip). It requires implementing a few more opcodes and changing a few elements of the original CHIP-8 VM, such as its resolution. Look up documentation for SCHIP and try turning our CHIP-8 VM into an SCHIP VM. Then, try playing some SCHIP games!

3. Try writing a very simple game that just displays a couple letters on the screen using CHIP-8's machine code instructions. You'll need a hex editor to do this. It's gratifying to see binary code you wrote running in a VM you understand.

Notes

1. Joe Weisbecker, "A Practical, Low-Cost, Home/School Microprocessor System," *Computer* 7, no. 08 (August 1974): 20–31.

2. Katianne Williams, "Joyce Weisbecker: The First Indie Game Developer," *IEEE Women in Engineering Magazine* 16, no. 2 (December 2022): 15–20, doi:10.1109/MWIE.2022.3203181.

3. RCA COSMAC VIP CDP18S711 Instruction Manual (RCA Corporation, 1978).

4. RCA COSMAC VIP CDP18S711 Instruction Manual (RCA Corporation, 1978).

5. RCA COSMAC VIP CDP18S711 Instruction Manual (RCA Corporation, 1978).

6

EMULATING THE NES GAME CONSOLE

In this chapter, we'll build a limited emulator for a beloved 1980s video game console, the Nintendo Entertainment System (NES). In other words, we'll create a piece of software that pretends to be NES hardware so that software written for the NES can be "fooled" into running on a modern platform. Building this project provides experience with emulating a full computer system. While the NES is a relatively simple computer, it features all the same basic components (microprocessor, memory, graphics, and so on) that more complex emulation projects do. And unlike CHIP-8 in Chapter 5, we'll be emulating more than just a software specification—we'll be simulating real hardware!

Our emulator won't be a 100 percent accurate reimplementation of the original hardware. We'll make several simplifications to make building the emulator manageable in one book chapter. Despite these simplifications, our emulator will still be capable of playing some basic NES games, including a few hobbyist free and open source games that are included in the book's source code repository. We won't be testing our emulator with any commercial games, although it will be capable of playing some simple ones. Our motivation is to learn about emulators, not to achieve full game compatibility. I'll leave it as an exercise for the reader to further enhance the emulator's game compatibility.

We'll build the emulator in pure Python, which at the time of writing isn't fast enough on a modern PC to emulate the NES at full speed. The code we produce can be enhanced with Cython, C extensions, or other kinds of native-code layers to run at full speed. This, too, will be left as an exercise for the reader.

This is the most challenging project in the book. I assume in this chapter that you already have the experience of completing the projects in Chapters 1, 2, and especially 5. You should at least complete the CHIP-8 project from Chapter 5 before beginning this chapter, but concepts explained in almost all the prior chapters show up in this project.

WARNING   *If you have legal concerns about completing this project, research the laws where you live or consult a lawyer. Note that the information used to develop the NES emulator in this chapter isn't based on any proprietary Nintendo documents. Keep in mind that most ROM files for commercial games are protected by copyright law. There's no need to download any protected ROM files to test your emulator, as the book's source code repository includes several noncommercial ROMs that are under open source licenses or released into the public domain.*

About the NES

The NES was one of the best-selling video game consoles of all time. First released in Japan in 1983 as the Famicom, the NES captivated a global generation of gamers with its 1985 international release.[1] At the time of its debut, the video game industry was only about a decade old. The microprocessors and other hardware in video game consoles were still quite primitive. Despite this, the NES managed 60 FPS of colorful sprites and backgrounds, played catchy chip tune music, and was the host platform for some of the most iconic games of all time.

NOTE   *Many of the hardware specifications for the NES and much of the information about its functionality that I present in this chapter come from NesDev, a community of NES homebrew developers and emulator writers that exists at* https://www.nesdev .org. *While I think this chapter is the best overview and tutorial about how to write an NES emulator, I strongly recommend checking out the NesDev website for the details. In lieu of a large corpus of citations of the site, I'm presenting you with this prominent note. In addition, several of the images in this chapter also came from*

NesDev and were released into the public domain, as noted on the copyright page of this book. Thank you to the folks at NesDev for being such a fantastic resource and releasing so much reference material into the public domain.

The Hardware

The central processing unit (CPU) in the NES was a clone of the MOS Technology 6502 microprocessor, manufactured by Ricoh, running at just below 2 MHz. The 6502 is the same microprocessor that was in popular home computers of the time, such as the Apple II and the Commodore 64. Built out of around 3,500 transistors, the 6502 was a particularly simple microprocessor; for example, it lacked instructions for multiplication and division.[2] Those arithmetic operations had to be implemented in software out of many simpler instructions like addition, subtraction, and bit shifts. When you think about just how slow and simple the 6502 was compared to a modern microprocessor, it's incredible what was accomplished with it.

The 6502 on the NES was combined with an audio chip in the same package. In NES development parlance, this chip is known as the *audio processing unit (APU)*. The APU supported five different channels of sound. To keep things simple, we won't implement the APU in our emulator. When implementing audio, timing is critical, and our emulator won't be timing accurate.

The NES's CPU could access 2KB of built-in RAM in the machine. Yes, you read that correctly. The working memory of the NES's CPU was just 2KB, not even enough memory to store the text of this section of this chapter. It's also less RAM than CHIP-8 systems typically had, which came out in the prior decade. Some cartridges included additional RAM.

The key to the NES's performance was the *picture processing unit (PPU)*, manufactured by Ricoh as the 2C02, based on an earlier design by Texas Instruments. The PPU not only could output tiled background graphics, but also had built-in support for sprites. It featured 2KB of memory for background tile information, 256 bytes of memory for keeping track of up to 64 sprites, and 28 bytes to hold color palette information. The NES supported 54 different colors, but only 25 could be used at the same time. The PPU even had some primitive support for collision detection.

The CPU communicated with the APU and PPU via *memory-mapped hardware registers*. These are particular memory addresses that, when written to, may modify the operation of the other hardware chip or, when read, will provide an update on the other chip's current flags or status. For instance, the CPU may write data to a PPU register to change the location of a sprite. Later, it may read from a different PPU register to see if the sprite collided with anything. The CPU also has memory-mapped registers for reading from the game controllers.

Let me make this concept of a memory-mapped register concrete with an example. When a game needs to check the status of the first joypad (player 1's controller), it uses a memory-mapped register. That register is at memory address 0x4016. If the game reads from 0x4016, it gets back 1 byte that indicates if a particular button on the joypad is pressed. Memory address 0x4016 can't be used for anything else; it's hooked up in hardware to lines coming from the joypad. To work properly, our emulator will need to do the right thing when several of these special memory addresses are either read or written to. Some are read-only, some are write-only, and some can be read or written. These are the memory-mapped hardware registers.

The other key piece of NES hardware was the game cartridges. Game cartridges, especially the early ones, mainly consisted of a large ROM chip containing the graphics and program code for a game. Game cartridges could also have RAM (sometimes backed by a battery so that game states could be saved), simple logic chips, and even so-called bank switching to allow for more total memory (RAM + ROM) than the 6502 could address in its default configuration. That 2KB of RAM figure is therefore slightly misleading because the program's code would reside on the ROM cartridge rather than in the game console's limited memory. Instead, that 2KB of memory could be used almost exclusively for holding onto state. Early game cartridges typically consisted of 24KB to 40KB of ROM, while later game cartridges may have had something like 128KB of ROM and 8KB of RAM. The largest mainstream cartridge for the NES featured 768KB of memory.[3]

The Software

The NES had no BIOS or operating system. The bare NES hardware had no software that came with it. All software was provided by the game cartridges. The programs on the game cartridges would directly control the CPU, PPU, and APU, with no layers of abstraction between them and the hardware.

NES games were typically written in 6502 assembly language. That may sound hardcore, but it was typical for the era; most programs that needed to be high performance on personal computers or gaming consoles were programmed in assembly language through to the early 1990s. Beyond an assembler, development tools were often built in-house. There was no NES Game Maker that one could download.

In fact, this was an era before downloads were a thing at all. The NES was a couple of console generations before any kind of internet connectivity existed. The first mainstream console with a built-in modem was the Sega Dreamcast, which came out in the late 1990s. What shipped on an NES cartridge was the final version of the game; there would be no updates. If there was a bug, then there was a bug, so games had to be near perfect for version 1.0. Contrast that with the typical game you purchase today, where developers are often working on the first major patch before the game has even been released. Back then, a whole other level of attention to detail was required, but on the other hand, the games were much less complex than they are today.

It's amazing to think that in this primitive environment, some of the most influential and genre-defining games of all time were developed. The technical aptitude required of the programmers on the teams was in a very different niche than what game developers occupy today. Most games today are built using prepacked frameworks or engines like Unreal or Unity. Developers can spend most of their time writing game-specific mechanics.

NES developers had to write their own engines in assembly. They had to directly manage the APU to play every sound and the PPU to show every graphic, and they had to squeeze every cycle out of the CPU to get anything done. Larger companies built their own internal frameworks and tooling that could be reused from title to title, but programmers were still working at a relatively low level.

Building the Emulator

It's time to write some code. Before we do, though, a note about direction and managing expectations: the emulator we're writing has been simplified at every corner. As mentioned earlier, it won't be compatible with many games, due to a very simplified PPU. It also won't have any sound, since we aren't implementing the APU. And it won't run fast enough to play games at their intended speed. It will, however, run real games, and they'll be playable. Our work here will also provide a firm foundation for making improvements and adding more features if you so choose.

Planning the Structure

The general plan for the emulator's execution isn't dissimilar to that of the CHIP-8 VM from Chapter 5. Like with CHIP-8, we'll read each instruction one at a time from the ROM file and interpret it. Like with CHIP-8, we'll use Pygame to display graphics and handle user input. Like with CHIP-8, we'll have one big loop that fetches each instruction and responds to each event. However, the structure of the code will be more sophisticated. In particular, we'll divide the emulator into three classes, each representing one physical component of the hardware. We'll have classes for the CPU, the PPU, and the cartridge. Here's a breakdown of each file we'll write and its purpose:

__main__.py   Handles command line arguments and implements the main emulator loop, which dispatches instructions, displays graphics, and responds to user input.

rom.py   Reads a ROM file and pretends to be a cartridge.

cpu.py   Maintains CPU state, interprets instructions, and handles main memory accesses.

ppu.py   Manages PPU state and draws backgrounds and sprites.

We'll tackle these files in the order listed here.

Creating the Main Loop

Our main file (*__main__.py*) is where the various components of the system (CPU, PPU, cartridge) come together. Its "run loop" gives the emulator life by keeping everything moving forward and coordinating between the different components, delegating to Pygame as needed to display graphics and read user input. The run() function receives a ROM object and the name of the ROM file as arguments. In our first snippet, we initialize Pygame, get a window on the screen, and create CPU and PPU objects:

NESEmulator/
__main__.py

```python
import sys
from argparse import ArgumentParser
from NESEmulator.rom import ROM
from NESEmulator.ppu import PPU, NES_WIDTH, NES_HEIGHT
from NESEmulator.cpu import CPU
import pygame
from timeit import default_timer as timer
import os


def run(rom: ROM, name: str):
    pygame.init()
    screen = pygame.display.set_mode((NES_WIDTH, NES_HEIGHT), 0, 24)
    pygame.display.set_caption(f"NES Emulator - {os.path.basename(name)}")
    ppu = PPU(rom)
    cpu = CPU(ppu, rom)
    ticks = 0
    start = None
```

As the calls to their constructors indicate, both the PPU and the CPU need to access the ROM. The CPU needs to read program instructions, and the PPU needs to read graphical data. The CPU also needs to access the PPU because when certain memory addresses are read or written, they're really proxies for PPU registers.

The ticks variable keeps track of how many cycles the CPU has run. For every CPU cycle, the PPU runs exactly three. In other words, the PPU is clocked three times faster than the CPU, so while the CPU is about 1.8 MHz, the PPU is about 5.4 MHz. Our code will need to simulate this, so in the next snippet, which is the main game loop, we keep track of how many cycles (or ticks) each CPU instruction takes (different instructions require different numbers of cycles) and then run the PPU for three times that number of cycles:

```python
while True:
    cpu.step()
    new_ticks = cpu.cpu_ticks - ticks
    # 3 PPU cycles for every CPU tick
    for _ in range(new_ticks * 3):
        ppu.step()
        # Draw, once per frame, everything onto the screen
        if (ppu.scanline == 240) and (ppu.cycle == 257): ❶
            pygame.surfarray.blit_array(screen, ppu.display_buffer)
            pygame.display.flip()
            end = timer()
            if start is not None:
                print(end - start)
            start = timer()
        if (ppu.scanline == 241) and (ppu.cycle == 2) and ppu.generate_nmi:
            cpu.trigger_NMI() ❷
    ticks += new_ticks
```

At the end of every frame, the graphics that the user sees are updated via the same Pygame methods that we used in Chapter 5. But how do we know a frame is over? The NES had a resolution of 256 pixels wide by 240 pixels high. Each row of pixels is known as a *scanline*, a term that comes from the cathode ray tube (CRT) televisions that the NES would be hooked up to. On the real NES, a single pixel would be updated with each PPU cycle. Because the PPU runs at three times the speed of the CPU (5.4 MHz versus 1.8 MHz), for every CPU cycle, the PPU draws three dots. When we get to the 257th dot on the 240th scanline, we should therefore be done with one frame ❶.

Highly accurate NES emulators simulate the real hardware's behavior by doing what the PPU is supposed to do every cycle: figuring out the color of the next dot. We use a much simpler technique of just drawing all the correct tiles and sprites in the right places once per frame. In other words, instead of thinking about one dot every cycle, we just think about what the whole screen is supposed to look like once per frame. While this technique is faster and doesn't require us to emulate as many details about the PPU's internal workings, it won't work with every game. More advanced NES games will make changes to the graphics even while a frame is being drawn to the screen (that is, between scanlines or even between dots).

Note that the PPU actually does additional processing between scanlines. This period is known as *hblank*. More important, the PPU has additional off-screen scanlines (it goes all the way up to scanline 261, counting the first as scanline 0). The time during the processing of these additional not-rendered scanlines is known as *vblank*. During vblank, it's safe for the CPU to modify any of the PPU's memory, since the PPU's memory isn't actively being accessed to render visible scanlines. The PPU sends a signal to the CPU when vblank begins (after it's done with all the visible scanlines) for this purpose ❷. The signal is a type of *non-maskable interrupt (NMI)*.

Think of an NMI as an interruption to a program that can't be stopped. In other words, it's a signal that says to the microprocessor, "Stop what you're doing immediately, because we're doing this other thing now." In the case of the NES, the other thing is updating the game's graphical display. Every NES game has an NMI handler that updates the game's graphics during vblank.

The rest of the loop just handles events:

```
for event in pygame.event.get():
    if event.type == pygame.QUIT:
        sys.exit()
    # Handle keyboard events as joypad changes
    if event.type not in {pygame.KEYDOWN, pygame.KEYUP}:
        continue
    is_keydown = event.type == pygame.KEYDOWN
    match event.key:
        case pygame.K_LEFT:
            cpu.joypad1.left = is_keydown
```

```
                case pygame.K_RIGHT:
                    cpu.joypad1.right = is_keydown
                case pygame.K_UP:
                    cpu.joypad1.up = is_keydown
                case pygame.K_DOWN:
                    cpu.joypad1.down = is_keydown
                case pygame.K_x:
                    cpu.joypad1.a = is_keydown
                case pygame.K_z:
                    cpu.joypad1.b = is_keydown
                case pygame.K_s:
                    cpu.joypad1.start = is_keydown
                case pygame.K_a:
                    cpu.joypad1.select = is_keydown

if __name__ == "__main__":
    # Parse the file argument
    file_parser = ArgumentParser("NESEmulator")
    file_parser.add_argument("rom_file",
                            help="An NES game file in iNES format.")
    arguments = file_parser.parse_args()
    game = ROM(arguments.rom_file)
    run(game, arguments.rom_file)
```

We recognize certain keys being pressed as equivalents of buttons on
an NES joypad. We mark the buttons that are pressed so that the CPU can
read them. Our main file finishes by handling a command line argument
to read a ROM file. The actual reading is done by the ROM class, which we'll
come to next.

Emulating the Cartridge

NES game cartridges were mainly composed of ROM chips in a plastic
shell. Those ROM chips held the game's code and graphical assets. The
code was in a ROM chip known as the PRG ROM, and the graphics were in
a ROM chip known as the CHR ROM. While cartridges were mainly composed of ROM chips, they could also have quite a bit more. As hinted earlier, one of the most common enhancements were logic chips that enabled
bank switching, a technique for having more ROM than the NES could typically address, but switched in a scheme so that the program could access a
particular memory-mapped address and say, "I'm done with the first 8KB of
CHR ROM, please switch my memory reads to be from the next 8KB."

Some cartridges went even further by providing additional RAM to
supplement the main CPU's measly 2KB. This is known as PRG RAM. Some
cartridges even had batteries so that the RAM's content wouldn't get erased
when the console was turned off. There was no other way to permanently
store user data on the NES, since there was no disk. Battery-backed RAM
enabled longer games. Nobody wants to play a 40-hour game if their prog-
ress is going to be erased after they shut down their console.

The longer the NES was on the market, the more sophisticated the cartridges got. The same advanced cartridge designs would be manufactured

for reuse across many games. As an emulator author, to support all games you need to support all of the different chipsets that cartridges could contain. However, there were a few particularly popular chipset designs that account for the majority of all games.

Each of these cartridge chipset designs is known in the NES emulator world as a *mapper* because the main use of cartridge chipsets was for switching between different memory banks, which in programming parlance can be thought of as mapping an address to a bank. One of the first NES emulators developed, iNES by Marat Fayzullin,[4] defined a numbering scheme for the many mappers. In addition, iNES defined a ROM file format that's used by almost all NES emulators today.

Unlike CHIP-8, which has ROM files that just consist of the raw game's memory, the NES requires a more sophisticated file format due to the variability of its game cartridges. In particular, the iNES format defines a header that we must pay attention to when reading a ROM file. Luckily, we have past experience with headers thanks to our work with the MacBinary header in Chapter 3. The header of the iNES file format is defined in Table 6-1.[5]

Table 6-1: iNES File Format Header

Bytes	Description
0–3	Constant 0x4E45531A (ASCII "NES" followed by MS-DOS end-of-file)
4	Size of PRG ROM in 16KB units
5	Size of CHR ROM in 8KB units (value 0 means the board uses CHR RAM)
6	Flags 6: mapper, mirroring, battery, trainer
7	Flags 7: mapper, VS/Playchoice, NES 2.0
8	Flags 8: PRG RAM size (rarely used extension)
9	Flags 9: TV system (rarely used extension)
10	Flags 10: TV system, PRG RAM presence (unofficial, rarely used extension)
11–15	Unused padding (should be filled with zeros, but some rippers put their name here)

As you can see, part of the header defines the mapper number of the game. Each flags byte can contain multiple individual flag bits, which is why some of the descriptions list multiple things. Our emulator won't make use of any of the information in flags 8, 9, or 10.

NOTE *The iNES file format has been extended by a newer format known as NES 2.0. Much of the iNES header fields are still valid in NES 2.0, with additional information in bytes 11 through 15 and some changes to the flags bytes.*

The emulator we build in this chapter is only capable of playing games using the simplest mapper, mapper 0, known as NROM. NROM cartridges feature no bank switching, so they're the easiest to emulate. An NROM cartridge will always have either 16KB or 32KB of PRG ROM and 8KB of CHR ROM. It can optionally have PRG RAM.

In our code, we define a namedtuple called Header to hold the contents of the ROM file's header, as well as declaring some standard constants:

NESEmulator/
rom.py

```
from pathlib import Path
from struct import unpack
from collections import namedtuple
from array import array

Header = namedtuple("Header", "signature prg_rom_size chr_rom_size "
                              "flags6 flags7 flags8 flags9 flags10 unused")
HEADER_SIZE = 16
TRAINER_SIZE = 512
PRG_ROM_BASE_UNIT_SIZE = 16384
CHR_ROM_BASE_UNIT_SIZE = 8192
PRG_RAM_SIZE = 8192
```

The constructor of the ROM class first utilizes the unpack() function from the struct standard library module to read the header from the ROM file and distribute it into appropriately sized fields, specified by a format string:

```
class ROM:
    def __init__(self, file_name: str | Path):
        with open(file_name, "rb") as file:
            # Read header and check signature "NES"
            self.header = Header._make(unpack("!LBBBBBBB5s",
                                              file.read(HEADER_SIZE)))
```

The ._make() class method on namedtuple can be used to construct an instance of that namedtuple out of an iterable, like the one we get back from unpack(). The specific item types in the unpack() format string are listed in Table 6-2. Each item in the format string corresponds to a header element from Table 6-1. For more details on the format string, see the struct module's documentation at *https://docs.python.org/3/library/struct.html#struct-format-strings*.

Table 6-2: Format String Characters for the struct Module

Item	# of bytes	C type	Python type
!	N/A	Indicates what follows is in big-endian format	N/A
L	4	unsigned long	int
B	1	unsigned char	int
5s	5	char[]	bytes

After this wrangling, self.header contains the proper pieces of the iNES header in nicely labeled segments. Next, we check a couple pieces of information from the header:

```
if self.header.signature != 0x4E45531A:
    print("Invalid ROM Header Signature")
else:
```

```
        print("Valid ROM Header Signature")
        # Untangle Mapper - one nibble in flags6 and one nibble in flags7
        self.mapper = (self.header.flags7 & 0xF0) | (
                (self.header.flags6 & 0xF0) >> 4)
        print(f"Mapper {self.mapper}")
        if self.mapper != 0:
                print("Invalid Mapper: Only Mapper 0 is Implemented")
```

Every iNES header is supposed to begin with the same 4-byte signature. Meanwhile, the mapper number is constructed from part of flags 7 and 8. Our emulator only works with games that use mapper 0.

Here's the rest of the constructor:

```
        self.read_cartridge = self.read_mapper0
        self.write_cartridge = self.write_mapper0
        # Check if there's a trainer (4th bit flags6) and read it
        self.has_trainer = bool(self.header.flags6 & 4)
        if self.has_trainer:
            self.trainer_data = file.read(TRAINER_SIZE)
        # Check mirroring from flags6 bit 0
        self.vertical_mirroring = bool(self.header.flags6 & 1)
        print(f"Has vertical mirroring {self.vertical_mirroring}")
        # Read PRG_ROM & CHR_ROM, in multiples of 16K and 8K, respectively
        self.prg_rom = file.read(PRG_ROM_BASE_UNIT_SIZE *
                                    self.header.prg_rom_size)
        self.chr_rom = file.read(CHR_ROM_BASE_UNIT_SIZE *
                                    self.header.chr_rom_size)
        self.prg_ram = array('B', [0] * PRG_RAM_SIZE)  # RAM
```

This code is concerned with setting up other properties of the game cartridge. How do we read and write from it (this can differ by the mapper, although we only support mapper 0)? Does it have a trainer (an esoteric feature that we'll ignore)? Does it utilize a particular type of mirroring for the graphics? Finally, based on sizes indicated by the header, the appropriate amount of data for the PRG ROM, CHR ROM, and (optionally) PRG RAM is read.

Notice how read_cartridge and write_cartridge are assigned as aliases for the read_mapper0() and write_mapper0() methods. If we supported more than one mapper, we would handle this differently. As it stands, here are the definitions for the mapper 0 methods:

```
def read_mapper0(self, address: int) -> int:
    if address < 0x2000:
        return self.chr_rom[address]
    elif 0x6000 <= address < 0x8000:
        return self.prg_ram[address % PRG_RAM_SIZE]
    elif address >= 0x8000:
        if self.header.prg_rom_size > 1:
            return self.prg_rom[address - 0x8000]
        else:
            return self.prg_rom[(address - 0x8000) % PRG_ROM_BASE_UNIT_SIZE]
```

```
        else:
            raise LookupError(f"Tried to read at invalid address {address:X}")

    def write_mapper0(self, address: int, value: int):
        if address >= 0x6000:
            self.prg_ram[address % PRG_RAM_SIZE] = value
```

Looking at read_mapper0() you'll note three distinct areas of memory on the cartridge. Addresses below 0x2000 are mapped to CHR ROM, which is directly accessed by the PPU. The CPU accesses PRG ROM with addresses greater than or equal to 0x8000, and it can read or write to PRG RAM (if the cartridge has any) with addresses greater than or equal to 0x6000 but below 0x8000.

That wraps up the cartridge portion of our code. In short, a ROM file is converted into areas of CHR ROM and PRG ROM that our PPU and CPU, respectively, can access. This is why both the PPU and CPU classes within our emulator need to be able to access the ROM class.

Emulating the CPU

CPUs can ultimately be thought of as sophisticated finite state machines. They maintain state in their registers and the finite amount of memory they have access to. They make state transitions via the instructions they can handle. This insight accounts for the key work our CPU emulator needs to do: maintain registers, access memory, and modify registers and memory correctly based on instructions.

The 6502 is one of the simplest CPU cores that ever found wide industry acceptance, and the version of the 6502 in the NES is even simpler than a standard 6502. It lacks instructions for BCD that most 6502s had. There are only 56 different types of instructions that we need to implement in order to have a working NES CPU, and many of them can be implemented in just a couple lines of code. In addition, the 6502 has just three main registers (A, X, and Y) along with a few specialized registers (SP, PC, and various flags). The only real complexity in the 6502 comes from the multiple different memory access methods that the various instructions can utilize, but we'll abstract them away in a helper function.

The Setup

The code for our 6502 implementation begins by setting up some helper constructs and constants:

NESEmulator/
cpu.py
```
from __future__ import annotations
from enum import Enum
from dataclasses import dataclass
from array import array
from typing import Callable
from NESEmulator.ppu import PPU, SPR_RAM_SIZE
from NESEmulator.rom import ROM
```

```
MemMode = Enum("MemMode", "DUMMY ABSOLUTE ABSOLUTE_X ABSOLUTE_Y ACCUMULATOR "
                          "IMMEDIATE IMPLIED INDEXED_INDIRECT INDIRECT "
                          "INDIRECT_INDEXED RELATIVE ZEROPAGE ZEROPAGE_X "
                          "ZEROPAGE_Y")

InstructionType = Enum("InstructionType", "ADC AHX ALR ANC AND ARR ASL AXS "
                                          "BCC BCS BEQ BIT BMI BNE BPL BRK "
                                          "BVC BVS CLC CLD CLI CLV CMP CPX "
                                          "CPY DCP DEC DEX DEY EOR INC INX "
                                          "INY ISC JMP JSR KIL LAS LAX LDA "
                                          "LDX LDY LSR NOP ORA PHA PHP PLA "
                                          "PLP RLA ROL ROR RRA RTI RTS SAX "
                                          "SBC SEC SED SEI SHX SHY SLO SRE "
                                          "STA STX STY TAS TAX TAY TSX TXA "
                                          "TXS TYA XAA")

@dataclass(frozen=True)
class Instruction:
    type: InstructionType
    method: Callable[[Instruction, int], None]
    mode: MemMode
    length: int
    ticks: int
    page_ticks: int

@dataclass
class Joypad:
    strobe: bool = False
    read_count: int = 0
    a: bool = False
    b: bool = False
    select: bool = False
    start: bool = False
    up: bool = False
    down: bool = False
    left: bool = False
    right: bool = False

STACK_POINTER_RESET = 0xFD
STACK_START = 0x100
RESET_VECTOR = 0xFFFC
NMI_VECTOR = 0xFFFA
IRQ_BRK_VECTOR = 0xFFFE
MEM_SIZE = 2048
```

The MemMode enum lists all the various different memory access schemes
in the 6502. On some basic microprocessors, retrieving a byte from memory
is as simple as specifying an address and getting back the byte stored there.
For example, if I say "read 0x1940," I get back whatever byte is stored in
memory at address 0x1940. The 6502 can do this with its ABSOLUTE memory
mode, but it has other memory modes that are helpful in certain situations.
Some of these modes access memory addresses that are calculated on the
fly instead of being specified literally. For example, mode ABSOLUTE_X adds

the value in the X register to the provided address and accesses the resulting memory location. In this mode, if we were to execute the same instruction again after incrementing X, we'd automatically read the next byte in memory. When programming at a low level, this can be a real convenience and even improve performance if the hardware is optimized for certain modes of access. We'll discuss the NES memory modes in more detail later in the chapter—thankfully, many of them are quite similar to one another.

The `InstructionType` enum lists all the different kinds of instructions that the 6502 can handle. Some of these instruction types are for BCD operations that, as mentioned earlier, the NES version of the 6502 didn't have. Some of them are "unofficial" instruction types that weren't actually documented as part of the 6502 but were found to exist through trial and error. Very few games use them. The remaining 56 are the instruction types that we'll actually implement. We list all of the possible instruction types in this enum—even the unimplemented ones—because we'll be using an auto-generated table of all 256 possible 6502 opcodes, and we want every entry in the table to have a valid instruction type value.

An `Instruction` refers to one of the 256 possible opcodes that the 6502 could understand. Every instruction has information about its type (`type`), its associated function in our program that handles it (`method`), its memory access mode (`mode`), its expected number of bytes (`length`), the number of CPU cycles it takes to run (`ticks`), and the additional number of cycles it takes to run if a memory page is crossed while it executes (`page_ticks`). A *memory page* is a portion of RAM that the memory controller can access any part of in quick succession to another part. In the 6502, memory pages are 256 bytes. If an instruction crosses those 256-byte boundaries, it may take longer to execute.

The fact that every instruction has an associated function to handle it is a hint that we'll be using quite a different design than in the CHIP-8 project. For the CHIP-8 VM, we used a giant `match` statement to process each instruction, but for the 6502 and its slightly more complex set of instructions, we'll utilize a cleaner design. Instead of switching on every instruction, we'll look it up in an array based on its opcode and then execute the associated function. This kind of design is a variation on a common pattern known as a *jump table*. In essence, we index into an instructions array by opcode to find what function to jump to.

The `Joypad` class represents the state of a joypad during program execution. The CPU can directly poll the joypad through a couple memory-mapped registers, so it seemed appropriate to put `Joypad` here in the `cpu` module. Recall that our main loop sets the joypad's state based on events detected by Pygame.

Here's a breakdown of the remaining helper constants in the previous code listing:

STACK_POINTER_RESET   The memory address that the CPU's stack pointer initially points to.

STACK_START   Where the stack starts in memory, which is interestingly a different address from STACK_POINTER_RESET.

RESET_VECTOR An address in memory that contains another address in memory where program execution starts. The PRG ROM of every NES game has some kind of kickoff code to get things going at the address listed at RESET_VECTOR.

NMI_VECTOR The same thing as RESET_VECTOR but for NMIs and vblank. When a vblank hits, control will be moved to the address in memory listed at NMI_VECTOR.

IRQ_BRK_VECTOR An address for a less commonly used type of interrupt that won't factor into the games we test with our program. It's included here for completeness.

MEM_SIZE The size, in bytes, of the main RAM that the NES CPU has access to.

Next, let's look at the beginning of our CPU class's constructor, which sets up its memory, registers, and configurable state variables:

```
class CPU:
    def __init__(self, ppu: PPU, rom: ROM):
        # Connections to Other Parts of the Console
        self.ppu: PPU = ppu
        self.rom: ROM = rom
        # Memory on the CPU
        self.ram = array('B', [0] * MEM_SIZE)
        # Registers
        self.A: int = 0
        self.X: int = 0
        self.Y: int = 0
        self.SP: int = STACK_POINTER_RESET
        self.PC: int = self.read_memory(RESET_VECTOR, MemMode.ABSOLUTE) | \
                    (self.read_memory(RESET_VECTOR + 1,
                                      MemMode.ABSOLUTE) << 8)
        # Flags
        self.C: bool = False  # Carry
        self.Z: bool = False  # Zero
        self.I: bool = True   # Interrupt disable
        self.D: bool = False  # Decimal mode
        self.B: bool = False  # Break command
        self.V: bool = False  # oVerflow
        self.N: bool = False  # Negative
        # Miscellaneous State
        self.jumped: bool = False
        self.page_crossed: bool = False
        self.cpu_ticks: int = 0
        self.stall: int = 0  # number of cycles to stall
        self.joypad1 = Joypad()
```

To better understand this setup code, let's do a deep dive on the 6502's registers. Table 6-3 lists all of them.

Table 6-3: 6502 Registers

Name	Size (in bytes)	Purpose
A	1	The main register used for arithmetic operations. Sometimes known as the *accumulator*.
X	1	An *index register*, often used as a loop counter. It can also be used as a general-purpose register, although not all instructions work with it as they do with A.
Y	1	The same as X.
PC	2	The *program counter*, which keeps track of where in memory the next instruction to execute resides. It's 2 bytes because the 6502 can address up to 64KB of memory (without bank switching).
SP	1	The *stack pointer*, which keeps track of where on the stack the program currently is. Since it's only 1 byte, the stack can hold a maximum of 256 bytes.
P	1	The *status* or *flags* register. Its individual bits indicate different things, such as something about an arithmetic operation (is the result zero, for example?) or whether a break happened or the interrupt is enabled (IRQ).

Since Python has only a single type for all integers regardless of size, we represent all of these registers except the flags with the int type. Instead of fiddling with the individual bits for each of the flags in the status register, we divide them into separate Booleans using the lettered nomenclature common in 6502 documentation. These are the C, Z, I, D, B, V, and N member variables. Most of them are set as a result of arithmetic operations, I is set when a program wants to not be interrupted by an IRQ signal, and B is set when flags are pushed to the stack after a break instruction. The D flag, used for BCD code, isn't relevant to the NES, since the NES doesn't have BCD instructions.

The jumped variable keeps track of whether a jump instruction altered the PC register, and page_crossed is for bookkeeping when accessing memory across a memory page, which, as discussed, can be more expensive than accessing memory close by. The NES CPU may need to wait a certain number of cycles for some tasks to complete. This is the purpose of stall. In our emulator, it's only used when a direct memory access (DMA) transfer occurs to send a bunch of data from main memory to object attribute memory (OAM), where the PPU stores information about sprites.

The Jump Table

Next, we'll declare the jump table, the list containing all of the potential instructions that the 6502 can process. Since thc 6502 uses 1-byte opcodes, and there are 256 possible values for a byte, there are potentially 256 different instructions. Later, in our step() method, we'll index into this list to get the specific instruction and its corresponding function for a given opcode that we decode. We won't actually implement every instruction (some are BCD or unofficial), so some are attached to a self.unimplemented() method.

All 256 lines of the jump table are included here for completeness:

```
self.instructions = [
    Instruction(InstructionType.BRK, self.BRK, MemMode.IMPLIED, 1, 7, 0),  # 00
    Instruction(InstructionType.ORA, self.ORA, MemMode.INDEXED_INDIRECT, 2, 6, 0),
    Instruction(InstructionType.KIL, self.unimplemented, MemMode.IMPLIED, 0, 2, 0),
    Instruction(InstructionType.SLO, self.unimplemented, MemMode.INDEXED_INDIRECT, 0, 8, 0),
    Instruction(InstructionType.NOP, self.NOP, MemMode.ZEROPAGE, 2, 3, 0),  # 04
    Instruction(InstructionType.ORA, self.ORA, MemMode.ZEROPAGE, 2, 3, 0),  # 05
    Instruction(InstructionType.ASL, self.ASL, MemMode.ZEROPAGE, 2, 5, 0),  # 06
    Instruction(InstructionType.SLO, self.unimplemented, MemMode.ZEROPAGE, 0, 5, 0),
    Instruction(InstructionType.PHP, self.PHP, MemMode.IMPLIED, 1, 3, 0),  # 08
    Instruction(InstructionType.ORA, self.ORA, MemMode.IMMEDIATE, 2, 2, 0),  # 09
    Instruction(InstructionType.ASL, self.ASL, MemMode.ACCUMULATOR, 1, 2, 0),  # 0a
    Instruction(InstructionType.ANC, self.unimplemented, MemMode.IMMEDIATE, 0, 2, 0),
    Instruction(InstructionType.NOP, self.NOP, MemMode.ABSOLUTE, 3, 4, 0),  # 0c
    Instruction(InstructionType.ORA, self.ORA, MemMode.ABSOLUTE, 3, 4, 0),  # 0d
    Instruction(InstructionType.ASL, self.ASL, MemMode.ABSOLUTE, 3, 6, 0),  # 0e
    Instruction(InstructionType.SLO, self.unimplemented, MemMode.ABSOLUTE, 0, 6, 0),
    Instruction(InstructionType.BPL, self.BPL, MemMode.RELATIVE, 2, 2, 1),  # 10
    Instruction(InstructionType.ORA, self.ORA, MemMode.INDIRECT_INDEXED, 2, 5, 1),
    Instruction(InstructionType.KIL, self.unimplemented, MemMode.IMPLIED, 0, 2, 0),
    Instruction(InstructionType.SLO, self.unimplemented, MemMode.INDIRECT_INDEXED, 0, 8, 0),
    Instruction(InstructionType.NOP, self.NOP, MemMode.ZEROPAGE_X, 2, 4, 0),  # 14
    Instruction(InstructionType.ORA, self.ORA, MemMode.ZEROPAGE_X, 2, 4, 0),  # 15
    Instruction(InstructionType.ASL, self.ASL, MemMode.ZEROPAGE_X, 2, 6, 0),  # 16
    Instruction(InstructionType.SLO, self.unimplemented, MemMode.ZEROPAGE_X, 0, 6, 0),
    Instruction(InstructionType.CLC, self.CLC, MemMode.IMPLIED, 1, 2, 0),  # 18
    Instruction(InstructionType.ORA, self.ORA, MemMode.ABSOLUTE_Y, 3, 4, 1),  # 19
    Instruction(InstructionType.NOP, self.NOP, MemMode.IMPLIED, 1, 2, 0),  # 1a
    Instruction(InstructionType.SLO, self.unimplemented, MemMode.ABSOLUTE_Y, 0, 7, 0),
    Instruction(InstructionType.NOP, self.NOP, MemMode.ABSOLUTE_X, 3, 4, 1),  # 1c
    Instruction(InstructionType.ORA, self.ORA, MemMode.ABSOLUTE_X, 3, 4, 1),  # 1d
    Instruction(InstructionType.ASL, self.ASL, MemMode.ABSOLUTE_X, 3, 7, 0),  # 1e
    Instruction(InstructionType.SLO, self.unimplemented, MemMode.ABSOLUTE_X, 0, 7, 0),
    Instruction(InstructionType.JSR, self.JSR, MemMode.ABSOLUTE, 3, 6, 0),  # 20
    Instruction(InstructionType.AND, self.AND, MemMode.INDEXED_INDIRECT, 2, 6, 0),
    Instruction(InstructionType.KIL, self.unimplemented, MemMode.IMPLIED, 0, 2, 0),
    Instruction(InstructionType.RLA, self.unimplemented, MemMode.INDEXED_INDIRECT, 0, 8, 0),
    Instruction(InstructionType.BIT, self.BIT, MemMode.ZEROPAGE, 2, 3, 0),  # 24
    Instruction(InstructionType.AND, self.AND, MemMode.ZEROPAGE, 2, 3, 0),  # 25
    Instruction(InstructionType.ROL, self.ROL, MemMode.ZEROPAGE, 2, 5, 0),  # 26
    Instruction(InstructionType.RLA, self.unimplemented, MemMode.ZEROPAGE, 0, 5, 0),
    Instruction(InstructionType.PLP, self.PLP, MemMode.IMPLIED, 1, 4, 0),  # 28
    Instruction(InstructionType.AND, self.AND, MemMode.IMMEDIATE, 2, 2, 0),  # 29
    Instruction(InstructionType.ROL, self.ROL, MemMode.ACCUMULATOR, 1, 2, 0),  # 2a
    Instruction(InstructionType.ANC, self.unimplemented, MemMode.IMMEDIATE, 0, 2, 0),
    Instruction(InstructionType.BIT, self.BIT, MemMode.ABSOLUTE, 3, 4, 0),  # 2c
    Instruction(InstructionType.AND, self.AND, MemMode.ABSOLUTE, 3, 4, 0),  # 2d
    Instruction(InstructionType.ROL, self.ROL, MemMode.ABSOLUTE, 3, 6, 0),  # 2e
    Instruction(InstructionType.RLA, self.unimplemented, MemMode.ABSOLUTE, 0, 6, 0),
    Instruction(InstructionType.BMI, self.BMI, MemMode.RELATIVE, 2, 2, 1),  # 30
    Instruction(InstructionType.AND, self.AND, MemMode.INDIRECT_INDEXED, 2, 5, 1),
    Instruction(InstructionType.KIL, self.unimplemented, MemMode.IMPLIED, 0, 2, 0),
```

```
Instruction(InstructionType.RLA, self.unimplemented, MemMode.INDIRECT_INDEXED, 0, 8, 0),
Instruction(InstructionType.NOP, self.NOP, MemMode.ZEROPAGE_X, 2, 4, 0),   # 34
Instruction(InstructionType.AND, self.AND, MemMode.ZEROPAGE_X, 2, 4, 0),   # 35
Instruction(InstructionType.ROL, self.ROL, MemMode.ZEROPAGE_X, 2, 6, 0),   # 36
Instruction(InstructionType.RLA, self.unimplemented, MemMode.ZEROPAGE_X, 0, 6, 0),
Instruction(InstructionType.SEC, self.SEC, MemMode.IMPLIED, 1, 2, 0),   # 38
Instruction(InstructionType.AND, self.AND, MemMode.ABSOLUTE_Y, 3, 4, 1),   # 39
Instruction(InstructionType.NOP, self.NOP, MemMode.IMPLIED, 1, 2, 0),   # 3a
Instruction(InstructionType.RLA, self.unimplemented, MemMode.ABSOLUTE_Y, 0, 7, 0),
Instruction(InstructionType.NOP, self.NOP, MemMode.ABSOLUTE_X, 3, 4, 1),   # 3c
Instruction(InstructionType.AND, self.AND, MemMode.ABSOLUTE_X, 3, 4, 1),   # 3d
Instruction(InstructionType.ROL, self.ROL, MemMode.ABSOLUTE_X, 3, 7, 0),   # 3e
Instruction(InstructionType.RLA, self.unimplemented, MemMode.ABSOLUTE_X, 0, 7, 0),
Instruction(InstructionType.RTI, self.RTI, MemMode.IMPLIED, 1, 6, 0),   # 40
Instruction(InstructionType.EOR, self.EOR, MemMode.INDEXED_INDIRECT, 2, 6, 0),
Instruction(InstructionType.KIL, self.unimplemented, MemMode.IMPLIED, 0, 2, 0),
Instruction(InstructionType.SRE, self.unimplemented, MemMode.INDEXED_INDIRECT, 0, 8, 0),
Instruction(InstructionType.NOP, self.NOP, MemMode.ZEROPAGE, 2, 3, 0),   # 44
Instruction(InstructionType.EOR, self.EOR, MemMode.ZEROPAGE, 2, 3, 0),   # 45
Instruction(InstructionType.LSR, self.LSR, MemMode.ZEROPAGE, 2, 5, 0),   # 46
Instruction(InstructionType.SRE, self.unimplemented, MemMode.ZEROPAGE, 0, 5, 0),
Instruction(InstructionType.PHA, self.PHA, MemMode.IMPLIED, 1, 3, 0),   # 48
Instruction(InstructionType.EOR, self.EOR, MemMode.IMMEDIATE, 2, 2, 0),   # 49
Instruction(InstructionType.LSR, self.LSR, MemMode.ACCUMULATOR, 1, 2, 0),
Instruction(InstructionType.ALR, self.unimplemented, MemMode.IMMEDIATE, 0, 2, 0),
Instruction(InstructionType.JMP, self.JMP, MemMode.ABSOLUTE, 3, 3, 0),   # 4c
Instruction(InstructionType.EOR, self.EOR, MemMode.ABSOLUTE, 3, 4, 0),   # 4d
Instruction(InstructionType.LSR, self.LSR, MemMode.ABSOLUTE, 3, 6, 0),   # 4e
Instruction(InstructionType.SRE, self.unimplemented, MemMode.ABSOLUTE, 0, 6, 0),
Instruction(InstructionType.BVC, self.BVC, MemMode.RELATIVE, 2, 2, 1),   # 50
Instruction(InstructionType.EOR, self.EOR, MemMode.INDIRECT_INDEXED, 2, 5, 1),
Instruction(InstructionType.KIL, self.unimplemented, MemMode.IMPLIED, 0, 2, 0),
Instruction(InstructionType.SRE, self.unimplemented, MemMode.INDIRECT_INDEXED, 0, 8, 0),
Instruction(InstructionType.NOP, self.NOP, MemMode.ZEROPAGE_X, 2, 4, 0),   # 54
Instruction(InstructionType.EOR, self.EOR, MemMode.ZEROPAGE_X, 2, 4, 0),   # 55
Instruction(InstructionType.LSR, self.LSR, MemMode.ZEROPAGE_X, 2, 6, 0),   # 56
Instruction(InstructionType.SRE, self.unimplemented, MemMode.ZEROPAGE_X, 0, 6, 0),
Instruction(InstructionType.CLI, self.CLI, MemMode.IMPLIED, 1, 2, 0),   # 58
Instruction(InstructionType.EOR, self.EOR, MemMode.ABSOLUTE_Y, 3, 4, 1),   # 59
Instruction(InstructionType.NOP, self.NOP, MemMode.IMPLIED, 1, 2, 0),   # 5a
Instruction(InstructionType.SRE, self.unimplemented, MemMode.ABSOLUTE_Y, 0, 7, 0),
Instruction(InstructionType.NOP, self.NOP, MemMode.ABSOLUTE_X, 3, 4, 1),   # 5c
Instruction(InstructionType.EOR, self.EOR, MemMode.ABSOLUTE_X, 3, 4, 1),   # 5d
Instruction(InstructionType.LSR, self.LSR, MemMode.ABSOLUTE_X, 3, 7, 0),   # 5e
Instruction(InstructionType.SRE, self.unimplemented, MemMode.ABSOLUTE_X, 0, 7, 0),
Instruction(InstructionType.RTS, self.RTS, MemMode.IMPLIED, 1, 6, 0),   # 60
Instruction(InstructionType.ADC, self.ADC, MemMode.INDEXED_INDIRECT, 2, 6, 0),
Instruction(InstructionType.KIL, self.unimplemented, MemMode.IMPLIED, 0, 2, 0),
Instruction(InstructionType.RRA, self.unimplemented, MemMode.INDEXED_INDIRECT, 0, 8, 0),
Instruction(InstructionType.NOP, self.NOP, MemMode.ZEROPAGE, 2, 3, 0),   # 64
Instruction(InstructionType.ADC, self.ADC, MemMode.ZEROPAGE, 2, 3, 0),   # 65
Instruction(InstructionType.ROR, self.ROR, MemMode.ZEROPAGE, 2, 5, 0),   # 66
Instruction(InstructionType.RRA, self.unimplemented, MemMode.ZEROPAGE, 0, 5, 0),
Instruction(InstructionType.PLA, self.PLA, MemMode.IMPLIED, 1, 4, 0),   # 68
```

```
Instruction(InstructionType.ADC, self.ADC, MemMode.IMMEDIATE, 2, 2, 0),  # 69
Instruction(InstructionType.ROR, self.ROR, MemMode.ACCUMULATOR, 1, 2, 0),  # 6a
Instruction(InstructionType.ARR, self.unimplemented, MemMode.IMMEDIATE, 0, 2, 0),
Instruction(InstructionType.JMP, self.JMP, MemMode.INDIRECT, 3, 5, 0),  # 6c
Instruction(InstructionType.ADC, self.ADC, MemMode.ABSOLUTE, 3, 4, 0),  # 6d
Instruction(InstructionType.ROR, self.ROR, MemMode.ABSOLUTE, 3, 6, 0),  # 6e
Instruction(InstructionType.RRA, self.unimplemented, MemMode.ABSOLUTE, 0, 6, 0),
Instruction(InstructionType.BVS, self.BVS, MemMode.RELATIVE, 2, 2, 1),  # 70
Instruction(InstructionType.ADC, self.ADC, MemMode.INDIRECT_INDEXED, 2, 5, 1),
Instruction(InstructionType.KIL, self.unimplemented, MemMode.IMPLIED, 0, 2, 0),
Instruction(InstructionType.RRA, self.unimplemented, MemMode.INDIRECT_INDEXED, 0, 8, 0),
Instruction(InstructionType.NOP, self.NOP, MemMode.ZEROPAGE_X, 2, 4, 0),  # 74
Instruction(InstructionType.ADC, self.ADC, MemMode.ZEROPAGE_X, 2, 4, 0),  # 75
Instruction(InstructionType.ROR, self.ROR, MemMode.ZEROPAGE_X, 2, 6, 0),  # 76
Instruction(InstructionType.RRA, self.unimplemented, MemMode.ZEROPAGE_X, 0, 6, 0),
Instruction(InstructionType.SEI, self.SEI, MemMode.IMPLIED, 1, 2, 0),  # 78
Instruction(InstructionType.ADC, self.ADC, MemMode.ABSOLUTE_Y, 3, 4, 1),  # 79
Instruction(InstructionType.NOP, self.NOP, MemMode.IMPLIED, 1, 2, 0),  # 7a
Instruction(InstructionType.RRA, self.unimplemented, MemMode.ABSOLUTE_Y, 0, 7, 0),
Instruction(InstructionType.NOP, self.NOP, MemMode.ABSOLUTE_X, 3, 4, 1),  # 7c
Instruction(InstructionType.ADC, self.ADC, MemMode.ABSOLUTE_X, 3, 4, 1),  # 7d
Instruction(InstructionType.ROR, self.ROR, MemMode.ABSOLUTE_X, 3, 7, 0),  # 7e
Instruction(InstructionType.RRA, self.unimplemented, MemMode.ABSOLUTE_X, 0, 7, 0),
Instruction(InstructionType.NOP, self.NOP, MemMode.IMMEDIATE, 2, 2, 0),  # 80
Instruction(InstructionType.STA, self.STA, MemMode.INDEXED_INDIRECT, 2, 6, 0),
Instruction(InstructionType.NOP, self.NOP, MemMode.IMMEDIATE, 0, 2, 0),  # 82
Instruction(InstructionType.SAX, self.unimplemented, MemMode.INDEXED_INDIRECT, 0, 6, 0),
Instruction(InstructionType.STY, self.STY, MemMode.ZEROPAGE, 2, 3, 0),  # 84
Instruction(InstructionType.STA, self.STA, MemMode.ZEROPAGE, 2, 3, 0),  # 85
Instruction(InstructionType.STX, self.STX, MemMode.ZEROPAGE, 2, 3, 0),  # 86
Instruction(InstructionType.SAX, self.unimplemented, MemMode.ZEROPAGE, 0, 3, 0),
Instruction(InstructionType.DEY, self.DEY, MemMode.IMPLIED, 1, 2, 0),  # 88
Instruction(InstructionType.NOP, self.NOP, MemMode.IMMEDIATE, 0, 2, 0),  # 89
Instruction(InstructionType.TXA, self.TXA, MemMode.IMPLIED, 1, 2, 0),  # 8a
Instruction(InstructionType.XAA, self.unimplemented, MemMode.IMMEDIATE, 0, 2, 0),
Instruction(InstructionType.STY, self.STY, MemMode.ABSOLUTE, 3, 4, 0),  # 8c
Instruction(InstructionType.STA, self.STA, MemMode.ABSOLUTE, 3, 4, 0),  # 8d
Instruction(InstructionType.STX, self.STX, MemMode.ABSOLUTE, 3, 4, 0),  # 8e
Instruction(InstructionType.SAX, self.unimplemented, MemMode.ABSOLUTE, 0, 4, 0),
Instruction(InstructionType.BCC, self.BCC, MemMode.RELATIVE, 2, 2, 1),  # 90
Instruction(InstructionType.STA, self.STA, MemMode.INDIRECT_INDEXED, 2, 6, 0),
Instruction(InstructionType.KIL, self.unimplemented, MemMode.IMPLIED, 0, 2, 0),
Instruction(InstructionType.AHX, self.unimplemented, MemMode.INDIRECT_INDEXED, 0, 6, 0),
Instruction(InstructionType.STY, self.STY, MemMode.ZEROPAGE_X, 2, 4, 0),  # 94
Instruction(InstructionType.STA, self.STA, MemMode.ZEROPAGE_X, 2, 4, 0),  # 95
Instruction(InstructionType.STX, self.STX, MemMode.ZEROPAGE_Y, 2, 4, 0),  # 96
Instruction(InstructionType.SAX, self.unimplemented, MemMode.ZEROPAGE_Y, 0, 4, 0),
Instruction(InstructionType.TYA, self.TYA, MemMode.IMPLIED, 1, 2, 0),  # 98
Instruction(InstructionType.STA, self.STA, MemMode.ABSOLUTE_Y, 3, 5, 0),  # 99
Instruction(InstructionType.TXS, self.TXS, MemMode.IMPLIED, 1, 2, 0),  # 9a
Instruction(InstructionType.TAS, self.unimplemented, MemMode.ABSOLUTE_Y, 0, 5, 0),
Instruction(InstructionType.SHY, self.unimplemented, MemMode.ABSOLUTE_X, 0, 5, 0),
Instruction(InstructionType.STA, self.STA, MemMode.ABSOLUTE_X, 3, 5, 0),  # 9d
Instruction(InstructionType.SHX, self.unimplemented, MemMode.ABSOLUTE_Y, 0, 5, 0),
```

```
Instruction(InstructionType.AHX, self.unimplemented, MemMode.ABSOLUTE_Y, 0, 5, 0),
Instruction(InstructionType.LDY, self.LDY, MemMode.IMMEDIATE, 2, 2, 0),  # a0
Instruction(InstructionType.LDA, self.LDA, MemMode.INDEXED_INDIRECT, 2, 6, 0),
Instruction(InstructionType.LDX, self.LDX, MemMode.IMMEDIATE, 2, 2, 0),  # a2
Instruction(InstructionType.LAX, self.unimplemented, MemMode.INDEXED_INDIRECT, 0, 6, 0),
Instruction(InstructionType.LDY, self.LDY, MemMode.ZEROPAGE, 2, 3, 0),  # a4
Instruction(InstructionType.LDA, self.LDA, MemMode.ZEROPAGE, 2, 3, 0),  # a5
Instruction(InstructionType.LDX, self.LDX, MemMode.ZEROPAGE, 2, 3, 0),  # a6
Instruction(InstructionType.LAX, self.unimplemented, MemMode.ZEROPAGE, 0, 3, 0),
Instruction(InstructionType.TAY, self.TAY, MemMode.IMPLIED, 1, 2, 0),  # a8
Instruction(InstructionType.LDA, self.LDA, MemMode.IMMEDIATE, 2, 2, 0),  # a9
Instruction(InstructionType.TAX, self.TAX, MemMode.IMPLIED, 1, 2, 0),  # aa
Instruction(InstructionType.LAX, self.unimplemented, MemMode.IMMEDIATE, 0, 2, 0),
Instruction(InstructionType.LDY, self.LDY, MemMode.ABSOLUTE, 3, 4, 0),  # ac
Instruction(InstructionType.LDA, self.LDA, MemMode.ABSOLUTE, 3, 4, 0),  # ad
Instruction(InstructionType.LDX, self.LDX, MemMode.ABSOLUTE, 3, 4, 0),  # ae
Instruction(InstructionType.LAX, self.unimplemented, MemMode.ABSOLUTE, 0, 4, 0),
Instruction(InstructionType.BCS, self.BCS, MemMode.RELATIVE, 2, 2, 1),  # b0
Instruction(InstructionType.LDA, self.LDA, MemMode.INDIRECT_INDEXED, 2, 5, 1),
Instruction(InstructionType.KIL, self.unimplemented, MemMode.IMPLIED, 0, 2, 0),
Instruction(InstructionType.LAX, self.unimplemented, MemMode.INDIRECT_INDEXED, 0, 5, 1),
Instruction(InstructionType.LDY, self.LDY, MemMode.ZEROPAGE_X, 2, 4, 0),  # b4
Instruction(InstructionType.LDA, self.LDA, MemMode.ZEROPAGE_X, 2, 4, 0),  # b5
Instruction(InstructionType.LDX, self.LDX, MemMode.ZEROPAGE_Y, 2, 4, 0),  # b6
Instruction(InstructionType.LAX, self.unimplemented, MemMode.ZEROPAGE_Y, 0, 4, 0),
Instruction(InstructionType.CLV, self.CLV, MemMode.IMPLIED, 1, 2, 0),  # b8
Instruction(InstructionType.LDA, self.LDA, MemMode.ABSOLUTE_Y, 3, 4, 1),  # b9
Instruction(InstructionType.TSX, self.TSX, MemMode.IMPLIED, 1, 2, 0),  # ba
Instruction(InstructionType.LAS, self.unimplemented, MemMode.ABSOLUTE_Y, 0, 4, 1),
Instruction(InstructionType.LDY, self.LDY, MemMode.ABSOLUTE_X, 3, 4, 1),  # bc
Instruction(InstructionType.LDA, self.LDA, MemMode.ABSOLUTE_X, 3, 4, 1),  # bd
Instruction(InstructionType.LDX, self.LDX, MemMode.ABSOLUTE_Y, 3, 4, 1),  # be
Instruction(InstructionType.LAX, self.unimplemented, MemMode.ABSOLUTE_Y, 0, 4, 1),
Instruction(InstructionType.CPY, self.CPY, MemMode.IMMEDIATE, 2, 2, 0),  # c0
Instruction(InstructionType.CMP, self.CMP, MemMode.INDEXED_INDIRECT, 2, 6, 0),
Instruction(InstructionType.NOP, self.NOP, MemMode.IMMEDIATE, 0, 2, 0),  # c2
Instruction(InstructionType.DCP, self.unimplemented, MemMode.INDEXED_INDIRECT, 0, 8, 0),
Instruction(InstructionType.CPY, self.CPY, MemMode.ZEROPAGE, 2, 3, 0),  # c4
Instruction(InstructionType.CMP, self.CMP, MemMode.ZEROPAGE, 2, 3, 0),  # c5
Instruction(InstructionType.DEC, self.DEC, MemMode.ZEROPAGE, 2, 5, 0),  # c6
Instruction(InstructionType.DCP, self.unimplemented, MemMode.ZEROPAGE, 0, 5, 0),
Instruction(InstructionType.INY, self.INY, MemMode.IMPLIED, 1, 2, 0),  # c8
Instruction(InstructionType.CMP, self.CMP, MemMode.IMMEDIATE, 2, 2, 0),  # c9
Instruction(InstructionType.DEX, self.DEX, MemMode.IMPLIED, 1, 2, 0),  # ca
Instruction(InstructionType.AXS, self.unimplemented, MemMode.IMMEDIATE, 0, 2, 0),
Instruction(InstructionType.CPY, self.CPY, MemMode.ABSOLUTE, 3, 4, 0),  # cc
Instruction(InstructionType.CMP, self.CMP, MemMode.ABSOLUTE, 3, 4, 0),  # cd
Instruction(InstructionType.DEC, self.DEC, MemMode.ABSOLUTE, 3, 6, 0),  # ce
Instruction(InstructionType.DCP, self.unimplemented, MemMode.ABSOLUTE, 0, 6, 0),
Instruction(InstructionType.BNE, self.BNE, MemMode.RELATIVE, 2, 2, 1),  # d0
Instruction(InstructionType.CMP, self.CMP, MemMode.INDIRECT_INDEXED, 2, 5, 1),
Instruction(InstructionType.KIL, self.unimplemented, MemMode.IMPLIED, 0, 2, 0),
Instruction(InstructionType.DCP, self.unimplemented, MemMode.INDIRECT_INDEXED, 0, 8, 0),
Instruction(InstructionType.NOP, self.NOP, MemMode.ZEROPAGE_X, 2, 4, 0),  # d4
```

```
Instruction(InstructionType.CMP, self.CMP, MemMode.ZEROPAGE_X, 2, 4, 0),   # d5
Instruction(InstructionType.DEC, self.DEC, MemMode.ZEROPAGE_X, 2, 6, 0),   # d6
Instruction(InstructionType.DCP, self.unimplemented, MemMode.ZEROPAGE_X, 0, 6, 0),
Instruction(InstructionType.CLD, self.CLD, MemMode.IMPLIED, 1, 2, 0),   # d8
Instruction(InstructionType.CMP, self.CMP, MemMode.ABSOLUTE_Y, 3, 4, 1),   # d9
Instruction(InstructionType.NOP, self.NOP, MemMode.IMPLIED, 1, 2, 0),   # da
Instruction(InstructionType.DCP, self.unimplemented, MemMode.ABSOLUTE_Y, 0, 7, 0),
Instruction(InstructionType.NOP, self.NOP, MemMode.ABSOLUTE_X, 3, 4, 1),   # dc
Instruction(InstructionType.CMP, self.CMP, MemMode.ABSOLUTE_X, 3, 4, 1),   # dd
Instruction(InstructionType.DEC, self.DEC, MemMode.ABSOLUTE_X, 3, 7, 0),   # de
Instruction(InstructionType.DCP, self.unimplemented, MemMode.ABSOLUTE_X, 0, 7, 0),
Instruction(InstructionType.CPX, self.CPX, MemMode.IMMEDIATE, 2, 2, 0),   # e0
Instruction(InstructionType.SBC, self.SBC, MemMode.INDEXED_INDIRECT, 2, 6, 0),
Instruction(InstructionType.NOP, self.NOP, MemMode.IMMEDIATE, 0, 2, 0),   # e2
Instruction(InstructionType.ISC, self.unimplemented, MemMode.INDEXED_INDIRECT, 0, 8, 0),
Instruction(InstructionType.CPX, self.CPX, MemMode.ZEROPAGE, 2, 3, 0),   # e4
Instruction(InstructionType.SBC, self.SBC, MemMode.ZEROPAGE, 2, 3, 0),   # e5
Instruction(InstructionType.INC, self.INC, MemMode.ZEROPAGE, 2, 5, 0),   # e6
Instruction(InstructionType.ISC, self.unimplemented, MemMode.ZEROPAGE, 0, 5, 0),
Instruction(InstructionType.INX, self.INX, MemMode.IMPLIED, 1, 2, 0),   # e8
Instruction(InstructionType.SBC, self.SBC, MemMode.IMMEDIATE, 2, 2, 0),   # e9
Instruction(InstructionType.NOP, self.NOP, MemMode.IMPLIED, 1, 2, 0),   # ea
Instruction(InstructionType.SBC, self.SBC, MemMode.IMMEDIATE, 0, 2, 0),   # eb
Instruction(InstructionType.CPX, self.CPX, MemMode.ABSOLUTE, 3, 4, 0),   # ec
Instruction(InstructionType.SBC, self.SBC, MemMode.ABSOLUTE, 3, 4, 0),   # ed
Instruction(InstructionType.INC, self.INC, MemMode.ABSOLUTE, 3, 6, 0),   # ee
Instruction(InstructionType.ISC, self.unimplemented, MemMode.ABSOLUTE, 0, 6, 0),
Instruction(InstructionType.BEQ, self.BEQ, MemMode.RELATIVE, 2, 2, 1),   # f0
Instruction(InstructionType.SBC, self.SBC, MemMode.INDIRECT_INDEXED, 2, 5, 1),
Instruction(InstructionType.KIL, self.unimplemented, MemMode.IMPLIED, 0, 2, 0),
Instruction(InstructionType.ISC, self.unimplemented, MemMode.INDIRECT_INDEXED, 0, 8, 0),
Instruction(InstructionType.NOP, self.NOP, MemMode.ZEROPAGE_X, 2, 4, 0),   # f4
Instruction(InstructionType.SBC, self.SBC, MemMode.ZEROPAGE_X, 2, 4, 0),   # f5
Instruction(InstructionType.INC, self.INC, MemMode.ZEROPAGE_X, 2, 6, 0),   # f6
Instruction(InstructionType.ISC, self.unimplemented, MemMode.ZEROPAGE_X, 0, 6, 0),
Instruction(InstructionType.SED, self.SED, MemMode.IMPLIED, 1, 2, 0),   # f8
Instruction(InstructionType.SBC, self.SBC, MemMode.ABSOLUTE_Y, 3, 4, 1),   # f9
Instruction(InstructionType.NOP, self.NOP, MemMode.IMPLIED, 1, 2, 0),   # fa
Instruction(InstructionType.ISC, self.unimplemented, MemMode.ABSOLUTE_Y, 0, 7, 0),
Instruction(InstructionType.NOP, self.NOP, MemMode.ABSOLUTE_X, 3, 4, 1),   # fc
Instruction(InstructionType.SBC, self.SBC, MemMode.ABSOLUTE_X, 3, 4, 1),   # fd
Instruction(InstructionType.INC, self.INC, MemMode.ABSOLUTE_X, 3, 7, 0),   # fe
Instruction(InstructionType.ISC, self.unimplemented, MemMode.ABSOLUTE_X, 0, 7, 0),
]
```

Hand-coding this jump table would have been incredibly tedious. Instead, I wrote an external script to automatically create the table from public sources. The script was a hack I threw together to generate the table, so I didn't include it in the repository. Sometimes those quick and dirty scripts save you a lot of typing, though!

The Instructions

Next, we need to declare all the methods that bring the 6502 instructions to life. As discussed, we have 56 unique methods to implement, ranging alphabetically from ADC to TYA, handling tasks such as arithmetic, control flow, and the like.

As with the CHIP-8 project, this is a good place for you to stop and try to write some of the methods on your own before looking at the implementations here. In order to do that, you'll need a good 6502 instruction reference. There are many available online, and the aforementioned *https://nesdev.org* links to several. A good reference should include the following:

- The name of the instruction, including its common mnemonic
- The opcode for various forms of the instruction
- The memory modes it supports
- What flags, if any, the instruction affects
- How many cycles it takes
- What register(s) it operates on
- An example of what it does

If you choose to implement the instructions yourself, you'll first want to look through the rest of the CPU class to see what helper methods are available to you. There are methods for modifying the stack, reading from memory, and writing to memory, and there are a couple other utility methods as well. See "Memory Access" on page 170 and "Helper Methods" on page 175 for these methods.

You'll find that many of the instructions are quite simple. For example, AND is exactly the logical AND operation you'd expect. We take the accumulator (self.A), do a bitwise AND operation between it and whatever we read from memory, and then store the result back in the accumulator:

```
def AND(self, instruction: Instruction, data: int):
    src = self.read_memory(data, instruction.mode)
    self.A = self.A & src
    self.setZN(self.A)
```

Note how two things have been abstracted away. Reading from memory is done by another method, self.read_memory(), which is passed the instruction's memory mode. We'll come back to that method's implementation later. Second, many different instructions affect flags, so we have methods like self.setZN() to handle flag changes. This is the classic don't repeat yourself (DRY) principle.

What follows are implementations for all 56 needed methods. We're writing in Python what the 6502 would be doing in hardware, and it's really not rocket science. Python has operators for completing most tasks. The other skill set that helps most with this sort of work is a strong understanding of bitwise operators, as there are several places where the instruction explicitly asks for them or we need to cut off a result to make sure it's still

8 bits so that it fits in the register. We cover how these bitwise operators work in the appendix.

```python
# Add memory to accumulator with carry
def ADC(self, instruction: Instruction, data: int):
    src = self.read_memory(data, instruction.mode)
    signed_result = src + self.A + self.C
    self.V = bool(~(self.A ^ src) & (self.A ^ signed_result) & 0x80)
    self.A = (self.A + src + self.C) % 256
    self.C = signed_result > 0xFF
    self.setZN(self.A)

# Bitwise AND with accumulator
def AND(self, instruction: Instruction, data: int):
    src = self.read_memory(data, instruction.mode)
    self.A = self.A & src
    self.setZN(self.A)

# Arithmetic shift left
def ASL(self, instruction: Instruction, data: int):
    src = self.A if instruction.mode == MemMode.ACCUMULATOR else (
        self.read_memory(data, instruction.mode))
    self.C = bool(src >> 7)  # carry is set to 7th bit
    src = (src << 1) & 0xFF
    self.setZN(src)
    if instruction.mode == MemMode.ACCUMULATOR:
        self.A = src
    else:
        self.write_memory(data, instruction.mode, src)

# Branch if carry clear
def BCC(self, instruction: Instruction, data: int):
    if not self.C:
        self.PC = self.address_for_mode(data, instruction.mode)
        self.jumped = True

# Branch if carry set
def BCS(self, instruction: Instruction, data: int):
    if self.C:
        self.PC = self.address_for_mode(data, instruction.mode)
        self.jumped = True

# Branch on result zero
def BEQ(self, instruction: Instruction, data: int):
    if self.Z:
        self.PC = self.address_for_mode(data, instruction.mode)
        self.jumped = True

# Bit test bits in memory with accumulator
def BIT(self, instruction: Instruction, data: int):
    src = self.read_memory(data, instruction.mode)
    self.V = bool((src >> 6) & 1)
    self.Z = ((src & self.A) == 0)
    self.N = ((src >> 7) == 1)
```

```python
# Branch on result minus
def BMI(self, instruction: Instruction, data: int):
    if self.N:
        self.PC = self.address_for_mode(data, instruction.mode)
        self.jumped = True

# Branch on result not zero
def BNE(self, instruction: Instruction, data: int):
    if not self.Z:
        self.PC = self.address_for_mode(data, instruction.mode)
        self.jumped = True

# Branch on result plus
def BPL(self, instruction: Instruction, data: int):
    if not self.N:
        self.PC = self.address_for_mode(data, instruction.mode)
        self.jumped = True

# Force break
def BRK(self, instruction: Instruction, data: int):
    self.PC += 2
    # Push PC to stack
    self.stack_push((self.PC >> 8) & 0xFF)
    self.stack_push(self.PC & 0xFF)
    # Push status to stack
    self.B = True
    self.stack_push(self.status)
    self.B = False
    self.I = True
    # Set PC to reset vector
    self.PC = (self.read_memory(IRQ_BRK_VECTOR, MemMode.ABSOLUTE)) | \
              (self.read_memory(IRQ_BRK_VECTOR + 1, MemMode.ABSOLUTE) << 8)
    self.jumped = True

# Branch on overflow clear
def BVC(self, instruction: Instruction, data: int):
    if not self.V:
        self.PC = self.address_for_mode(data, instruction.mode)
        self.jumped = True

# Branch on overflow set
def BVS(self, instruction: Instruction, data: int):
    if self.V:
        self.PC = self.address_for_mode(data, instruction.mode)
        self.jumped = True

# Clear carry
def CLC(self, instruction: Instruction, data: int):
    self.C = False

# Clear decimal
def CLD(self, instruction: Instruction, data: int):
    self.D = False
```

```python
# Clear interrupt
def CLI(self, instruction: Instruction, data: int):
    self.I = False

# Clear overflow
def CLV(self, instruction: Instruction, data: int):
    self.V = False

# Compare accumulator
def CMP(self, instruction: Instruction, data: int):
    src = self.read_memory(data, instruction.mode)
    self.C = self.A >= src
    self.setZN(self.A - src)

# Compare X register
def CPX(self, instruction: Instruction, data: int):
    src = self.read_memory(data, instruction.mode)
    self.C = self.X >= src
    self.setZN(self.X - src)

# Compare Y register
def CPY(self, instruction: Instruction, data: int):
    src = self.read_memory(data, instruction.mode)
    self.C = self.Y >= src
    self.setZN(self.Y - src)

# Decrement memory
def DEC(self, instruction: Instruction, data: int):
    src = self.read_memory(data, instruction.mode)
    src = (src - 1) & 0xFF
    self.write_memory(data, instruction.mode, src)
    self.setZN(src)

# Decrement X
def DEX(self, instruction: Instruction, data: int):
    self.X = (self.X - 1) & 0xFF
    self.setZN(self.X)

# Decrement Y
def DEY(self, instruction: Instruction, data: int):
    self.Y = (self.Y - 1) & 0xFF
    self.setZN(self.Y)

# Exclusive or memory with accumulator
def EOR(self, instruction: Instruction, data: int):
    self.A ^= self.read_memory(data, instruction.mode)
    self.setZN(self.A)

# Increment memory
def INC(self, instruction: Instruction, data: int):
    src = self.read_memory(data, instruction.mode)
    src = (src + 1) & 0xFF
    self.write_memory(data, instruction.mode, src)
    self.setZN(src)
```

```python
# Increment X
def INX(self, instruction: Instruction, data: int):
    self.X = (self.X + 1) & 0xFF
    self.setZN(self.X)

# Increment Y
def INY(self, instruction: Instruction, data: int):
    self.Y = (self.Y + 1) & 0xFF
    self.setZN(self.Y)

# Jump
def JMP(self, instruction: Instruction, data: int):
    self.PC = self.address_for_mode(data, instruction.mode)
    self.jumped = True

# Jump to subroutine
def JSR(self, instruction: Instruction, data: int):
    self.PC += 2
    # Push PC to stack
    self.stack_push((self.PC >> 8) & 0xFF)
    self.stack_push(self.PC & 0xFF)
    # Jump to subroutine
    self.PC = self.address_for_mode(data, instruction.mode)
    self.jumped = True

# Load accumulator with memory
def LDA(self, instruction: Instruction, data: int):
    self.A = self.read_memory(data, instruction.mode)
    self.setZN(self.A)

# Load X with memory
def LDX(self, instruction: Instruction, data: int):
    self.X = self.read_memory(data, instruction.mode)
    self.setZN(self.X)

# Load Y with memory
def LDY(self, instruction: Instruction, data: int):
    self.Y = self.read_memory(data, instruction.mode)
    self.setZN(self.Y)

# Logical shift right
def LSR(self, instruction: Instruction, data: int):
    src = self.A if instruction.mode == MemMode.ACCUMULATOR else (
        self.read_memory(data, instruction.mode))
    self.C = bool(src & 1)  # carry is set to 0th bit
    src >>= 1
    self.setZN(src)
    if instruction.mode == MemMode.ACCUMULATOR:
        self.A = src
    else:
        self.write_memory(data, instruction.mode, src)

# No op
def NOP(self, instruction: Instruction, data: int):
    pass
```

```python
# Or memory with accumulator
def ORA(self, instruction: Instruction, data: int):
    self.A |= self.read_memory(data, instruction.mode)
    self.setZN(self.A)


# Push accumulator
def PHA(self, instruction: Instruction, data: int):
    self.stack_push(self.A)


# Push status
def PHP(self, instruction: Instruction, data: int):
    # https://nesdev.org/the%20'B'%20flag%20&%20BRK%20instruction.txt
    self.B = True
    self.stack_push(self.status)
    self.B = False


# Pull accumulator
def PLA(self, instruction: Instruction, data: int):
    self.A = self.stack_pop()
    self.setZN(self.A)


# Pull status
def PLP(self, instruction: Instruction, data: int):
    self.set_status(self.stack_pop())


# Rotate one bit left
def ROL(self, instruction: Instruction, data: int):
    src = self.A if instruction.mode == MemMode.ACCUMULATOR else (
        self.read_memory(data, instruction.mode))
    old_c = self.C
    self.C = bool((src >> 7) & 1)  # carry is set to 7th bit
    src = ((src << 1) | old_c) & 0xFF
    self.setZN(src)
    if instruction.mode == MemMode.ACCUMULATOR:
        self.A = src
    else:
        self.write_memory(data, instruction.mode, src)


# Rotate one bit right
def ROR(self, instruction: Instruction, data: int):
    src = self.A if instruction.mode == MemMode.ACCUMULATOR else (
        self.read_memory(data, instruction.mode))
    old_c = self.C
    self.C = bool(src & 1)  # carry is set to 0th bit
    src = ((src >> 1) | (old_c << 7)) & 0xFF
    self.setZN(src)
    if instruction.mode == MemMode.ACCUMULATOR:
        self.A = src
    else:
        self.write_memory(data, instruction.mode, src)


# Return from interrupt
def RTI(self, instruction: Instruction, data: int):
    # Pull status out
```

```python
        self.set_status(self.stack_pop())
        # Pull PC out
        lb = self.stack_pop()
        hb = self.stack_pop()
        self.PC = ((hb << 8) | lb)
        self.jumped = True

    # Return from subroutine
    def RTS(self, instruction: Instruction, data: int):
        # Pull PC out
        lb = self.stack_pop()
        hb = self.stack_pop()
        self.PC = ((hb << 8) | lb) + 1  # 1 past last instruction
        self.jumped = True

    # Subtract with carry
    def SBC(self, instruction: Instruction, data: int):
        src = self.read_memory(data, instruction.mode)
        signed_result = self.A - src - (1 - self.C)
        # Set overflow
        self.V = bool((self.A ^ src) & (self.A ^ signed_result) & 0x80)
        self.A = (self.A - src - (1 - self.C)) % 256
        self.C = not (signed_result < 0)  # set carry
        self.setZN(self.A)

    # Set carry
    def SEC(self, instruction: Instruction, data: int):
        self.C = True

    # Set decimal
    def SED(self, instruction: Instruction, data: int):
        self.D = True

    # Set interrupt
    def SEI(self, instruction: Instruction, data: int):
        self.I = True

    # Store accumulator
    def STA(self, instruction: Instruction, data: int):
        self.write_memory(data, instruction.mode, self.A)

    # Store X register
    def STX(self, instruction: Instruction, data: int):
        self.write_memory(data, instruction.mode, self.X)

    # Store Y register
    def STY(self, instruction: Instruction, data: int):
        self.write_memory(data, instruction.mode, self.Y)

    # Transfer A to X
    def TAX(self, instruction: Instruction, data: int):
        self.X = self.A
        self.setZN(self.X)
```

```
# Transfer A to Y
def TAY(self, instruction: Instruction, data: int):
    self.Y = self.A
    self.setZN(self.Y)

# Transfer stack pointer to X
def TSX(self, instruction: Instruction, data: int):
    self.X = self.SP
    self.setZN(self.X)

# Transfer X to A
def TXA(self, instruction: Instruction, data: int):
    self.A = self.X
    self.setZN(self.A)

# Transfer X to SP
def TXS(self, instruction: Instruction, data: int):
    self.SP = self.X

# Transfer Y to A
def TYA(self, instruction: Instruction, data: int):
    self.A = self.Y
    self.setZN(self.A)

def unimplemented(self, instruction: Instruction, data: int):
    print(f"{instruction.type.name} is unimplemented.")
```

While most instructions are fairly simple, I found handling add with carry (ADC) and subtract with carry (SBC) a little tricky. The 6502's main registers are just 8 bits, so carries are going to happen a lot and you need to get the flags right. But we have a trick: the Python int type isn't limited to 8 bits. We can therefore do the arithmetic as if we're working with normal int values and then just mod off anything above 255.

The step() Method

With implementations for all of the instructions in place, we're ready to step through executing actual 6502 machine code. The step() method reads the next opcode at PC and pulls the instruction from the jump table. Here's the start of the method:

```
def step(self):
    if self.stall > 0:
        self.stall -= 1
        self.cpu_ticks += 1
        return

    opcode = self.read_memory(self.PC, MemMode.ABSOLUTE)
    self.page_crossed = False
    self.jumped = False
    instruction = self.instructions[opcode]
    data = 0
```

```
        for i in range(1, instruction.length):
            data |= (self.read_memory(self.PC + i,
                                MemMode.ABSOLUTE) << ((i - 1) * 8))
```

Most 6502 instructions also have some data that comes with them, and the number of bytes can vary. For example, the TAY instruction (transfer A to Y) takes no data, so it's just 1 byte, but any instruction that reads from memory will need additional data to specify the memory address. The amount of data to be read is specified by instruction.length.

The step() method continues as follows:

```
instruction.method(instruction, data)

if not self.jumped:
    self.PC += instruction.length
elif instruction.type in {InstructionType.BCC, InstructionType.BCS,
                            InstructionType.BEQ, InstructionType.BMI,
                            InstructionType.BNE, InstructionType.BPL,
                            InstructionType.BVC, InstructionType.BVS}:
    # Branch instructions are +1 ticks if they succeeded
    self.cpu_ticks += 1
self.cpu_ticks += instruction.ticks
if self.page_crossed:
    self.cpu_ticks += instruction.page_ticks
```

We call the instruction's actual method to execute the instruction, then increment the program counter as needed. We finish with some bookkeeping regarding ticks (CPU cycles).

Memory Access

The next few methods we'll write help with reading and writing to memory. Memory access is one of the more complicated areas of the 6502 because it has a dozen different memory access modes. The method address_for_mode() is responsible for translating the data associated with an instruction into a specific memory address based on the instruction's mode (MemMode):

```
def address_for_mode(self, data: int, mode: MemMode) -> int:
    def different_pages(address1: int, address2: int) -> bool:
        return (address1 & 0xFF00) != (address2 & 0xFF00)

    address = 0
    match mode:
        case MemMode.ABSOLUTE:
            address = data
        case MemMode.ABSOLUTE_X:
            address = (data + self.X) & 0xFFFF
            self.page_crossed = different_pages(address, address - self.X)
        case MemMode.ABSOLUTE_Y:
            address = (data + self.Y) & 0xFFFF
            self.page_crossed = different_pages(address, address - self.Y)
```

```
        case MemMode.INDEXED_INDIRECT:
            # OxFF for zero-page wrapping in next two lines
            ls = self.ram[(data + self.X) & 0xFF]
            ms = self.ram[(data + self.X + 1) & 0xFF]
            address = (ms << 8) | ls
        case MemMode.INDIRECT:
            ls = self.ram[data]
            ms = self.ram[data + 1]
            if (data & 0xFF) == 0xFF:
                ms = self.ram[data & 0xFF00]
            address = (ms << 8) | ls
        case MemMode.INDIRECT_INDEXED:
            # OxFF for zero-page wrapping in next two lines
            ls = self.ram[data & 0xFF]
            ms = self.ram[(data + 1) & 0xFF]
            address = (ms << 8) | ls
            address = (address + self.Y) & 0xFFFF
            self.page_crossed = different_pages(address, address - self.Y)
        case MemMode.RELATIVE:
            address = (self.PC + 2 + data) & 0xFFFF if (data < 0x80) \
                else (self.PC + 2 + (data - 256)) & 0xFFFF  # signed
        case MemMode.ZEROPAGE:
            address = data
        case MemMode.ZEROPAGE_X:
            address = (data + self.X) & 0xFF
        case MemMode.ZEROPAGE_Y:
            address = (data + self.Y) & 0xFF
    return address
```

To understand this code, here's a breakdown of the 6502's memory access modes and their relationship to the data associated with the instruction:

ABSOLUTE   The address is data.

ABSOLUTE_X   The X register is added to data to form the address.

ABSOLUTE_Y   The Y register is added to data to form the address.

ACCUMULATOR   The A register is being used, not memory. We handle this mode directly in the individual instruction methods, so it doesn't appear in address_for_mode().

IMMEDIATE   data is the final item; we're not actually accessing memory. We handle this mode directly in the methods for reading and writing to memory.

INDEXED_INDIRECT   The 2-byte address is in RAM at data + X.

INDIRECT   The 2-byte address is in RAM at data.

INDIRECT_INDEXED   The address at data in RAM is added to the Y register to form the final address.

RELATIVE   data is added to PC to form the address.

ZEROPAGE   This is like ABSOLUTE, but within the first 256 bytes of memory (the *zero page*).

ZEROPAGE_X   This is like ABSOLUTE_X, but within the first 256 bytes of memory.

ZEROPAGE_Y   This is like ABSOLUTE_Y, but within the first 256 bytes of memory.

The ZEROPAGE modes may seem redundant to the ABSOLUTE modes, but there's a nice optimization here: since the zero page in memory is only 256 bytes, it requires only a single data byte to specify an address within it. This saves a cycle of CPU time (a second address byte doesn't need to be fetched) when executing an instruction that utilizes the zero page. Instructions in ZEROPAGE mode are therefore faster than other instructions that access memory. In fact, 6502 programmers sometimes treat the 256 memory slots in the zero page like additional registers since they're so fast to read and write. This helps make up for how few actual registers the 6502 has.

Now that we can form memory addresses, we're closer to reading and writing memory, but we also need some knowledge of the NES's different memory regions—which addresses map to RAM, which to the PPU, and so on. It's important to note that many NES memory regions contain extensive mirroring. For example, the first 2KB in the memory map, or addresses up to 0x800 in hexadecimal, are mapped to the CPU's RAM, but any address accessed below 0x2000 maps to that same RAM because the 2KB repeats four times up until 0x2000. In other words, address 0x801 is the same as address 0x001, and so are addresses 0x1001 and 0x1801 ($2 \times 0x800$ in hexadecimal is 0x1000, and $3 \times 0x800$ is 0x1800).

This mirroring was a result of hardware peculiarities of the NES in order to cut costs. For example, not all of the 6502's memory hardware lines, which you can think of as wires, were needed to address that measly 2KB of RAM, so some of the hardware lines were simply ignored. To illustrate, 0x800 is 2,048 in decimal and 100000000000 in binary. Each digit in the binary can be thought of as a signal carried by a hardware line. To address the first 2,048 addresses, you only need 11 hardware lines, which correspond to the 11 trailing 0s in our number. Those 11 hardware lines are enough for 2,048 different values, decimal values 0 through 2,047. The 12th hardware line, represented by the 1 in the binary, can just be ignored. In other words, 0x800 maps to 12 hardware lines, but only 11 of those hardware lines actually existed, so 0x800 was essentially the same as 0x0.

Table 6-4 shows the NES CPU's memory map, as seen by our emulator. It includes both regions and individual memory-mapped addresses. Regions and addresses that our emulator ignores or doesn't implement aren't shown. The table also indicates whether a region or address is readable, writable, or both. Finally, it mentions if there's any mirroring.

There are many addresses and details missing from Table 6-4. For example, our simple emulator doesn't have an APU, but a real NES has memory-mapped addresses in the 0x4000 range for the APU and other I/O devices (like a second joypad). We also don't specify the individual PPU registers between 0x2000 and 0x2007, which we'll come back to when we implement the PPU. The cartridge memory space can vary quite a bit depending on the mapper. That's beyond the scope of this section; we discussed some of the

Table 6-4: A Simplified NES Memory Map

Address or region	Length	Description	Read/ write	Mirroring?
0x0000–0x1FFF	0x800	Main 2KB of CPU memory	RW	Yes, first 0x800 is mirrored up to 0x2000
0x2000–0x3FFF	0x8	8 PPU registers	Varies	0x2000 through 0x2007 are mirrored every 8 bytes
0x4014	0x1	DMA transfer of sprite data	W	No
0x4016	0x1	Joypad 1 status	RW	No
0x6000–0xFFFF	Varies by cartridge	Cartridge memory	Varies	Varies

specifics of cartridge memory in "Emulating the Cartridge" on page 148. Finally, the CPU's measly 2KB of RAM actually has two important subregions: the fast zero page region from 0x0000 to 0x00FF already discussed, and the space typically used for the stack from 0x0100 to 0x01FF.

Now that we have some understanding of how the memory is divided, we can look at our methods for reading and writing it. We'll start with the read_memory() method. It takes a location to read and a memory mode, and returns a byte (represented as an int in Python) from that location:

```python
def read_memory(self, location: int, mode: MemMode) -> int:
    if mode == MemMode.IMMEDIATE:
        return location  # location is actually data in this case
    address = self.address_for_mode(location, mode)

    # Memory map at https://wiki.nesdev.org/w/index.php/CPU_memory_map
    if address < 0x2000:  # main RAM 2KB goes up to 0x800
        return self.ram[address % 0x800]  # mirrors for next 6KB
    elif address < 0x4000:  # 2000-2007 is PPU, mirrors every 8 bytes
        temp = ((address % 8) | 0x2000)  # get data from PPU register
        return self.ppu.read_register(temp)
    elif address == 0x4016:  # joypad 1 status
        if self.joypad1.strobe:
            return self.joypad1.a
        self.joypad1.read_count += 1
        match self.joypad1.read_count:
            case 1:
                return 0x40 | self.joypad1.a
            case 2:
                return 0x40 | self.joypad1.b
            case 3:
                return 0x40 | self.joypad1.select
            case 4:
                return 0x40 | self.joypad1.start
            case 5:
                return 0x40 | self.joypad1.up
```

```
            case 6:
                return 0x40 | self.joypad1.down
            case 7:
                return 0x40 | self.joypad1.left
            case 8:
                return 0x40 | self.joypad1.right
            case _:
                return 0x41
    elif address < 0x6000:
        return 0  # unimplemented other kinds of IO
    else:  # addresses from 0x6000 to 0xFFFF are from the cartridge
        return self.rom.read_cartridge(address)
```

If the memory mode is IMMEDIATE, that means the actual data associated with the instruction is what's meant to be "read." Remember, our code is abstracted to the point where a method for a single instruction is supposed to work with any memory mode. In the case of IMMEDIATE mode, we don't need to do any actual lookups, so we just return the data associated with the instruction. (The name location is a little weird here, but it's a good name for everything but IMMEDIATE mode.) Otherwise, the location associated with the instruction is converted to a memory address using address_for_mode().

After obtaining the memory address, we use a series of if statements to determine where the memory should actually be read from, as per Table 6-4. We account for mirroring by using a modulus. Depending on the region, the CPU, the PPU, the joypad, or the cartridge may be accessed. The NES had a peculiar way of reading the joypad. Every time address 0x4016 is read, the status of a different button of the joypad is returned. You therefore need to complete eight reads to know the status of every button.

Next, let's look at writing to memory:

```
def write_memory(self, location: int, mode: MemMode, value: int):
    if mode == MemMode.IMMEDIATE:
        self.ram[location] = value
        return

    address = self.address_for_mode(location, mode)
    # Memory map at https://wiki.nesdev.org/w/index.php/CPU_memory_map
    if address < 0x2000:  # main RAM 2KB goes up to 0x800
        self.ram[address % 0x800] = value  # mirrors for next 6KB
    elif address < 0x3FFF:  # 2000-2007 is PPU, mirrors every 8 bytes
        temp = ((address % 8) | 0x2000)  # write data to PPU register
        self.ppu.write_register(temp, value)
    elif address == 0x4014:  # DMA transfer of sprite data
        from_address = value * 0x100  # address to start copying from
        for i in range(SPR_RAM_SIZE):  # copy all 256 bytes to sprite RAM
            self.ppu.spr[i] = self.read_memory((from_address + i),
                                                MemMode.ABSOLUTE)
        # Stall for 512 cycles while this completes
        self.stall = 512
    elif address == 0x4016:  # joypad 1
        if self.joypad1.strobe and (not bool(value & 1)):
```

```
        self.joypad1.read_count = 0
      self.joypad1.strobe = bool(value & 1)
      return
  elif address < 0x6000:
      return  # unimplemented other kinds of IO
  else:  # addresses from 0x6000 to 0xFFFF are from the cartridge
      # We haven't implemented support for cartridge RAM
      return self.rom.write_cartridge(address, value)
```

The write_memory() method is quite similar to read_memory(). It handles IMMEDIATE mode, then exchanges a location for an address for the other modes and writes to the appropriate location.

Helper Methods

We'll round out the CPU class with a series of helper methods, starting with these three:

```
def setZN(self, value: int):
    self.Z = (value == 0)
    self.N = bool(value & 0x80) or (value < 0)

def stack_push(self, value: int):
    self.ram[(0x100 | self.SP)] = value
    self.SP = (self.SP - 1) & 0xFF

def stack_pop(self) -> int:
    self.SP = (self.SP + 1) & 0xFF
    return self.ram[(0x100 | self.SP)]
```

Many instructions need to set the zero (Z) and negative (N) flags. Instead of repeating those couple of lines in the instruction methods, we have setZN(). The stack_push() method puts a new value on the stack. This involves putting the value on the stack at the write address and moving the stack pointer. Similarly, stack_pop() gets a value back from the stack pointer, moves the stack pointer, and returns the value.

For convenience, our CPU class stores the various status flags in seven separate Boolean variables, but a real 6502 has one 8-bit status register where each flag is a single bit. The BRK, PHP, PLP, and RTI instructions need to work with the status register in its bit-centric format, so the methods that follow, status() and set_status(), use bitwise operations to translate between the two formats:

```
@property
def status(self) -> int:
    return (self.C | self.Z << 1 | self.I << 2 | self.D << 3 |
            self.B << 4 | 1 << 5 | self.V << 6 | self.N << 7)

def set_status(self, temp: int):
    self.C = bool(temp & 0b00000001)
    self.Z = bool(temp & 0b00000010)
```

```
    self.I = bool(temp & 0b00000100)
    self.D = bool(temp & 0b00001000)
    # https://nesdev.org/the%20'B'%20flag%20&%20BRK%20instruction.txt
    self.B = False
    self.V = bool(temp & 0b01000000)
    self.N = bool(temp & 0b10000000)
```

Finally, we have a method to handle what happens when an NMI is triggered, and a log() method for debugging:

```
def trigger_NMI(self):
    self.stack_push((self.PC >> 8) & 0xFF)
    self.stack_push(self.PC & 0xFF)
    # https://nesdev.org/the%20'B'%20flag%20&%20BRK%20instruction.txt
    self.B = True
    self.stack_push(self.status)
    self.B = False
    self.I = True
    # Set PC to NMI vector
    self.PC = (self.read_memory(NMI_VECTOR, MemMode.ABSOLUTE)) | \
              (self.read_memory(NMI_VECTOR + 1, MemMode.ABSOLUTE) << 8)

def log(self) -> str:
    opcode = self.read_memory(self.PC, MemMode.ABSOLUTE)
    instruction = self.instructions[opcode]
    data1 = "  " if instruction.length < 2 else f"{self.read_memory(self.PC + 1,
                                                    MemMode.ABSOLUTE):02X}"
    data2 = "  " if instruction.length < 3 else f"{self.read_memory(self.PC + 2,
                                                    MemMode.ABSOLUTE):02X}"
    return f"{self.PC:04X}  {opcode:02X} {data1} {data2}  {instruction.type.name}{29 * ' '}" \
           f"A:{self.A:02X} X:{self.X:02X} Y:{self.Y:02X} P:{self.status:02X} SP:{self.SP:02X}"
```

An NMI sends execution to a code block at the address specified in NMI_VECTOR. When an NMI is triggered, similar to BRK and JSR instructions, we need to put a bookmark down so that we can come back to where we were before the NMI took us away. That's the purpose of pushing PC and status to the stack.

Implementing the CPU involved writing a lot of code to a specification—a specification that's long but made of many small, relatively easy-to-digest pieces. The last part of the emulator that we need to implement is the PPU, and it will feel quite different. There's still a specification with a lot of details, but those details come together to essentially do just two big things: draw background tiles and draw sprites.

Understanding the PPU

Implementing the PPU is the most complex part of an NES emulation project. The PPU is responsible for drawing the graphics on the screen. For the purposes of our simple emulator, we can think about the graphics as having two aspects: the background and the sprites.

The background is the back layer of the graphics where the individual pieces typically either don't move at all or only scroll together as a group. The NES hardware draws the background using *tiles*. In a platform game, for example, a tile might be a part of a platform, a part of an artistic background (a mountain, perhaps), a ladder, or a door. These elements typically can't move on their own.

By contrast, *sprites* are individual game objects that can move anywhere on the screen independently. Think of the player and enemies in a platform game. The NES has specialized hardware for handling up to 64 8×8 or 8×16 (in pixels) sprites on the screen at a time.

There are many different ways to implement the PPU. The most accurate is to simulate what the real PPU does: generate each pixel of the screen, one at a time. If this implementation is done properly, any game written for the NES should work correctly. This approach is also the most performance intensive. A popular alternative is to implement graphics one scanline at a time. Instead of doing updates for every pixel, the updates occur when each scanline's processing is complete.

We won't be doing either of these. As discussed earlier, we'll implement the PPU using the even simpler approach of updating the entire screen one frame at a time. This is the least accurate technique, because if the game somehow changes the graphics between pixels or between scanlines, those updates won't appear. Compatibility will still be good, but it won't extend to all games.

While our method is the furthest away from how the real PPU works, it's the most performant technique, since it requires the fewest updates per frame (just one big update instead of many small updates). It's also the least conceptually difficult, since it doesn't require understanding all the details of how the real PPU works. Because our emulator is being written in a relatively slow programming language, Python, and is intended to be as simple as possible for demonstration purposes, per-frame rendering is arguably the best choice.

While we don't need to understand every detail of the PPU to implement our frame-by-frame approach, we still need to understand some fundamentals about where the data for the backgrounds and the sprites comes from. We'll dive into that in the coming sections. Some of the information was already scattered throughout earlier parts of the chapter, but here it's all woven together with many new ideas and details to cohesively explain how the PPU operates.

CHR ROM

The data for both the background tiles and the sprites is initially located on the cartridge in a region of memory known as CHR ROM. The size of this memory could range quite a bit. Early games typically had just 8KB of CHR ROM, but later games with mappers could have hundreds of kilobytes, with the ability to swap in any other 8KB region for the first so as to be compatible with the expectations of the PPU hardware (which can only address 8KB of CHR ROM directly).

Some games replaced CHR ROM with CHR RAM, which is modifiable during game operation. However, most games had fixed CHR ROM. If a game had CHR RAM, the game had to load the graphics into the CHR RAM as needed from the PRG ROM, instead of it just always being there. Some rare games had both CHR ROM and CHR RAM in different banks.

Pattern Tables and Tiles

At any given time the PPU can be "hooked up" to either of two 4KB portions of the CHR ROM on the cartridge. These portions are known as *pattern tables*. The NES pulls all of its graphics data for a given frame from the selected pattern table. Note that some documentation refers to all 8KB of addressable CHR ROM as a single overall pattern table rather than calling each 4KB section a separate pattern table.

Each pattern table is divided into 256 16-byte tiles, and each tile defines potential graphics for an 8×8 pixel region of the screen. Together, the predefined tiles in the pattern tables represent all the different things you might see in the game. For example, Figure 6-1 shows the pattern tables for the open source game *BrickBreaker* by Aleff Correa, which we'll run in our emulator later in the chapter.

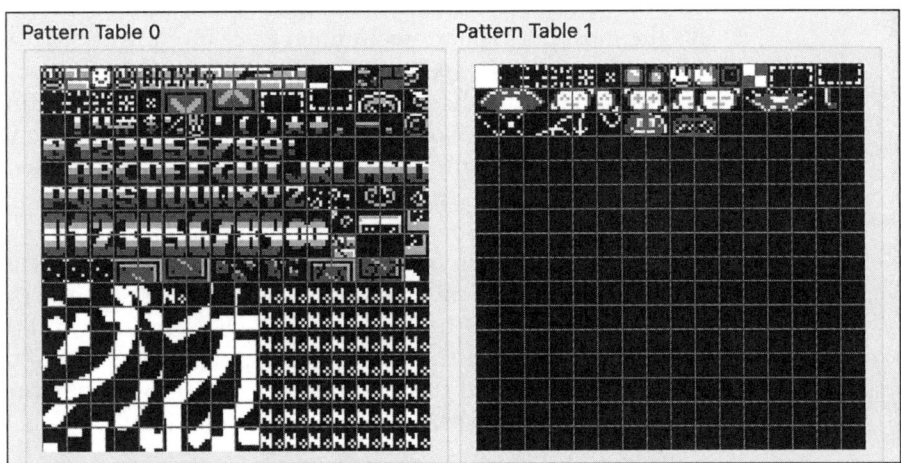

Figure 6-1: The pattern tables of BrickBreaker, *as displayed by the FCEUX emulator's PPU Viewer*

You can see how some of the tiles in the pattern tables represent sprites, some represent text, and some represent background patterns. Many of the tiles in the pattern tables are blank because *BrickBreaker* doesn't have the need to use them (it has more space in CHR ROM for graphical assets than it actually needs).

NOTE *Figure 6-1 was generated using the PPU Viewer feature of the FCEUX emulator, which allows you to see the contents of CHR ROM, separate from actual gameplay. Adding debug features like a pattern table viewer can be very helpful when writing an emulator. For example, you could compare the output of your PPU to that of an established emulator like FCEUX.*

As mentioned, each tile in a pattern table is 16 bytes. With 16 bytes defining $8 \times 8 = 64$ pixels, that leaves just 2 bits per pixel, and 2 bits can only represent four different values (00, 01, 10, 11). The PPU therefore only supports four colors within a given tile. In fact, one of those is always a preset background color or transparent (00), so there are essentially only three programmer-selected colors that can appear in a specific tile. This palette of colors is set for regions of four tiles at a time and is controlled in a separate part of memory from the pattern tables themselves. This is why all of the tiles appear in grayscale in Figure 6-1; the color palette of each tile isn't determined by the pattern table. We'll come back to how colors are selected shortly.

Unfortunately, the tiles get a little bit more complicated: the 2-bit values that define each pixel aren't laid out sequentially. Instead, the zeroth bit of each pixel is laid out in the first 8 bytes of the tile, and the first bit of each pixel is laid out in the second 8 bytes of the tile. Each 8 bytes forms a *bit plane*, and the two planes combine, two bits at a time, to determine each pixel's color.

Let me phrase that another way. The first 8 bytes (first bit plane) of a tile can be thought of as 64 halves of the color values for the 64 pixels in the 8×8 tile. They're laid out sequentially. The second 8-byte bit plane defines another 64 halves of the color values for the same 64 pixels. They're also laid out sequentially. The two planes need to be combined to get the 64 final color values. As an example, consider the following 16 bytes of tile data:[6]

```
    Bit Plane 1
Byte 1    01000001
Byte 2    11000010
Byte 3    01000100
Byte 4    01001000        Pixel Pattern
Byte 5    00010000
Byte 6    00100000        01000003
Byte 7    01000000        11000030
Byte 8    10000000  ===== 01000300
    Bit Plane 2           01003000
Byte 9    00000001  ===== 00030220
Byte 10   00000010        00300002
Byte 11   00000100        03000020
Byte 12   00001000        30000222
Byte 13   00010110
Byte 14   00100001
Byte 15   01000010
Byte 16   10000111
```

The matching bits from the two bit planes come together to form the pixel pattern shown in the listing and illustrated in Figure 6-2: an image of the fraction 1/2.

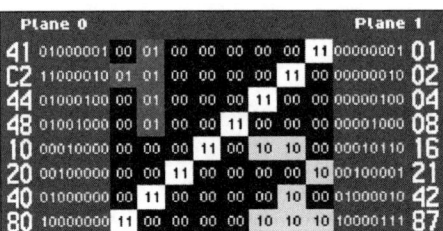

Figure 6-2: How a tile comes together from two bit planes

Where there's a 1 in the first bit plane and a 0 in the second, the bits combine to form 01, or color 1 in the color scheme. Likewise, a 0 from the first bit plane and a 1 from the second form 10, or color 2, and a 1 in both bit planes yields 11, or color 3.

Nametables

Nametables are where the actual tiles for the background of the screen are laid out. What does the background of the screen look like right now? What tiles is it composed of, and what colors are used in each? That's the job of a nametable and its accompanying attribute table (discussed next).

Each nametable, representing a single screen of the game, is 32 tiles wide and 30 tiles high. Each tile in the nametable is specified by a single byte—the index of a tile in the current pattern table. In this way, the pattern table tiles are directly mapped to the nametable, so you can think of a nametable as just a specific ordering of tiles from a pattern table.

How big is a nametable? Well, $32 \times 30 = 960$, so there are 960 locations in a nametable. And each location in the table is occupied by a 1-byte index, so a nametable is 960 bytes.

We now have enough information to understand why the NES had a 256×240 resolution. Each tile is 8 pixels wide and 8 pixels tall. If the nametable represents the background of the screen and is 32 tiles wide, it follows that $8 \times 32 = 256$. And the height of the screen in pixels is found with $8 \times 30 = 240$.

The PPU only has 2KB of memory, which is only enough for two nametables (and their attribute tables). Those two nametables can be mirrored, so there are a total of four logical nametables. Figure 6-3 shows the nametables for the title screen of *BrickBreaker* laid out.

Figure 6-3: The nametables of the BrickBreaker title screen

Only one nametable is set with meaningful data in Figure 6-3. You can observe *horizontal mirroring* in the way the right half of the image is a copy of the left half.

Color Palettes and Attribute Tables

The PPU has *palette memory* for four different background color palettes. Recall from "Pattern Tables and Tiles" on page 178 that each tile is composed of pixels in one of four colors, with one of those being the background color or transparent. That means that only three colors are actually specific to a tile. Each palette in the PPU's palette memory therefore defines a set of three colors. (We'll discuss palette memory further in the next section.)

To specify which color palette applies to which tile, each nametable is followed by an *attribute table*. The attribute table is 8×8, and each entry in it is just 1 byte. How can there be 960 tiles and just 64 1-byte attribute table entries? Each entry actually defines the colors for a 2×2 set of *areas*, and each of those areas represents a 2×2 grid of tiles. Therefore, each 1-byte entry in the attribute table actually covers 16 tiles. How does that work out?

Every 2 bits of that 1-byte entry is for one area, and 2 bits can represent up to four values. Each 2-bit value is a selector between one of the four different background color palettes. Every 2×2 region of tiles on the screen can therefore have a single palette out of the four possible background palettes. That means all four of the tiles in each area must use the same three colors (and background/transparent).

That's no easy feat. Artists working on graphics for the NES had to paint significant areas of the screen (four-tile areas) using just three non-background colors. And then each of those areas using just three non-background colors had to blend in with the adjacent areas that may be using different three-color palettes.

Figures 6-4, 6-5, and 6-6, created for *https://nesdev.org*, showcase attribute tables in action. (If you're reading this in print, see the *figures* directory of the companion repository for color versions of the images.) First, Figure 6-4 shows the background of a game (*Thwaite* by Damian Yerrick) broken up into the areas the attribute table can select colors for.

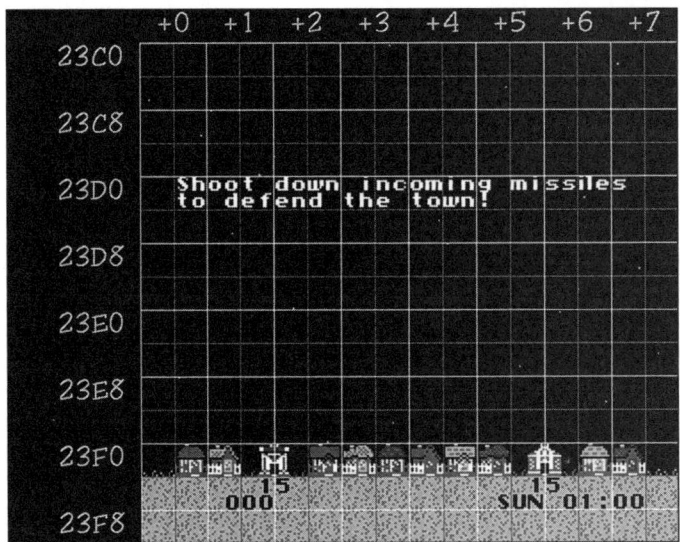

Figure 6-4: The attribute table layout across the screen in Thwaite

Figure 6-5 shows the actual palette selection (which background palette, 0–3) for each area from Figure 6-4.

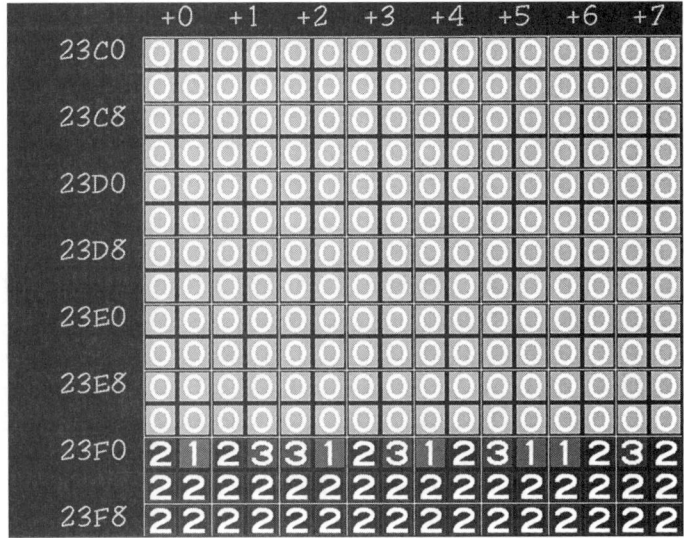

Figure 6-5: The attribute table color palette mapping in Thwaite

Finally, Figure 6-6 shows the four background palettes that can be selected. There's some color overlap between the palettes, which allows the different areas of the screen to blend with each other.

Figure 6-6: The background color palettes in Thwaite

Each attribute table is 64 bytes, and each nametable is 960 bytes. One nametable and its corresponding attribute table therefore take up 960 + 64 = 1,024 bytes, or 1KB. This is how the 2KB of RAM on the PPU fill up with two pattern table/attribute table combinations.

Palette Memory

The PPU's palette memory has room for four background palettes and four sprite palettes. As we've discussed, a palette consists of three colors (along with the background/transparent color). It can be used to paint a four-tile background area of the screen (see the prior section on attribute tables) or a sprite. In other words, each four-tile area of the background can be colored using one out of four palettes, and each sprite can be colored using one out of four palettes.

A palette is defined using 3 bytes. Each byte specifies one of the three colors of the palette, although only 6 bits of each byte are actually used for selecting a color. Since 6 bits can select from among 64 values, this tells us that NES artists only had 64 colors to work with. In practice, 10 of these 64 possible colors amounted to essentially black, so really the NES had 54 colors. Figure 6-7 shows these colors for an NTSC NES. The colors differed a bit for PAL NES machines. (Different countries used different video standards—NTSC in North America versus PAL in much of Europe and Asia, for instance—which would affect how the PPU of the NES operated.)

0x00	0x01	0x02	0x03	0x04	0x05	0x06	0x07	0x08	0x09	0x0A	0x0B	0x0C	**0x0D**	0x0E	0x0F
0x10	0x11	0x12	0x13	0x14	0x15	0x16	0x17	0x18	0x19	0x1A	0x1B	0x1C	0x1D	0x1E	0x1F
0x20	0x21	0x22	0x23	0x24	0x25	0x26	0x27	0x28	0x29	0x2A	0x2B	0x2C	0x2D	0x2E	0x2F
0x30	0x31	0x32	0x33	0x34	0x35	0x36	0x37	0x38	0x39	0x3A	0x3B	0x3C	0x3D	0x3E	0x3F

Figure 6-7: The colors available on an NTSC NES

As an example, say your background area is painted using background palette 1, and background palette 1 specifies the colors 0x11, 0x0A, and 0x3D. That means you can paint that area using shades of blue, green, and gray, as well as the background color.

Object Attribute Memory

OAM stores information about the sprites on the screen. Sprites are essentially the moving objects in a game—for example, the player, the enemies, and the projectiles. The NES supports 64 sprites at a time and uses 4 bytes to describe each one, so there are 256 bytes of OAM.

The images for sprites come from the same CHR ROM on the cartridge as the background tiles—that is, the pattern tables. Unlike the background, however, sprites aren't constrained to tile locations; they can be drawn at any position on the screen. Each sprite can also be flipped horizontally or vertically, placed in front of or behind the background, and colored using any of four different palettes. The 4 bytes for each sprite and what they do are briefly described in Table 6-5.

Table 6-5: Sprite Specification in OAM

Byte #	Description
0	The y-axis position of the sprite
1	The index into the pattern table where the sprite's graphical data is located
2	Sprite attributes including palette (bits 0–1), front or back (bit 5), horizontal flip (bit 6), and vertical flip (bit 7)
3	The x-axis position of the sprite

Why the bytes for the y-axis position and the x-axis position aren't next to each other is a question I have for the NES's creators. Perhaps it has to do with the physical wiring order of the lines in the PPU.

Frame Creation and Timing

The PPU in a real NES draws the screen from the top left to the bottom right, one pixel at a time. This reflected the "gun" in the CRT televisions that the NES would be hooked up to. Its electron beam "shot" behind the screen from left to right, one scanline at a time from top to bottom. The NTSC NES draws the entire screen 60 times per second (60 frames per second, or 60 FPS). A PAL NES draws at a slower 50 FPS. A *frame* is the gun completing its journey across the entire screen. As mentioned earlier in the chapter, the gun would also sometimes be temporarily off-screen during hblank (between scanlines) and vblank (between frames) periods. These were therefore the safest times for an NES program to change the memory that the pixels were being read from.

Since the NES resolution is 256×240, we know that there must be at least 256 dots drawn per scanline and 240 scanlines in total. There's a prerender scanline, which we'll call scanline 0. Then, scanlines 1 through 240 are the "visible" scanlines that represent what the program actually displays on the screen. Scanlines 241 through 261 are during the vblank phase. The NMI, mentioned earlier in the chapter, is therefore triggered at the start of scanline 241 to tell the program it's safe to change PPU memory. Dots 0 through 255 represent the 256 visible dots on each scanline. Dots 256 through 340 are "silent" dots during which the hblank phase between scanlines occurs.

Each dot represents one PPU cycle. If you do the math, 341 dots per scanline times 262 scanlines means it takes 89,342 PPU cycles to draw each frame. Recall that there are 3 PPU cycles for every 1 CPU cycle. If we divide the PPU cycles by 3 and round, we get 29,781 CPU cycles per frame. The CPU in the NES runs at about 1.79 MHz, or 1,790,000 cycles per second. If you divide 1,790,000 by 29,781, you get a number close to 60. That's the 60 frames per second!

To create a cycle-accurate NES emulator, it's important to understand the details of how the PPU figures out what color to draw for each pixel, one pixel at a time. Since we're using the simpler but less accurate approach of drawing one frame at a time, we can leave those details out as beyond the scope of our project. What we do know based on the timing just discussed is that at some point during every 89,342 PPU cycles we need to draw the whole frame. To me, the logical time to do that is when the visible scanlines are done. In the code we'll look at shortly, you'll therefore see all of the background and all of the sprites being drawn at once at the timing of scanline 240, dot 256 (the last visible dot in the last visible scanline). Our simplified renderer does no drawing except during that PPU cycle, once per frame.

Implementing the PPU

Implementing our PPU starts with some important constants, including various memory sizes, the screen resolution, and the full palette of available colors:

NESEmulator/
ppu.py
```
from array import array
from NESEmulator.rom import ROM
import numpy as np
```

```
SPR_RAM_SIZE = 256
NAMETABLE_SIZE = 2048
PALETTE_SIZE = 32
NES_WIDTH = 256
NES_HEIGHT = 240
NES_PALETTE = [0x7C7C7C, 0x0000FC, 0x0000BC, 0x4428BC, 0x940084, 0xA80020,
               0xA81000, 0x881400, 0x503000, 0x007800, 0x006800, 0x005800,
               0x004058, 0x000000, 0x000000, 0x000000, 0xBCBCBC, 0x0078F8,
               0x0058F8, 0x6844FC, 0xD800CC, 0xE40058, 0xF83800, 0xE45C10,
               0xAC7C00, 0x00B800, 0x00A800, 0x00A844, 0x008888, 0x000000,
               0x000000, 0x000000, 0xF8F8F8, 0x3CBCFC, 0x6888FC, 0x9878F8,
               0xF878F8, 0xF85898, 0xF87858, 0xFCA044, 0xF8B800, 0xB8F818,
               0x58D854, 0x58F898, 0x00E8D8, 0x787878, 0x000000, 0x000000,
               0xFCFCFC, 0xA4E4FC, 0xB8B8F8, 0xD8B8F8, 0xF8B8F8, 0xF8A4C0,
               0xF0D0B0, 0xFCE0A8, 0xF8D878, 0xD8F878, 0xB8F8B8, 0xB8F8D8,
               0x00FCFC, 0xF8D8F8, 0x000000, 0x000000]
```

The colors are specified in hexadecimal RGB values. Different websites have slight variations on what the exact color values should be, and there were real differences in these colors between the different variations of the NES hardware (NTSC versus PAL, for example). The same game may therefore have slightly different colors when played on different NES hardware or different emulators.

The PPU class has instance variables for its sprite memory (OAM), nametable memory, and palette memory:

```
class PPU:
    def __init__(self, rom: ROM):
        self.rom = rom
        # PPU memory
        self.spr = array('B', [0] * SPR_RAM_SIZE)  # sprite RAM
        self.nametables = array('B', [0] * NAMETABLE_SIZE)  # nametable RAM
        self.palette = array('B', [0] * PALETTE_SIZE)  # palette RAM
```

The rest of the PPU class's constructor sets up default values for its various program-settable PPU registers and many helper variables (we'll go into more detail about what some of these are for as our implementation progresses):

```
# Registers
self.addr = 0  # main PPU address register
self.addr_write_latch = False
self.status = 0
self.spr_address = 0
# Variables controlled by PPU control registers
self.nametable_address = 0
self.address_increment = 1
self.spr_pattern_table_address = 0
self.background_pattern_table_address = 0
self.generate_nmi = False
self.show_background = False
self.show_sprites = False
```

```
self.left_8_sprite_show = False
self.left_8_background_show = False
# Internal helper variables
self.buffer2007 = 0
self.scanline = 0
self.cycle = 0
# Pixels for screen
self.display_buffer = np.zeros((NES_WIDTH, NES_HEIGHT), dtype=np.uint32)
```

Next, we have the rendering method, step():

```
def step(self):
    # Our simplified PPU draws just once per frame
    if (self.scanline == 240) and (self.cycle == 256):
        if self.show_background:
            self.draw_background()
        if self.show_sprites:
            self.draw_sprites(False)
    if (self.scanline == 241) and (self.cycle == 1):
        self.status |= 0b10000000  # set vblank
    if (self.scanline == 261) and (self.cycle == 1):
        # Vblank off, clear sprite zero, clear sprite overflow
        self.status |= 0b00011111

    self.cycle += 1
    if self.cycle > 340:
        self.cycle = 0
        self.scanline += 1
        if self.scanline > 261:
            self.scanline = 0
```

Each call to step() from the emulator's main loop represents one PPU cycle. Because our strategy is to draw everything once per frame, and not to be pixel or scanline accurate, step() is remarkably simple. It just draws the background and sprites all at once at the end of each visible portion of a frame. It also sets the status register when vblank starts and ends so that the CPU can coordinate with the PPU. Finally, it does some bookkeeping to keep track of the current scanline and current cycle on each scanline.

The heavy lifting is done by the draw_background() and draw_sprites() methods, which are called by step(). We'll look at these methods next.

Drawing the Background

We begin the draw_background() background method by calculating the address of the attribute table:

```
def draw_background(self):
    attribute_table_address = self.nametable_address + 960
```

The attribute table is always right after the nametable, and recall from earlier in the chapter that the nametable is 960 bytes. I also mentioned earlier in the chapter that the nametable is composed of 960 bytes because it uses 1 byte to represent the index of each of 960 tiles. The screen is 32 tiles wide and 30 tiles tall, with each tile representing an 8×8 pixel area. We draw these tiles from the top left to the bottom right of the screen, one row at a time, going from left to right:

```
for y in range(30):
    for x in range(32):
        tile_address = self.nametable_address + y * 32 + x
        nametable_entry = self.read_memory(tile_address)
```

Each tile_address is calculated by adding the base nametable_address to the current tile's offset. Since each row is 32 tiles long, we multiple the row (y) by 32 and add the x component, which can be thought of as the column. To get the actual index byte (nametable_entry) we read a byte of memory at the tile_address. Later in the method we'll use nametable_entry to retrieve the tile's pixel content from the pattern table.

Next, we get the attribute table entry corresponding to the current nametable entry:

```
attrx = x // 4
attry = y // 4
attribute_address = attribute_table_address + attry * 8 + attrx
attribute_entry = self.read_memory(attribute_address)
```

Because each entry in the 8×8 attribute table is for 16 tiles, we divide both x and y by 4 to get the attribute entry connected to the tile in question. (See "Color Palettes and Attribute Tables" on page 181 to better make sense of this code.) Since each attribute_entry is for four 2×2 tile areas (hence 16 tiles in total), we need to drill down to the specific tile area:

```
block = (y & 0x02) | ((x & 0x02) >> 1)
attribute_bits = 0
if block == 0:
    attribute_bits = (attribute_entry & 0b00000011) << 2
elif block == 1:
    attribute_bits = (attribute_entry & 0b00001100)
elif block == 2:
    attribute_bits = (attribute_entry & 0b00110000) >> 2
elif block == 3:
    attribute_bits = (attribute_entry & 0b11000000) >> 4
else:
    print("Invalid block")
```

The attribute_entry is 1 byte, and every 2 bits of that byte correspond to a different tile area. The variable block represents the tile area for the current tile; it can be 0, 1, 2, or 3. Depending on the value of block, we use the appropriate bitwise operations to retrieve the two specific bits for that tile area from attribute_entry and store them in attribute_bits.

Now we need to retrieve the individual pixels of each tile from the pattern table:

```
for fine_y in range(8):
    low_order = self.read_memory(self.background_pattern_table_address +
                                 nametable_entry * 16 + fine_y)
    high_order = self.read_memory(self.background_pattern_table_address +
                                  nametable_entry * 16 + 8 + fine_y)
    for fine_x in range(8):
        pixel = ((low_order >> (7 - fine_x)) & 1) | (
                  ((high_order >> (7 - fine_x)) & 1) << 1) | attribute_bits
```

Recall from "Pattern Tables and Tiles" on page 178 that each pattern table is composed of 16-byte tiles. Therefore, to calculate the address of a tile, we need to multiply its index (nametable_entry) by 16 and add it to the background_pattern_table_address. In addition, the pattern table tiles are divided into two bit planes, with each color being 2 bits and each of those 2 bits being 8 bytes apart in the separate planes (see Figure 6-2).

Our strategy is to read 2 bytes, one for the low_order plane and one for the high_order plane. Each byte holds half of the pixel entries for one row of the tile. We use fine_y to represent each row of the tile, then zero in on the individual bits using fine_x, which represents each column. The combination of the bits from each plane with the attribute_bits produces an address in palette memory where the color of the current pixel is stored.

Finally, we draw each pixel from the tile one at a time in the appropriate screen location using the predefined colors in NES_PALETTE:

```
x_screen_loc = x * 8 + fine_x
y_screen_loc = y * 8 + fine_y
transparent = ((pixel & 3) == 0)
# If the background is transparent, use the first color in the palette
color = self.palette[0] if transparent else self.palette[pixel]
self.display_buffer[x_screen_loc, y_screen_loc] = NES_PALETTE[color]
```

Setting pixels for the screen means setting values in display_buffer, which is a NumPy array because that's what Pygame accepts.

Drawing Sprites

Drawing sprites has some similarity to drawing background tiles. However, instead of reading from a nametable, we read from OAM (self.spr). Each sprite's entry in memory is 4 bytes, representing the sprite's y position, pattern table index, attributes, and x position (see Table 6-5). There's room for up to 64 sprite entries in OAM. If the y position is 0xFF, then the entry isn't being used. We start draw_sprites() by moving 4 bytes at a time through OAM to find all of the valid entries:

```
def draw_sprites(self, background_transparent: bool):
    for i in range(SPR_RAM_SIZE - 4, -4, -4):
        y_position = self.spr[i]
```

```
if y_position == 0xFF:  # 0xFF is a marker for no sprite data
    continue
background_sprite = bool((self.spr[i + 2] >> 5) & 1)
x_position = self.spr[i + 3]
```

We retrieve each valid sprite's y position and x position. We also look at bit 5 of its attributes to see if it's a background sprite. Background sprites are drawn only if the background is transparent. Note that we are traversing sprite memory backward because, as we'll see at the end of this section, the zeroth sprite has special significance.

Just as we drew background tiles one pixel at a time, we do the same for sprites:

```
for x in range(x_position, x_position + 8):
    if x >= NES_WIDTH:
        break
    for y in range(y_position, y_position + 8):
        if y >= NES_HEIGHT:
            break
```

Here, x and y are analogous to fine_x and fine_y in draw_background(). We're careful not to draw any pixels that are off-screen.

Another attribute a sprite can have is the ability to be flipped vertically (flip_y), which is determined by the seventh bit in the sprite's attribute byte:

```
flip_y = bool((self.spr[i + 2] >> 7) & 1)
sprite_line = y - y_position
if flip_y:
    sprite_line = 7 - sprite_line
```

If a sprite is flipped vertically, we read its pixels in reverse vertical order. We use the magic number 7 because every sprite is 8×8 pixels.

Reading the actual pixel bits from the pattern table, based on the pattern table index, is very similar to the work done in draw_background():

```
index = self.spr[i + 1]
bit0s_address = self.spr_pattern_table_address + (index * 16) + sprite_line
bit1s_address = self.spr_pattern_table_address + (index * 16) + sprite_line + 8
bit0s = self.read_memory(bit0s_address)
bit1s = self.read_memory(bit1s_address)
bit3and2 = ((self.spr[i + 2]) & 3) << 2
```

I used some different terminology here (bit0s_address and bit1s_address instead of low_order and high_order) because I thought different naming might resonate with different readers. The attribute color bits are bits 0 and 1 in the sprite's attribute byte, and they're stored in bit3and2 for the final color.

Sprites can also be flipped horizontally based on bit 6 in the attribute byte:

```
flip_x = bool((self.spr[i + 2] >> 6) & 1)
x_loc = x - x_position  # position within sprite
if not flip_x:
        x_loc = 7 - x_loc
```

We put the two bit planes together and skip over drawing pixels that are transparent:

```
bit1and0 = (((bit1s >> x_loc) & 1) << 1) | (
            ((bit0s >> x_loc) & 1) << 0)
if bit1and0 == 0:  # transparent pixel... skip
        continue
```

The PPU keeps track of whether the zeroth sprite (the first entry in OAM) is colliding with any non-transparent background pixels. This is called a *sprite-zero hit*. We implement this simple form of collision detection here:

```
# This is not transparent. Is it a sprite-zero hit therefore?
# Check that left 8 pixel clipping is not off.
if (i == 0) and (not background_transparent) and (not (x < 8 and (
        not self.left_8_sprite_show or not self.left_8_background_show))
            and self.show_background and self.show_sprites):
    self.status |= 0b01000000
# Need to do this after sprite-zero checking so we still count background
# sprites for sprite-zero checks
if background_sprite and not background_transparent:
    continue  # background sprite shouldn't draw over opaque pixels
```

When a sprite-zero hit occurs, we mark it in the status register. In this chunk of code, we also skip drawing background sprites if the background isn't transparent. There are flags that can be set in the PPU to clip the left 8 pixels of a background tile or sprite. That flag is also checked in this section to ensure if it's on that there aren't erroneous sprite-zero hits.

Finally, we retrieve the color of the individual pixel:

```
color = bit3and2 | bit1and0
color = self.read_memory(0x3F10 + color)  # from palette
self.display_buffer[x, y] = NES_PALETTE[color]
```

To retrieve the color, we combine bit3and2 with bit1and0 and read from the appropriate location in palette memory. Then, we put this pixel on the screen. Instead of reading from palette directly, we use read_memory() here because of the need to incorporate address mirroring.

Accessing Registers

The PPU has several memory-mapped registers, and there are some technicalities and peculiarities when reading or writing them. We'll tackle these through the read_register() and write_register() methods. In read_register(), we first handle address 0x2002, which is for reading the status register:

```
def read_register(self, address: int) -> int:
    if address == 0x2002:
        self.addr_write_latch = False
        current = self.status
        self.status &= 0b01111111  # clear vblank on read to 0x2002
        return current
```

When the status register is read, self.addr_write_latch is set to False, which modifies how addresses are written to 0x2006 (coming up later). Also, vblank is cleared on reads to the status register. Next, the current self.spr_address in OAM can be read through 0x2004:

```
    elif address == 0x2004:
        return self.spr[self.spr_address]
```

The PPU memory at self.addr can be read and written through register 0x2007. But it's read through a buffer (self.buffer2007), with the details varying depending on what address is being read:

```
    elif address == 0x2007:
        if (self.addr % 0x4000) < 0x3F00:
            value = self.buffer2007
            self.buffer2007 = self.read_memory(self.addr)
        else:
            value = self.read_memory(self.addr)
            self.buffer2007 = self.read_memory(self.addr - 0x1000)
        # Every read to 0x2007 there is an increment
        self.addr += self.address_increment
        return value
    else:
        raise LookupError(f"Error: Unrecognized PPU read {address:X}")
```

Notice how self.address_increment is added to self.addr after every read. This allows for subsequent reads to automatically get the next entry, either 1 byte or 32 bytes further.

In write_register(), we change the operation of the PPU by writing to its various memory-mapped registers. First, registers 0x2000 and 0x2001 are called *control registers*. They're used for changing various internal values that we've already seen in use throughout the rest of the PPU's implementation:

```
def write_register(self, address: int, value: int):
    if address == 0x2000:  # Control1
        self.nametable_address = (0x2000 + (value & 0b00000011) * 0x400)
        self.address_increment = 32 if (value & 0b00000100) else 1
        self.spr_pattern_table_address = (((value & 0b00001000) >> 3) * 0x1000)
        self.background_pattern_table_address = (((value & 0b00010000) >> 4) * 0x1000)
        self.generate_nmi = bool(value & 0b10000000)
    elif address == 0x2001:  # Control2
        self.show_background = bool(value & 0b00001000)
```

```
self.show_sprites = bool(value & 0b00010000)
self.left_8_background_show = bool(value & 0b00000010)
self.left_8_sprite_show = bool(value & 0b00000100)
```

Next, we handle registers 0x2003 through 0x2007:

```
elif address == 0x2003:
    self.spr_address = value
elif address == 0x2004:
    self.spr[self.spr_address] = value
    self.spr_address += 1
elif address == 0x2005:  # scroll
    pass
elif address == 0x2006:
    # Based on https://wiki.nesdev.org/w/index.php/PPU_scrolling
    if not self.addr_write_latch:  # first write
        self.addr = (self.addr & 0x00FF) | ((value & 0xFF) << 8)
    else:  # second write
        self.addr = (self.addr & 0xFF00) | (value & 0xFF)
    self.addr_write_latch = not self.addr_write_latch
elif address == 0x2007:
    self.write_memory(self.addr, value)
    self.addr += self.address_increment
else:
    raise LookupError(f"Error: Unrecognized PPU write {address:X}")
```

Register 0x2003 sets self.spr_address. Register 0x2004 sets the value at
self.spr_address and then increments self.spr_address by 1. Register 0x2005
is a scroll register; we haven't implemented it in our simple PPU, but a full
implementation would require it. As it stands, our emulator won't work
with games that require scrolling. Register 0x2006 is for modifying self.addr.
This is where self.addr_write_latch comes in: we need the latch because self
.addr is 16 bits (2 bytes) but can only be written to 1 byte at a time. Finally,
0x2007 is for writing to self.addr.

Accessing Memory

Our PPU implementation is basically done, but we need helper methods for
reading and writing to PPU memory. These read_memory() and write_memory()
methods are quite similar to their analogs in the CPU:

```
def read_memory(self, address: int) -> int:
    address = address % 0x4000  # mirror >0x4000
    if address < 0x2000:  # pattern tables
        return self.rom.read_cartridge(address)
    elif address < 0x3F00:  # nametables
        address = (address - 0x2000) % 0x1000  # 3000-3EFF is a mirror
        if self.rom.vertical_mirroring:
            address = address % 0x0800
        else:  # horizontal mirroring
            if (address >= 0x400) and (address < 0xC00):
                address = address - 0x400
```

```
            elif address >= 0xC00:
                address = address - 0x800
        return self.nametables[address]
    elif address < 0x4000:  # palette memory
        address = (address - 0x3F00) % 0x20
        if (address > 0x0F) and ((address % 0x04) == 0):
            address = address - 0x10
        return self.palette[address]
    else:
        raise LookupError(f"Error: Unrecognized PPU read at {address:X}")

def write_memory(self, address: int, value: int):
    address = address % 0x4000  # mirror >0x4000
    if address < 0x2000:  # pattern tables
        return self.rom.write_cartridge(address, value)
    elif address < 0x3F00:  # nametables
        address = (address - 0x2000) % 0x1000  # 3000-3EFF is a mirror
        if self.rom.vertical_mirroring:
            address = address % 0x0800
        else:  # horizontal mirroring
            if (address >= 0x400) and (address < 0xC00):
                address = address - 0x400
            elif address >= 0xC00:
                address = address - 0x800
        self.nametables[address] = value
    elif address < 0x4000:  # palette memory
        address = (address - 0x3F00) % 0x20
        if (address > 0x0F) and ((address % 0x04) == 0):
            address = address - 0x10
        self.palette[address] = value
    else:
        raise LookupError(f"Error: Unrecognized PPU write at {address:X}")
```

In these methods, different memory regions are mapped to their
respective areas—the pattern tables (which are actually on the cartridge),
nametables, and the like. The only complication is that the nametables and
palette memory can be mirrored. We handle this using the mod operator (%),
as we did in the CPU.

Testing the Emulator

Many test ROMs have been created for folks developing NES emulators.
Some are included in the repository for this book. These can test the 6502
CPU as well as the PPU. Thank you to Shay Green and Kevin Horton for
developing these tests.

Our 10 unit tests run these ROMs and then check that certain values in
the virtual NES's memory are set correctly, as specified by the test ROMs'
creators. Like all tests for the book, the file for these unit tests appears in
the *tests* directory in the root of the source code repository:

```
# tests/test_nesemulator.py
import unittest
from pathlib import Path
from NESEmulator.cpu import CPU
from NESEmulator.ppu import PPU
from NESEmulator.rom import ROM


class CPUTestCase(unittest.TestCase):
    def setUp(self) -> None:
        self.test_folder = (Path(__file__).resolve().parent.parent
                            / 'NESEmulator' / 'Tests')

    def test_nes_test(self):
        # Create machinery that we are testing
        rom = ROM(self.test_folder / "nestest" / "nestest.nes")
        ppu = PPU(rom)
        cpu = CPU(ppu, rom)
        # Set up tests
        cpu.PC = 0xC000  # special starting location for tests
        with open(self.test_folder / "nestest" / "nestest.log") as f:
            correct_lines = f.readlines()
        log_line = 1
        # Check every line of the log against our own produced logs
        while log_line < 5260:  # go until first unofficial opcode test
            our_line = cpu.log()
            correct_line = correct_lines[log_line - 1]
            self.assertEqual(correct_line[0:14], our_line[0:14],
                             f"PC/Opcode doesn't match at line {log_line}")
            self.assertEqual(correct_line[48:73], our_line[48:73],
                             f"Registers don't match at line {log_line}")
            cpu.step()
            log_line += 1

    def test_blargg_instr_test_v5_basics(self):
        # Create machinery that we are testing
        rom = ROM(self.test_folder / "instr_test-v5" / "rom_singles" / "01-basics.nes")
        ppu = PPU(rom)
        cpu = CPU(ppu, rom)
        # Tests run as long as 0x6000 is 80, and then 0x6000 is result code; 0 means success
        rom.prg_ram[0] = 0x80
        while rom.prg_ram[0] == 0x80:  # go until first unofficial opcode test
            cpu.step()
        self.assertEqual(0, rom.prg_ram[0],
                         f"Result code of basics test is {rom.prg_ram[0]} not 0")
        message = bytes(rom.prg_ram[4:]).decode("utf-8")
        print(message[0:message.index("\0")])  # message ends with null terminator

    def test_blargg_instr_test_v5_implied(self):
        # Create machinery that we are testing
        rom = ROM(self.test_folder / "instr_test-v5" / "rom_singles" / "02-implied.nes")
        ppu = PPU(rom)
        cpu = CPU(ppu, rom)
        # Tests run as long as 0x6000 is 80, and then 0x6000 is result code; 0 means success
        rom.prg_ram[0] = 0x80
```

```python
        while rom.prg_ram[0] == 0x80:  # go until first unofficial opcode test
            cpu.step()
        self.assertEqual(0, rom.prg_ram[0],
                         f"Result code of implied test is {rom.prg_ram[0]} not 0")
        message = bytes(rom.prg_ram[4:]).decode("utf-8")
        print(message[0:message.index("\0")])  # message ends with null terminator

    def test_blargg_instr_test_v5_branches(self):
        # Create machinery that we are testing
        rom = ROM(self.test_folder / "instr_test-v5" / "rom_singles" / "10-branches.nes")
        ppu = PPU(rom)
        cpu = CPU(ppu, rom)
        # Tests run as long as 0x6000 is 80, and then 0x6000 is result code; 0 means success
        rom.prg_ram[0] = 0x80
        while rom.prg_ram[0] == 0x80:  # go until first unofficial opcode test
            cpu.step()
        self.assertEqual(0, rom.prg_ram[0],
                         f"Result code of branches test is {rom.prg_ram[0]} not 0")
        message = bytes(rom.prg_ram[4:]).decode("utf-8")
        print(message[0:message.index("\0")])  # message ends with null terminator

    def test_blargg_instr_test_v5_stack(self):
        # Create machinery that we are testing
        rom = ROM(self.test_folder / "instr_test-v5" / "rom_singles" / "11-stack.nes")
        ppu = PPU(rom)
        cpu = CPU(ppu, rom)
        # Tests run as long as 0x6000 is 80, and then 0x6000 is result code; 0 means success
        rom.prg_ram[0] = 0x80
        while rom.prg_ram[0] == 0x80:  # go until first unofficial opcode test
            cpu.step()
        self.assertEqual(0, rom.prg_ram[0],
                         f"Result code of stack test is {rom.prg_ram[0]} not 0")
        message = bytes(rom.prg_ram[4:]).decode("utf-8")
        print(message[0:message.index("\0")])  # message ends with null terminator

    def test_blargg_instr_test_v5_jmp_jsr(self):
        # Create machinery that we are testing
        rom = ROM(self.test_folder / "instr_test-v5" / "rom_singles" / "12-jmp_jsr.nes")
        ppu = PPU(rom)
        cpu = CPU(ppu, rom)
        # Tests run as long as 0x6000 is 80, and then 0x6000 is result code; 0 means success
        rom.prg_ram[0] = 0x80
        while rom.prg_ram[0] == 0x80:  # go until first unofficial opcode test
            cpu.step()
        self.assertEqual(0, rom.prg_ram[0],
                         f"Result code of jmp_jsr test is {rom.prg_ram[0]} not 0")
        message = bytes(rom.prg_ram[4:]).decode("utf-8")
        print(message[0:message.index("\0")])  # message ends with null terminator

    def test_blargg_instr_test_v5_rts(self):
        # Create machinery that we are testing
        rom = ROM(self.test_folder / "instr_test-v5" / "rom_singles" / "13-rts.nes")
        ppu = PPU(rom)
        cpu = CPU(ppu, rom)
```

```
        # Tests run as long as 0x6000 is 80, and then 0x6000 is result code; 0 means success
        rom.prg_ram[0] = 0x80
        while rom.prg_ram[0] == 0x80:  # go until first unofficial opcode test
            cpu.step()
        self.assertEqual(0, rom.prg_ram[0],
                         f"Result code of rts test is {rom.prg_ram[0]} not 0")
        message = bytes(rom.prg_ram[4:]).decode("utf-8")
        print(message[0:message.index("\0")])  # message ends with null terminator

    def test_blargg_instr_test_v5_rti(self):
        # Create machinery that we are testing
        rom = ROM(self.test_folder / "instr_test-v5" / "rom_singles" / "14-rti.nes")
        ppu = PPU(rom)
        cpu = CPU(ppu, rom)
        # Tests run as long as 0x6000 is 80, and then 0x6000 is result code; 0 means success
        rom.prg_ram[0] = 0x80
        while rom.prg_ram[0] == 0x80:  # go until first unofficial opcode test
            cpu.step()
        self.assertEqual(0, rom.prg_ram[0],
                         f"Result code of rti test is {rom.prg_ram[0]} not 0")
        message = bytes(rom.prg_ram[4:]).decode("utf-8")
        print(message[0:message.index("\0")])  # message ends with null terminator

    def test_blargg_instr_test_v5_brk(self):
        # Create machinery that we are testing
        rom = ROM(self.test_folder / "instr_test-v5" / "rom_singles" / "15-brk.nes")
        ppu = PPU(rom)
        cpu = CPU(ppu, rom)
        # Tests run as long as 0x6000 is 80, and then 0x6000 is result code; 0 means success
        rom.prg_ram[0] = 0x80
        while rom.prg_ram[0] == 0x80:  # go until first unofficial opcode test
            cpu.step()
        message = bytes(rom.prg_ram[4:]).decode("utf-8")
        print(message[0:message.index("\0")])  # message ends with null terminator
        self.assertEqual(0, rom.prg_ram[0],
                         f"Result code of brk test is {rom.prg_ram[0]} not 0")

    def test_blargg_instr_test_v5_special(self):
        # Create machinery that we are testing
        rom = ROM(self.test_folder / "instr_test-v5" / "rom_singles" / "16-special.nes")
        ppu = PPU(rom)
        cpu = CPU(ppu, rom)
        # Tests run as long as 0x6000 is 80, and then 0x6000 is result code; 0 means success
        rom.prg_ram[0] = 0x80
        while rom.prg_ram[0] == 0x80:  # go until first unofficial opcode test
            cpu.step()
        message = bytes(rom.prg_ram[4:]).decode("utf-8")
        print(message[0:message.index("\0")])  # message ends with null terminator
        self.assertEqual(0, rom.prg_ram[0],
                         f"Result code of special test is {rom.prg_ram[0]} not 0")


if __name__ == "__main__":
    unittest.main()
```

It's important to have automated tests like this when developing an emulator. Even when you think your CPU is perfect, you may have missed a small bug that throws whole programs off. You also need to know that changing one part of your emulator doesn't break another part of it.

Playing Games

Unit tests are one thing, but the real test of our emulator is whether it can play actual NES software. For legal reasons, we won't be testing any commercial software in our NES emulator. Due to its simplicity, our emulator wouldn't be capable of playing most of the NES library anyway. Instead, the book's source code repository includes several open source or public domain games that our emulator is capable of running. These are real games in the sense that they can run on a real NES console.

Let's start with *BrickBreaker*, a *Breakout*-like game by Aleff Correa that I mentioned earlier. Assuming you have Pygame and NumPy installed, you can play this game by just running this command from the repository's home directory:

```
% python3 -m NESEmulator NESEmulator/Games/brix.nes
```

It looks pretty good (see Figure 6-8).

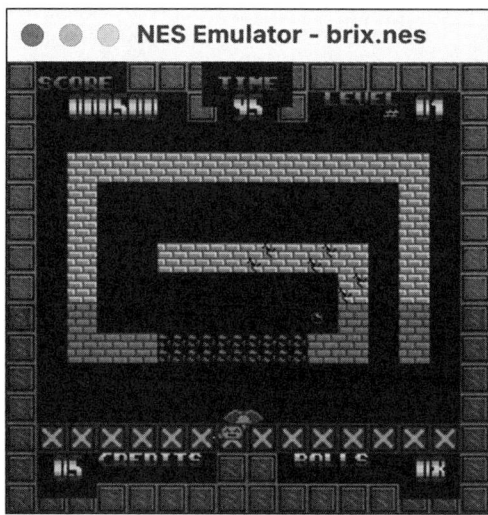

Figure 6-8: BrickBreaker *by Aleff Correa*

Next, let's try *Chase* by Shiru:

```
% python3 -m NESEmulator NESEmulator/Games/Chase.nes
```

Figure 6-9 shows the game.

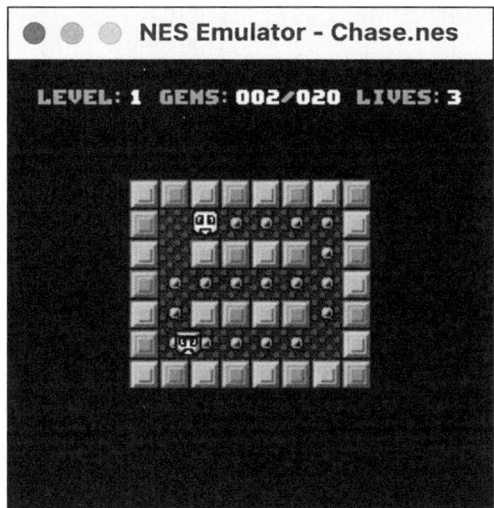

Figure 6-9: Chase *by Shiru*

Finally, let's try *Lan Master* by Shiru:

```
% python3 -m NESEmulator NESEmulator/Games/LanMaster.nes
```

This one's a puzzle game, shown in Figure 6-10.

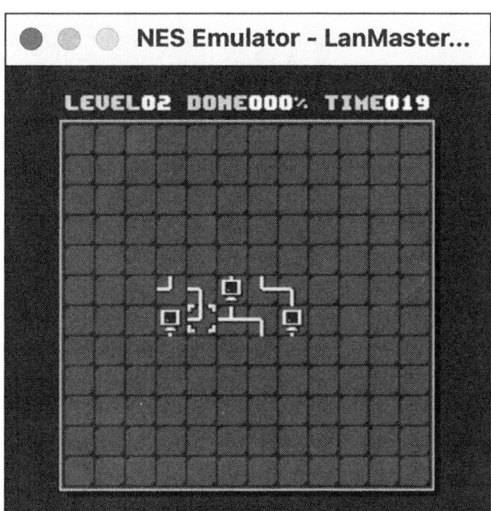

Figure 6-10: Lan Master *by Shiru*

Lan Master is very playable on our emulator, but the other two are not. Why? Well, you may have noticed all of them run pretty slowly. On my M1 MacBook Air running CPython 3.13, for example, they run at approximately 14 FPS. That's about one-quarter the speed of a real NES. Our emulator is correctly running these games, just very slowly.

What's the lesson? Python, and in particular the mainline version of Python, CPython, is slow. In recent years there have been efforts to improve the performance of CPython, but it's still very slow compared to most other programming language implementations and isn't tuned out of the box for writing low-level programs like emulators. To write more performant programs, you need to jump through some hoops: you can use particular libraries that are implemented in a lower-level language, use Cython, write a C extension, or use an alternative Python interpreter like PyPy.

I'll leave speeding up the emulator using something like Cython as an exercise for the reader. I'm confident that with the right solution you can get this NES emulator up to a real NES's 60 FPS.

CODE MEETS LIFE

When I started my emulator-programming journey by writing a CHIP-8 VM in Swift, my real dream was to write an emulator for the first game console I owned as a child, the NES. Two years later I got there, writing a basic NES emulator with no sound in C. While the CHIP-8 VM took me a day or two, the NES emulator took me about 30 days, spread over a year of off-and-on research and programming time. I found writing the CPU portion quite straightforward, but writing a pixel-perfect background renderer was much more challenging. I ended up porting the background renderer of the PPU of Michael Fogleman's excellent NES emulator[7] from Go to C and combining it with my own sprite-rendering code.

If the NES emulator took me about 30 days to write and the CHIP-8 VM took about two days, was the project 15 times harder? I don't think so. My challenge in writing the PPU was keeping all of the technical details in my mind at once. I was too focused on writing a pixel-perfect renderer when I should have started with a per-frame renderer as we did in this chapter. At the time there were also no great tutorials, although the documentation at NesDev was invaluable. I had first wanted to write an NES emulator as a teenager, so completing it was a dream come true, even if it was pretty basic and lacked sound. (I later added sound, as well as more mappers than just NROM.)

In this chapter, I tried to provide the tutorial that I wish I had when I was developing my NES emulator. I knew pixel-perfect rendering would be too complicated and too full of esoteric internal-register minutiae for a first-time emulator writer, so I went back and rewrote the PPU of my C NES emulator as simply as possible. That's the renderer I ported to Python for this chapter.

After finishing the NES emulator, I went on to write an emulator for the original IBM PC. That was a significantly more complicated project, largely because the Intel 8088/8086 is much more complicated than the MOS 6502. In that project, not writing automated tests very early on bit me. Eventually I got it working at a basic level, but I should have written the tests much earlier. The more complicated the microprocessor you're emulating, the more you need automated tests as early as possible.

Real-World Applications

Emulators are probably most commonly used to play video games for systems that are no longer in production, but they've also long been used at critical junctures in computing history. For example, when Bill Gates and Paul Allen started Microsoft in 1975 by writing a BASIC interpreter for the Altair 8800, as was discussed in Chapter 2, they didn't actually have an Altair 8800 available to them. Instead, they wrote an emulator for the Altair's Intel 8080 microprocessor on one of the minicomputers at Harvard, where Gates was going to college.[8]

Apple has transitioned the microprocessor family used in its Macintosh line of computers three times: from the Motorola 68K to the Motorola/IBM PowerPC, from the PowerPC to the Intel x86, and finally from the Intel x86 to Apple's own ARM-derived Apple Silicon. Does that mean Apple had to have developers recompile or rewrite all of their software several times? In the long run, yes, but in the short term during the transitions, Apple provided emulators. PowerPC Macs could run 68K Mac software, Intel Macs (at the beginning) could run PowerPC Mac software, and Apple Silicon Macs can run Intel Mac software too. Apple is an amazing emulator developer. In fact, PowerPC Macs would run 68K software faster than 68K Macs. The same was sometimes true of Apple Silicon Macs running Intel software.

Emulators are also important for the preservation of software. What happens when it's very hard to obtain the original hardware that a piece of software was written for? In those cases an emulator may be the only option. On the other end of the spectrum, emulators are sometimes used in the design phase of a new computing platform. Before the platform exists, the designers may utilize an emulator to simulate what it will be like and help flesh out its features in a realistic environment.

Finally, emulator writing is very educational. It's one of the best ways to teach how computers work at a low level, as I hope you discovered in this chapter.

Exercises

1. Try to get the performance of our emulator up to that of a real NES—in other words, 60 FPS. You'll likely need to use something like Cython, or Python in combination with a low-level language like C or Rust through an extension. It will be nearly impossible to get pure Python to run at 60 FPS as of CPython 3.13 and 2025 era microprocessors.

2. Add support for scrolling to our emulator using the documentation at *https://nesdev.org*.

3. Implement another mapper. Right now our emulator only implements NROM, the most basic mapper. Two other popular mappers are MMC1 and UxROM.

4. And now for the largest challenge of all: try writing an APU for our emulator so that you can play games with sound.

Notes

1. David Sheff, *Game Over: How Nintendo Conquered the World* (GamePress, 1999).

2. Russ Cox, "The MOS 6502 and the Best Layout Guy in the World," *research!rsc*, January 3, 2011, *https://research.swtch.com/6502*.

3. Steven Collier, "What Was the Biggest NES Game Ever Made?," DKoldies, March 24, 2016, *https://www.dkoldies.com/blog/what-was-the-biggest-nes-game-ever-made/*.

4. Marat Fayzullin, "iNES," accessed April 19, 2024, *http://fms.komkon.org/iNES*.

5. Table 6-1 is based on information from NesDev.org released into the public domain. See *https://www.nesdev.org/wiki/INES*.

6. The example is borrowed from user Damian Yerrick of NesDev.org. All the information on NesDev.org is released into the public domain. See *https://www.nesdev.org/wiki/PPU_pattern_tables*.

7. See *https://github.com/fogleman/nes*.

8. James Wallace and Jim Erickson, *Hard Drive: Bill Gates and the Making of the Microsoft Empire* (HarperBusiness, 1993).

PART IV

SUPER-SIMPLE MACHINE LEARNING

7

CLASSIFICATION WITH K-NEAREST NEIGHBORS

This chapter will introduce *k-nearest neighbors (KNN)*, an extraordinarily simple machine learning algorithm that can be highly effective for some applications. First developed in the 1950s and 1960s,[1] KNN can be used for both *classification* (deciding what category something belongs to) and *regression* (predicting a value). For readers daunted by the complexities of machine learning, KNN provides an accessible yet real-world entry point into the field. In this chapter, we'll use KNN to solve two classification problems with a high degree of accuracy: distinguishing between different types of fish and recognizing handwritten digits. Then, in Chapter 8, we'll extend KNN to some related regression problems.

The Rise of Machine Learning

Going back to the 1950s, traditional artificial intelligence (AI) research was chiefly concerned with utilizing algorithms to model human intelligence. Starting in the 1990s, however, and especially since the advent of neural networks backed by GPU computing in the 2000s, much of the focus of AI research and productization has turned to the subfield of machine learning, which uses large datasets to train models that can make decisions without needing to reference the human method of problem solving. To understand this shift, think of the difference between a chess program that evaluates a position based on well-understood heuristics from grandmasters and a chess program that evaluates a position based on auto-tuned weights assimilated from statistically analyzing millions of games. Indeed, machine learning is heavily based on statistics.

All the exciting machine learning applications we're familiar with, including LLMs, image recognition, and digital assistants, are built using sophisticated multilayer neural networks trained on GPUs or specialized neural processors. This is known as *deep learning*. To program a deep learning framework from scratch you would need a significant understanding of both calculus and statistics. Even if you dodge some of that by using a library, you still typically need a huge dataset, which is often hard to obtain, and powerful hardware.

Because of these barriers, programmers interested in getting started with machine learning are sometimes intimidated. They're afraid the math will be too hard or they'll lack the resources needed to develop the application they're interested in. What's more, some learning programmers like to build their projects from the ground up; they don't want to just `pip install` their way to a solution that offers them no understanding about how the underlying process actually works.

As you'll see in this chapter, however, machine learning can have a very approachable starting point if you don't jump right into the deep learning deep end. You can program the KNN algorithm from scratch and use it to solve real problems, and you don't need a background in mathematics beyond the middle school level to understand what you're doing. The only statistical concept required to implement KNN is the idea of a mean (average), and the only other formula you'll need is the Pythagorean theorem to find the Euclidean distance between two points. That's not asking much, right?

NOTE   *If you want to learn more about neural networks, you can check out Chapter 7, "Fairly Simple Neural Networks," of my prior book* Classic Computer Science Problems in Python *(Manning, 2019).*

How KNN Works

The KNN algorithm makes a simple assumption: the neighbors of a data point are likely to be the other data points that have the most in common with it. For example, if I'm trying to figure out the disease that a patient has, perhaps other patients with the same symptoms and same vital signs are the best clues. Incidentally, this is why you probably don't want a doctor straight out of medical school. More experienced doctors can use the obvious heuristic of "I've seen other patients like this before" to offer you better initial guidance.

Another way of putting it is that the data points that are closest to an unknown value are the likeliest ones to tell us what that unknown value is. Perhaps you're a car dealer, and you want to know if you should spend more marketing dollars trying to attract a potential repeat customer by sending her further mailers. The customer has filled in a customer satisfaction survey rating various aspects of your business. You have a lot of data from prior customers filling in the same survey, and you know whether or not they ended up buying another car with you. You can compare this potential repeat customer's survey ratings to the ratings of prior customers to find the customers that are the most similar to her in disposition. If those prior customers with similar ratings ended up buying another car, you know it's probably worthwhile to spend the money on sending her more marketing material. That's essentially the analysis that KNN does: it lets prior data "vote" on a likely value associated with some new data.

Let's look at the last example visually along two dimensions. Figure 7-1 is a fictionalized dataset of respondents' ratings on the dealer survey for "Car Happiness" and "Dealer Happiness." Crosses are survey respondents who purchased another car from the dealer, triangles are survey respondents who did not, and the round dot is the new survey respondent.

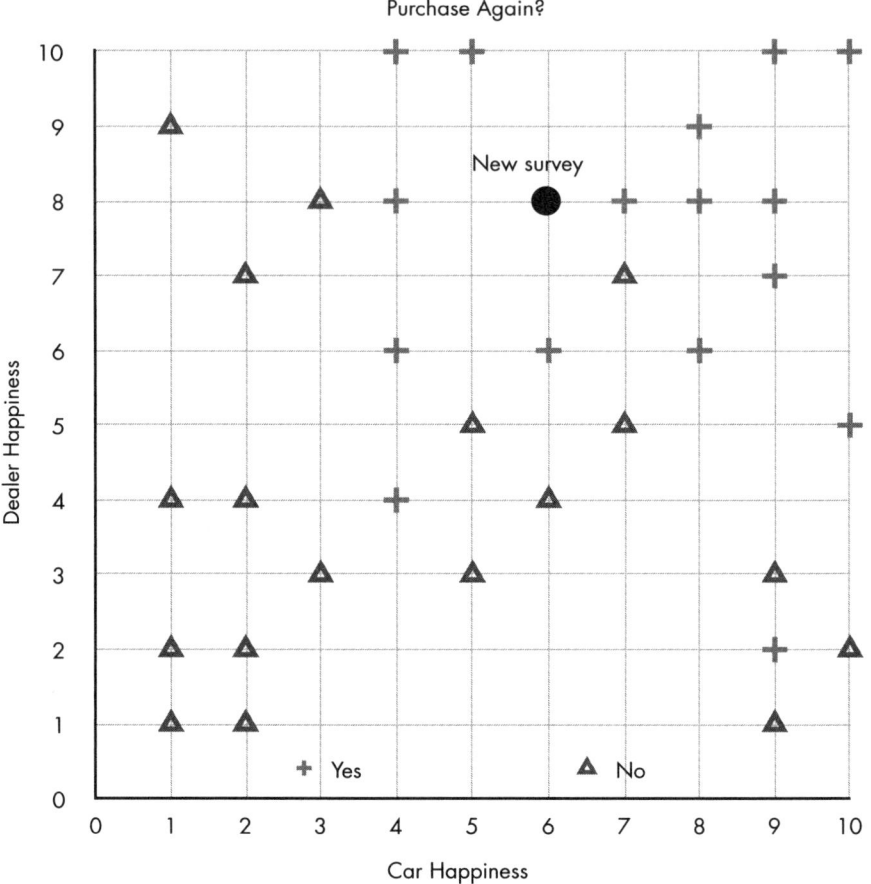

Figure 7-1: Car dealership survey respondents' data

How would we classify our new survey respondent? Is she likely to buy another car or not? Using KNN, we need to first choose a value for k, the *meta-heuristic*. This is simply the number of neighbors we'll look at. If we set k to 1, then we look at just the data point that's closest to our unknown value. In Figure 7-1, with our survey respondent at (6, 8), our next closest data point to compare is at (7, 8), and that's someone who did buy another car. With k set to 1, we would therefore conclude that it's worth spending the money to send our new respondent some more marketing material.

But what if k is set to a number greater than 1? The typical solution in the KNN algorithm is to "vote." For example, if k is 3 in our scenario, you can see that the three closest data points would be two that bought a new car and one that didn't. Since the majority bought another car, we would still conclude it's worth spending the money on marketing to the new survey respondent. If k is set to 2, we would have a problem since one decided to buy another car and one didn't. Then, we would have to have some kind of tie-breaking criterion.

And that's it. That's the whole KNN algorithm for classification. We look at k data points close to the data point in question, and we let them vote on what our unknown should be. We can thus summarize the KNN algorithm for classification as follows:

1. Choose k, the number of neighbors to compare to an unclassified data point.
2. Find the k-nearest neighbors to the data point.
3. Vote on the classification of the data point based on the classes of the k-nearest neighbors.

This simple algorithm requires three clarifications: What does it mean to be a "nearest" neighbor? How is the winner of the vote determined? And what is the right value for k? All these questions may have different answers for different applications of KNN.

"Nearest" is most commonly determined using Euclidean distance. In other words, if we drew straight lines on Figure 7-1 between our unclassified point (the round dot) and all the other data points on the graph, the shortest lines would determine the neighbors. However, for some applications that don't have numerical data points, something like *Hamming distance* (counting the differences) may apply. Distance functions other than Euclidean distance are beyond the scope of this chapter.

Voting usually means determining what class a plurality of the nearest neighbors belongs to. You need some kind of tie-breaking criterion, though, even if you stick to odd numbers for k. This is because many applications have more than two classes. For instance, what if you have three classes and k is set to 5? You may end up with two of the nearest neighbors belonging to class A, two belonging to class B, and one belonging to class C. Should the data point in question be classified as A or B?

Determining the right value for k is actually quite straightforward. Unless we have some specific domain knowledge to tell us otherwise, we should use the value that has been found to be the most accurate in testing. We can test KNN with several different values for k with a particular dataset and set of test points and see which value is the most useful.

Those are the basics of classification with KNN. Obviously, there are a lot of options and enhancements that can be made beyond this simple outline, but you already know enough to implement KNN!

Implementing Classification with KNN

Like the algorithm itself, our code to implement KNN will be quite simple. But before we can get to the algorithm, we need a generic type for representing a data point. We'll create a DataPoint class that's a *protocol*, meaning there will be no instances of this type itself, but only of its subclasses. It's an abstract template outlining the functionality that a more concrete data point type must have:

KNN/knn.py

```
from pathlib import Path
import csv
from typing import Protocol, Self
from collections import Counter
import numpy as np

class DataPoint(Protocol):
    kind: str

    @classmethod
    def from_string_data(cls, data: list[str]) -> Self: ...

    def distance(self, other: Self) -> float: ...
```

Our protocol specifies that a data point should have a kind attribute (or a *class* in the words of classification), a from_string_data() method for converting a line from a CSV (comma-separated values) file to an instance of the class, and distance() to find the distance between two of the same kind of data points. We'll create DataPoint subclasses for the two concrete datasets we work with in this chapter.

Our main KNN implementation is via a class not surprisingly called KNN:

```
class KNN[DP: DataPoint]:
    def __init__(self, data_point_type: type[DP], file_path: str | Path,
                 has_header: bool = True) -> None:
        self.data_point_type = data_point_type
        self.data_points = []
        self._read_csv(file_path, has_header)

    # Read a CSV file and return a list of data points
    def _read_csv(self, file_path: str | Path, has_header: bool) -> None:
        with open(file_path, 'r') as f:
            reader = csv.reader(f)
            if has_header:
                _ = next(reader)
            for row in reader:
                self.data_points.append(
                    self.data_point_type.from_string_data(row))
```

The type hint syntax class KNN[DP: DataPoint]: says that a generic type, DP, is associated with KNN and that a DP must be a subclass of DataPoint. We'll be loading all our datasets from CSV files. Our KNN class's _read_csv() method utilizes the built-in Python csv module to load these files. Each line in the CSV file is used to initialize one of our DataPoint subclasses via its from_string_data() class method. We'll come back to the specifics of CSV files in a bit when we look at our first dataset.

Now that we have a dataset loaded in the KNN class, we're ready to implement the actual KNN algorithm. Where do we start? Given a point that we want to classify, the first thing we need is to identify its *k*-nearest neighbors. All our data points have built-in `distance()` methods, so we can just calculate the distance from our unclassified data point to every data point in the dataset and find the *k* nearest:

```
def nearest(self, k: int, data_point: DP) -> list[DP]:
    return sorted(self.data_points, key=data_point.distance)[:k]
```

Yup, it is a one-liner. We just use the `distance()` method's results to sort all of the data points, and then we keep the k lowest values (the points with the least distance from data_point). The core of the KNN algorithm really is that simple.

Is this the most efficient way to find the nearest neighbors? No. Sorting is an $O(n \log n)$ operation, where n is the number of data points in the dataset. If the dataset is very large, this would be a significant bottleneck. We could improve this a bit by writing code to manually evaluate the distances of all the data points utilizing an ancillary data structure to only keep the k smallest. To take performance even further, we may need a more sophisticated data structure than an unsorted list for storing the dataset. In short, there's a trade-off here between algorithmic performance and data structure complexity.

Another alternative would be to not actually search the entire dataset for neighbors each time. There are various approaches to limit the search either through precomputation of a more limited subset of data points that are representative of the whole or sampling the dataset during the search through a so-called *approximate search*.[2] That said, our simple sorting technique is fast enough for our applications and is true to the title of this part of the book, "Super-Simple Machine Learning."

Next, we need to do the "voting." That involves counting how many of each class (or kind) there are in the nearest neighbors and returning the class that there are the most of:

```
def classify(self, k: int, data_point: DP) -> str:
    neighbors = self.nearest(k, data_point)
    return Counter(neighbor.kind for neighbor in neighbors).most_common(1)[0][0]
```

First, we find the `neighbors`. Then, we use Python's built-in `Counter` collection type to find the most common kind among the neighbors. The `most_common(1)` call returns the single most common item in the `Counter`, and the `[0][0]` says retrieve that first item from the collection and take its kind label. The `Counter` will internally be structured as key-value pairs that look something like `[("amphibian", 3), ("reptile", 4), ("mammal", 1)]`. In that example, the line would find the key-value pair with the highest value, `("reptile", 4)`, and return just its key, `"reptile"`. We don't handle tie-breakers in any systematic way here—we just leave it up to the whim of `Counter`. Again, remember the part title.

That's it. Thanks to some nice Python standard library routines, the actual algorithmic work behind KNN is effectively just three lines of code between nearest() and classify(). I told you it would be "super simple." With the algorithm in place, let's now apply KNN to two classification problems.

Classifying Fish

Suppose you work as a programmer for a company that makes a fish-finding device for anglers. It consists of a camera on the end of a pole that travels underneath a boat. It has image recognition built in, so when a fish passes by the underwater camera, it can automatically take a picture of it and recognize the rectangle within the photo that contains the fish. It can also estimate the dimensions of the fish in the photo. Your task is to write a layer of software on top of this image recognition system that tells the angler what type of fish it is. After all, not all fish are legal to catch.

Luckily, we have a dataset in the public domain that will help us with this fish classification task. It's originally from a 1917 Finnish paper by Pekka Brofeldt that in English was called "Contribution to the Knowledge of Fish Stocks in Dangerous Lakes."[3] It contains the dimensions and weights of 159 fish from a lake, classified by species (so our program may only work in that one lake). Figure 7-2 shows the fish in our dataset along just two dimensions, height and width.

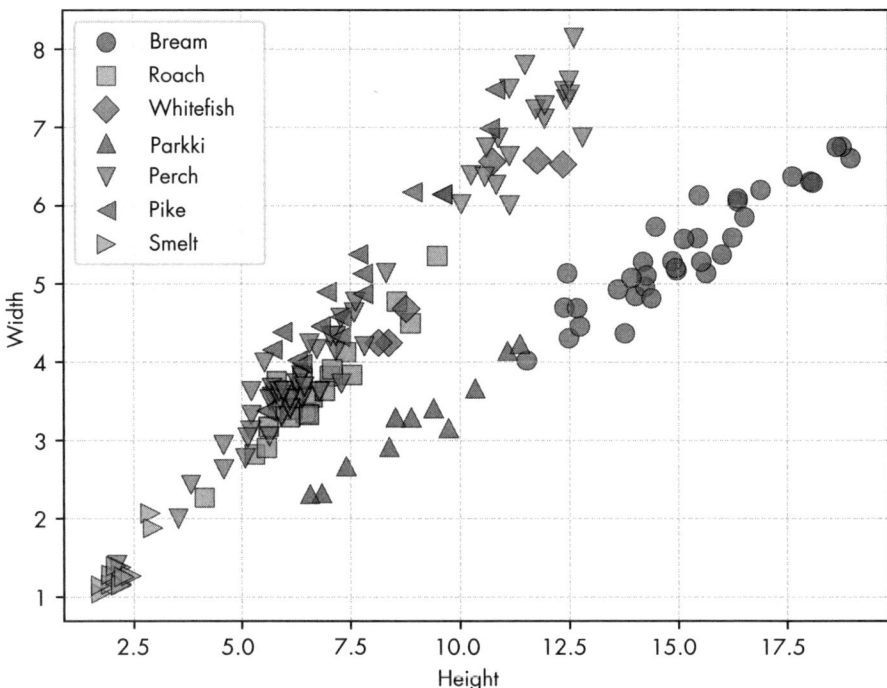

Figure 7-2: Fish categorized by species and plotted along the height and width dimensions

As you may expect, fish of a similar species tend to be close together when viewed in terms of height and width. That's a good indicator that KNN may be a useful algorithm for this problem.

Let's look at what the raw data looks like. Here's a sample of the first few lines of *fish.csv*:

```
Species,Weight,Length1,Length2,Length3,Height,Width
Bream,242,23.2,25.4,30,11.52,4.02
Bream,290,24,26.3,31.2,12.48,4.3056
Bream,340,23.9,26.5,31.1,12.3778,4.6961
Bream,363,26.3,29,33.5,12.73,4.4555
```

The first row is a header that describes each column. The three length dimensions, which represent the distances from the nose of each fish to various different body parts, are in centimeters, and the weight is in grams. There's some ambiguity in sources about the units of the height and width. As long as the units are consistent between samples, however, the data is still useful, even if we don't know if it's centimeters, some kind of percentage, or otherwise.

The Fish Class

To implement our fish classifier, we need to build a subclass of DataPoint to represent a fish:

```python
# KNN/fish.py
from dataclasses import dataclass
from KNN.knn import DataPoint
from typing import Self

@dataclass
class Fish(DataPoint):
    kind: str
    weight: float
    length1: float
    length2: float
    length3: float
    height: float
    width: float

    @classmethod
    def from_string_data(cls, data: list[str]) -> Self:
        return cls(kind=data[0], weight=float(data[1]), length1=float(data[2]),
                length2=float(data[3]), length3=float(data[4]),
                height=float(data[5]), width=float(data[6]))

    def distance(self, other: Self) -> float:
        return ((self.length1 - other.length1) ** 2 +
                (self.length2 - other.length2) ** 2 +
                (self.length3 - other.length3) ** 2 +
                (self.height - other.height) ** 2 +
                (self.width - other.width) ** 2) ** 0.5
```

Technically, we don't need to explicitly make Fish a subclass of DataPoint for protocol conformance in Python type hints. By fulfilling all the requirements of the DataPoint protocol, a Fish can substitute for a DataPoint without even subclassing it thanks to the concept of implicit subtypes.[4] Still, we declare

Fish as a subclass of DataPoint explicitly because it provides clarity to the reader of our code and aids in type checking.

Each line of a CSV is provided from the KNN class as a list of strings for the Fish class to convert into a Fish instance. The from_string_data() method does this conversion. The distance() calculates the Euclidean distance between the current instance and another Fish. We find the differences between each dimension in the dataset, square those differences, and sum them. Then, we return the square root (** 0.5) of that sum. Note that we don't consider the weight attribute from the dataset as part of the comparison. This is because we'll be using the dimensions of a fish to predict its weight in the next chapter, so the weight will be unknown for the fish in question.

The Unit Tests

We have unit tests to make sure we're getting the expected results from our fish detector. We start with a test that checks whether the fish nearest to a sample fish are the expected ones:

```python
# tests/test_knn.py
import unittest
from pathlib import Path
import csv
from KNN.knn import KNN
from KNN.fish import Fish
from KNN.digit import Digit

class FishTestCase(unittest.TestCase):
    def setUp(self) -> None:
        self.data_file = (Path(__file__).resolve().parent.parent
                          / "KNN" / "datasets" / "fish" / "fish.csv")

    def test_nearest(self):
        k: int = 3
        fish_knn = KNN(Fish, self.data_file)
        test_fish: Fish = Fish("", 0.0, 30.0, 32.5, 38.0, 12.0, 5.0)
        nearest_fish: list[Fish] = fish_knn.nearest(k, test_fish)
        self.assertEqual(len(nearest_fish), k)
        expected_fish = [Fish('Bream', 340.0, 29.5, 32.0, 37.3, 13.9129, 5.0728),
                         Fish('Bream', 500.0, 29.1, 31.5, 36.4, 13.7592, 4.368),
                         Fish('Bream', 700.0, 30.4, 33.0, 38.3, 14.8604, 5.2854)]
        self.assertEqual(nearest_fish, expected_fish)
```

Next, we try classifying a sample fish:

```python
    def test_classify(self):
        k: int = 5
        fish_knn = KNN(Fish, self.data_file)
        test_fish: Fish = Fish("", 0.0, 20.0, 23.5, 24.0, 10.0, 4.0)
        classify_fish: str = fish_knn.classify(k, test_fish)
        self.assertEqual(classify_fish, "Parkki")
--snip--
```

To run these unit tests we have our standard test-running code:

```
if __name__ == "__main__":
    unittest.main()
```

Note that we've skipped over about 40 lines in the *test_knn.py* file containing further tests that will appear later in this chapter and the next.

Classifying Handwritten Digits

Optical character recognition (OCR) is concerned with using computers to recognize the characters in images of typed or handwritten text. For example, the post office has sorting machines that use OCR to automatically read the addresses written on envelopes. A wide variety of techniques have been successfully deployed to perform OCR, KNN among them. In this section, we'll use KNN to develop a handwritten digit recognizer that will achieve 98 percent accuracy on the samples in a significant test set.

The dataset we'll use was developed by Cenk Kaynak and Ethem Alpaydin in 1998 at Bogazici University in Istanbul, Turkey, and was later submitted to the UC Irvine Machine Learning Repository under a Creative Commons Attribution 4.0 International license. It consists of 5,620 bitmaps of handwritten digits (0–9) created by 43 different people.[5] The digit images are downscaled to 8×8 pixels, with each pixel represented in a CSV file as an integer between 0 and 16 indicating its grayscale level. Each line in the CSV consists of the 64 integers representing the 64 pixels in the handwritten digit image, plus a 65th integer representing which digit (0–9) the image should be classified as. Figure 7-3 shows a sampling of these digits.

Figure 7-3: Some 8×8 handwritten digit images from the OCR dataset

The digits are artificially enlarged a bit in the figure, but you can see that the downscaling to 8×8 results in some loss of detail. That lower level of detail, and therefore a lower dimensionality in the dataset, makes our program faster to execute. Comparing 64 pixels between images is obviously much faster than comparing 1,024 pixels between images (they were originally 32×32 before being downscaled).

The Digit Class

To represent each digit, we define another subclass of DataPoint:

KNN/digit.py
```
from dataclasses import dataclass
from KNN.knn import DataPoint
from typing import Self
import numpy as np
```

```
@dataclass
class Digit(DataPoint):
    kind: str
    pixels: np.ndarray

    @classmethod
    def from_string_data(cls, data: list[str]) -> Self:
        return cls(kind=data[64],
                   pixels=np.array(data[:64], dtype=np.uint32))

    def distance(self, other: Self) -> float:
        tmp = self.pixels - other.pixels
        return np.sqrt(np.dot(tmp.T, tmp))
```

We store the pixel data as a NumPy array. This is convenient because in the next chapter, we'll use Pygame to work with our own handwritten digit scrawls, and Pygame can interface directly with NumPy arrays. Since the distance() method is calculating across NumPy arrays, we use built-in NumPy functions to implement a form of Euclidean distance.

The Unit Test

The dataset is divided between 3,823 digit images in a training set and 1,797 digit images in a test set. We'll use the training set as the dataset that our KNN implementation makes predictions based on, and we'll test how many digits in the test set can be correctly identified against it. Let's define another test case in *test_knn.py* for this, after the Fish test case but before the if __name__ == "__main__" line:

tests/test_knn.py
```
class DigitsTestCase(unittest.TestCase):
    def setUp(self) -> None:
        self.data_file = (Path(__file__).resolve().parent.parent
                          / "KNN" / "datasets" / "digits" / "digits.csv")
        self.test_file = (Path(__file__).resolve().parent.parent
                          / "KNN" / "datasets" / "digits" / "digits_test.csv")

    def test_digits_test_set(self):
        k: int = 1
        digits_knn = KNN(Digit, self.data_file, has_header=False)
        test_data_points: list[Digit] = []
        with open(self.test_file, 'r') as f:
            reader = csv.reader(f)
            for row in reader:
                test_data_points.append(Digit.from_string_data(row))
        correct_classifications = 0
        for test_data_point in test_data_points:
            predicted_digit: str = digits_knn.classify(k, test_data_point)
            if predicted_digit == test_data_point.kind:
                correct_classifications += 1
        correct_percentage = (correct_classifications
                              / len(test_data_points) * 100)
        print(f"Correct Classifications: "
              f"{correct_classifications} of {len(test_data_points)} "
```

```
            f"or {correct_percentage}%")
        self.assertGreater(correct_percentage, 97.0)
```

This test loads the training dataset (*digits.csv*) into an instance of the KNN class. It then opens the test set (*digits_test.csv*) and turns the CSV data into a list of data points, test_data_points. Then, it tries classifying each of the data points one at a time and records how many classifications it got right. Finally, it reports that percentage and fails if the accuracy is below 97 percent.

Let's run all the tests to see how we did. With the fish and OCR tests combined, this will take a little while. Classifying those 1,797 digit images takes about 11 seconds on my laptop:

```
% python3 -m tests.test_knn
Correct Classifications: 1761 out of 1797 or 97.9966611018364%
....
----------------------------------------------------------------------
Ran 4 tests in 10.826s

OK
```

From the documentation that came with the OCR dataset (see the bottom of *KNN/datasets/digits/readme.txt*), we know that the authors tested the accuracy of the dataset themselves using KNN with various different values of *k*. They found the highest accuracy, 98 percent, with *k* set to 1. The test output of our classifier matches that. That means it works!

CODE MEETS LIFE

A couple years ago I found myself teaching an introductory course on artificial intelligence to a group of senior undergraduates. I split the course into two halves. The first half covered what we termed at the beginning of this chapter "traditional AI," including algorithms like A* and MiniMax (both of which you can find in my prior book *Classic Computer Science Problems in Python*) and concepts like expert systems. The second half was dedicated to machine learning. I used KNN as the first example of a machine learning algorithm thanks to its extreme simplicity. It served as a great transition into the world of machine learning, which is why I came to believe it could do the same for the readers of this book.

Since then, my department has used KNN as a teaching demo presentation topic for candidates coming to campus to interview to become new computer science faculty. They're told the presentation topic at least a week before they come to campus and have a chance to prepare. KNN works well as a topic for this purpose because, while there are many possible extensions and improvements to the core algorithm, the core algorithm itself shouldn't take very long to explain, and even an audience of unfamiliar faculty or first-year students should be able to comprehend it. It's a great gauge of whether someone is ready to be a good instructor.

(continued)

As an aside, you'd be amazed how many PhDs with a background in machine learning aren't able to give a good introductory lecture on a topic like KNN. It's worth remembering that a PhD is a research degree, not a teaching degree. This is why, when you're advising your child on where to go to college, you should consider a teaching college. At a large research university, the student may be taught by research faculty who don't care about teaching, an adjunct for whom teaching is a part-time job, or in the worst case, a very inexperienced graduate student. Having a faculty full of PhDs doesn't mean much for an undergraduate student's experience in an introductory course when those faculty care more about research grants than teaching. By contrast, at a teaching college, you have an entire full-time faculty (most with PhDs anyway) who were hired because they're fully dedicated to the art of teaching and often actually like being in an introductory classroom. What you lose is a connection to cutting-edge research, but for an undergraduate, that connection generally isn't what will make the biggest impact on their trajectory anyway. But take what I'm saying with a grain of salt, since I've worked at a teaching college for the past nine years.

Real-World Applications

KNN has been widely used in the real world for everything from optical character recognition to recommendation systems and from text classification to financial modeling. Its simplicity and wide applicability make it universally taught in machine learning.

However, when utilizing KNN in practice, several issues that have already been alluded to in this chapter must be overcome. The first is finding the right value for k. This is typically done via cross validation using a test dataset. What's the value for k that worked best with the test data? Using too small a value can lead to *overfitting*, where the model is too close to one specific dataset. Meanwhile, too large a value can lead to *under-fitting*, where the model is too far away from being guided by the test data.[6]

The next challenge is the performance implications of the basic algorithm with large datasets of high dimensionality. As mentioned earlier in the chapter, two ways of approaching this problem are designing a better data structure for storing the dataset or using approximate searching. One of the most popular data structures for speeding up the finding of nearest neighbors is a k-d tree.[7] However, this is a fairly complex data structure and is only worth the headache if performance is critical.

Choosing the right distance function is also critical. Euclidean distance works for many applications, but Hamming distance is appropriate for boolean dimensions, and other distance functions are well studied in the research literature. The right distance function is application specific; there's no one-size-fits-all solution. Often, you also have to normalize the data to eliminate the possibility of different units or magnitudes, influencing results. We didn't normalize the data in the fish example in this chapter, and the data in the OCR example was all in the same units and scales and thus didn't require normalization.

While we saw that it's borderline trivial to implement KNN from scratch, many popular Python machine learning libraries have highly optimized built-in KNN functions anyway. For example, scikit-learn's implementation is widely used.

Exercises

1. Find another dataset of your own interest that our KNN implementation can accurately classify.

2. Try to speed up the unit tests by improving the performance of the `Digit` class's `distance()` method while retaining the 98 percent accuracy of the test. Feel free to move away from using NumPy arrays if you'd like. You can even move away from using pure Euclidean distance. Perhaps you don't even need to compare every pixel?

3. Reimplement our classifier using the scikit-learn library. Compare the performance of our classifier to the KNN classifier built into scikit-learn.

Notes

1. Thomas Cover and Peter E. Hart, "Nearest Neighbor Pattern Classification," *IEEE Transactions on Information Theory* 13, no. 1 (January 1967): 21–27.

2. Shichao Zhang, "Challenges in KNN Classification," *IEEE Transactions on Knowledge and Data Engineering* 34, no. 10 (October 2022): 4663–4675, *https://doi.org/10.1109/tkde.2021.3049250*.

3. Pekka Brofeldt, "Bidrag till kaennedom on fiskbestondet i vaara sjoear Laengelmaevesi," T.H.Jaervi: Finlands Fiskeriet Band 4, Meddelanden utgivna av fiskerifoereningen i Finland, Helsingfors, 1917.

4. "Protocols," typing Documentation, accessed May 8, 2024, *https://typing .readthedocs.io/en/latest/spec/protocol.html#explicitlydeclaring-implementation*.

5. Ethem Alpaydin and Cenk Kaynak, "Optical Recognition of Handwritten Digits," UCI Machine Learning Repository, accessed December 10, 2024, *https://doi.org/10.24432/C50P49*.

6. Stuart Russell and Peter Norvig, *Artificial Intelligence: A Modern Approach*, 4th ed. (Pearson, 2021), 688.

7. Russell and Norvig, *Artificial Intelligence*.

8

REGRESSION WITH K-NEAREST NEIGHBORS

In this chapter, we'll extend our KNN implementation to perform regression. For our purposes, *regression* simply means predicting a numeric value. With some small additions to our code from Chapter 7, we can use our same KNN class to not only classify but also make predictions about any numeric attribute value in our datasets.

We'll apply regression to the two KNN examples from the preceding chapter. First, we'll revisit the fish dataset and use regression to predict the weight of a fish based on its dimensions. Then, we'll write a program that allows the user to draw part of a digit and then predicts what the rest of the drawing could look like.

Unlike the other chapters in this book, this chapter doesn't stand alone. It builds off the prior chapter. Please be sure you've worked through Chapter 7 before diving into this one.

How KNN Regression Works

In KNN classification, we tried to predict the class or category that a data point belongs to, selecting the appropriate class from a limited set of options. In KNN regression, instead of predicting a class, we're trying to predict an attribute value. These attribute values will typically be numeric, meaning there's potentially an infinite range of values that could be assigned. Of course, it would make sense for the attribute value to be missing if it's something we want to predict.

As an example, say we're a hospital assigning patients to rooms. We may want to know how many days the patient will likely need to stay. We could look at past data from patients with similar diagnoses, symptoms, and vital signs to make the prediction. Let's look at this example visually with a scatterplot along two dimensions (Figure 8-1).

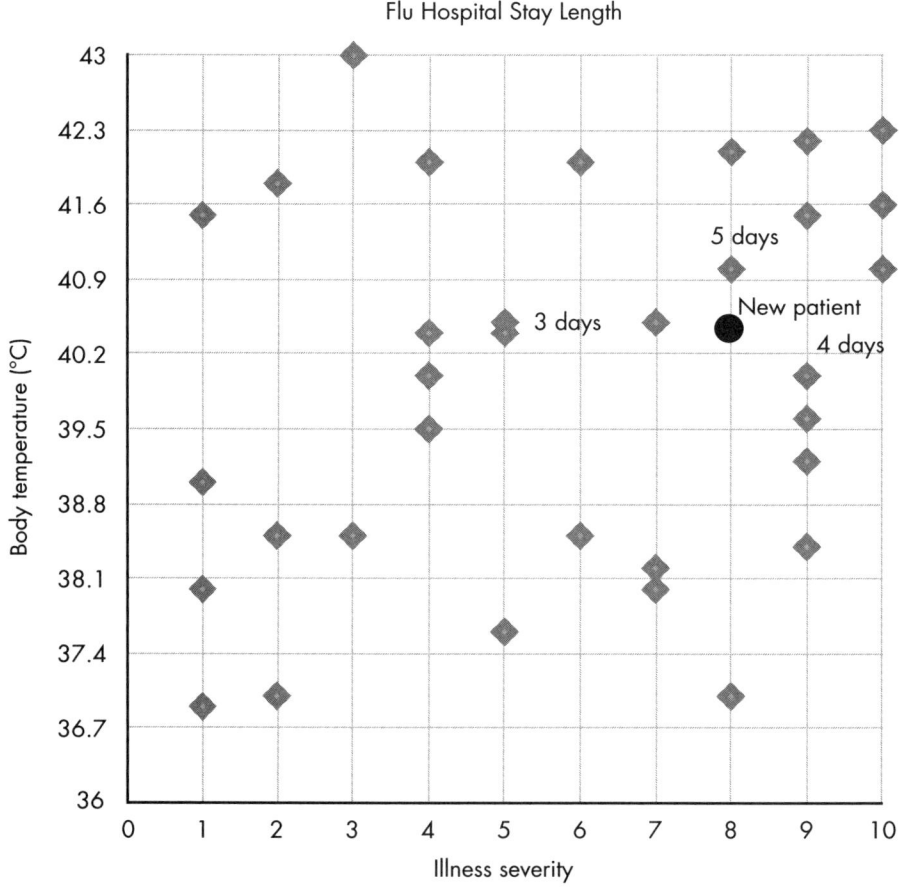

Figure 8-1: Hospital stay length for flu based on body temperature and illness severity

Suppose the diamonds in Figure 8-1 represent past patients who were admitted to the hospital with flu. Their illness was rated by a doctor on a severity scale from 1 to 10, and their temperature was noted at the time of admission. We also have data about how long they ended up staying at the hospital.

The round dot represents a patient who was just admitted. We have their severity rating and their body temperature, and we'd like to predict how long they will end up staying in the hospital so that we can put them in the appropriate room. If we use KNN with Euclidean distance and set *k* to 3, then we'll look at the three patients in the past data that are closest on the scatterplot to the new patient's dot. The figure notes their stays as three, four, and five days, respectively. Estimating the new patient's hospital stay length using this method can be as simple as averaging the three nearest neighbors. That average (whether mean or median) would be four, so we would predict that the new patient will stay in the hospital for four days.

More broadly, here are the steps for performing regression with KNN:

1. Choose *k*, the number of neighbors to compare to a data point with a missing attribute.
2. Find the *k*-nearest neighbors to the data point.
3. Average the corresponding attribute value across the *k*-nearest neighbors to predict what that missing attribute value should be for the data point in question.

As you can see, using KNN for regression is very similar to using KNN for classification. It's really just the last step that differs. We have some of the same questions and answers about this algorithm as we had in the prior chapter too: What's the right value for *k*? How do we calculate distance? See Chapter 7 for a discussion of those questions.

We also have a new question: What does it mean to take the average? Typically this is either the mean or the median. Like with the question of the right distance function, the best way to take the average can be application specific. It generally requires some domain knowledge to make the best determination.

Implementing Regression with KNN

To perform regression, we'll need to add just two methods to our KNN class from Chapter 7. One predicts a scalar numeric attribute, and one predicts an attribute that's an array of numbers. We'll use the latter for the handwriting example so that we can predict pixels. Here are the updates:

```
# KNN/knn.py
# Predict a numeric property of a data point based on the k-nearest neighbors.
# Find the average of that property from the neighbors and return it.
def predict(self, k: int, data_point: DP, property_name: str) -> float:
    neighbors = self.nearest(k, data_point)
    return (sum([getattr(neighbor, property_name) for neighbor in neighbors])
            / len(neighbors))
```

```
# Predict a NumPy array property of a data point based on the k-nearest neighbors.
# Find the average of that property from the neighbors and return it.
def predict_array(self, k: int, data_point: DP, property_name: str) -> np.ndarray:
    neighbors = self.nearest(k, data_point)
    return (np.sum([getattr(neighbor, property_name) for neighbor in neighbors], axis=0)
            / len(neighbors))
```

Like classify() from the preceding chapter, these methods start by finding the k nearest neighbors. Then, they calculate and return the mean of some property among those neighbors. We take advantage of the dynamic nature of Python here by allowing the caller to specify the property as a string and then using getattr() to retrieve that specified property (or *attribute*) by name.

The only real difference here between predict() and predict_array() is that the latter uses the NumPy sum() function instead of Python's built-in sum() function. NumPy arrays will actually work with the built-in sum() function too since they implement the plus operator, but NumPy's version is a bit faster.

That's it. Essentially it takes just two more lines of code (both functions are about the same) and we're making predictions.

Predicting Fish Weights

Let's add a unit test to FishTestCase to make sure our new predict() method is working. We want to answer the question, "If we know the dimensions of a fish, can we make an educated guess about what its weight could be?" The answer, of course, is yes:

tests/test_knn.py
```
def test_predict(self):
    k: int = 5
    fish_knn = KNN(Fish, self.data_file)
    test_fish: Fish = Fish("", 0.0, 20.0, 23.5, 24.0, 10.0, 4.0)
    predict_fish: float = fish_knn.predict(k, test_fish, "weight")
    self.assertEqual(predict_fish, 165.0)
```

In this method, we create a test_fish with no weight specified (0.0), and we compare it to the five closest fish to it in terms of their anatomical dimensions—length1, length2, length3, width, and height. (Recall from the preceding chapter that we don't compare fish by weight in the distance() method.) We then predict its weight by averaging the weights of these five nearest neighbors. Run the unit tests again, and you should find that the fish's weight is correctly predicted. To test if this prediction method is accurate more generally, we could try running it across the entire fish dataset. Since the dataset includes the known weights of each sample, we could measure how accurate our KNN results are compared to the actual fish weights.

Predicting the Rest of a Handwritten Digit

In the preceding chapter, we correctly classified 98 percent of a test set of images of handwritten digits against a training set of the same kind of

8×8 pixel images using KNN. In this final KNN example, we'll classify an 8×8 digit that the user draws and even predict what the rest of the pixels of the image could look like. Instead of implementing this as another set of unit tests, we'll create a fun interactive program using Pygame that allows the user to draw in a window housing an 8×8 grid.

Here's a preview of what we're building. Figure 8-2 shows the drawing window with a squiggly 7 that I tried to draw. I pressed the C key and the program correctly classified it as a 7 (that shows in the terminal, not pictured).

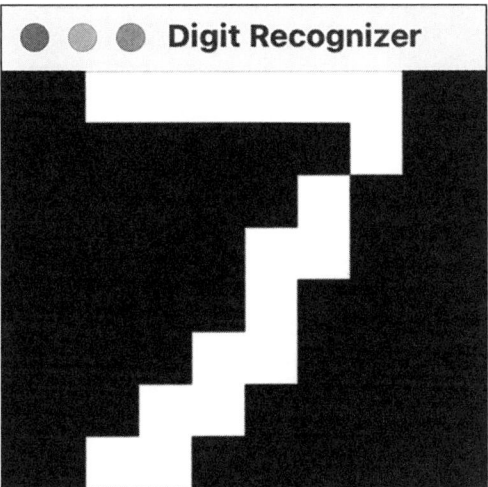

Figure 8-2: Drawing a 7 in the digit recognizer program

Figure 8-3 shows the window after pressing the P key, which triggers a prediction of what the rest of the digit's pixels may look like based on the average of the pixels of the nine nearest neighbors.

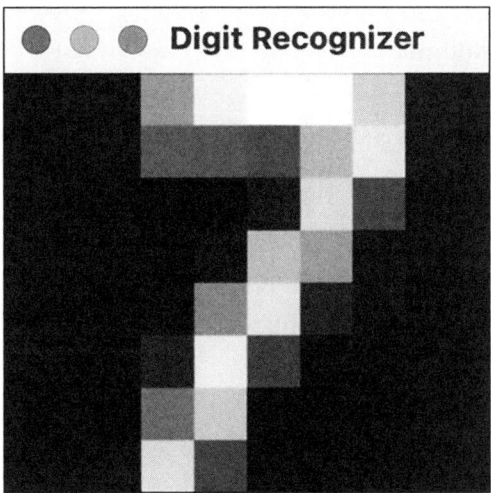

Figure 8-3: The predicted digit's pixels based on the nearest neighbors' pixels

In our simple program, we can only draw with white. The prediction yields a better-looking 7 since it can use more levels of gray. We start our program with some imports and constants:

```
from KNN.knn import KNN
from KNN.digit import Digit
from pathlib import Path
import sys
import pygame
import numpy as np

PIXEL_WIDTH = 8
PIXEL_HEIGHT = 8
P_TO_D = 16 / 255  # pixel to digit scale factor
D_TO_P = 255 / 16  # digit to pixel scale factor
K = 9
WHITE = (255, 255, 255)
```

The PIXEL_WIDTH and PIXEL_HEIGHT constants are the size of one image. The P_TO_D constant converts between the 255 shades of gray in the pixel representation we'll work with and the 16 shades of gray in the source dataset; D_TO_P is its inverse. We set K, the number of neighbors KNN will consider, to 9, and WHITE is a constant for the white color in the RGB pixel format.

This is a short program. We have just one central run() function that spends as much time handling the user interface as it does running KNN. Here's the start of the function:

```
def run():
    # Create a 2D array of pixels to represent the digit
    digit_pixels = np.zeros((PIXEL_HEIGHT, PIXEL_WIDTH, 3),
                            dtype=np.uint32)
    # Load the training data
    digits_file = (Path(__file__).resolve().parent
                    / "datasets" / "digits" / "digits.csv")
    digits_knn = KNN(Digit, digits_file, has_header=False)
    # Start up Pygame, create the window
    pygame.init()
    screen = pygame.display.set_mode(size=(PIXEL_WIDTH, PIXEL_HEIGHT),
                                     flags=pygame.SCALED | pygame.RESIZABLE)
    pygame.display.set_caption("Digit Recognizer")
```

In these first few lines, we create the pixel array, load the dataset, and initialize Pygame. The main window is initialized to be a "stretched out" 8×8 pixels. You can resize the window and it will maintain its 8×8 dimensions. This is set via the set_mode() flags (flags=pygame.SCALED | pygame .RESIZABLE).

Next, we need to set up the main loop:

```
while True:
    pygame.surfarray.blit_array(screen, digit_pixels)
    pygame.display.flip()
```

Since this a GUI program using Pygame, we effectively have an event loop. It listens for some action by the user and then responds. This action could be a keyboard or mouse event. To keep the screen in sync, we constantly blit digit_pixels to the screen at the beginning of the loop. Then, we handle keyboard events:

```
for event in pygame.event.get():
    if event.type == pygame.KEYDOWN:
        key_name = pygame.key.name(event.key)
        if key_name == "c":  # classify the digit
            pixels = digit_pixels.transpose((1, 0, 2))[:, :, 0].flatten() * P_TO_D
            classified_digit = digits_knn.classify(K, Digit("", pixels))
            print(f"Classified as {classified_digit}")
```

We start with the C key used for classification. This is similar to the classification we did in the preceding chapter. The result is printed to the console. The only tricky bit is the transformation of the pixels representing the picture to a form that our classifier can use. In essence, we're moving from a pixel format of 255 grays and multiple dimensions to a flat array of 16 grays. The keyboard handler continues:

```
    elif key_name == "e":  # erase the digit
        digit_pixels.fill(0)
    elif key_name == "p":  # predict what the digit should look like
        pixels = digit_pixels.transpose((1, 0, 2))[:, :, 0].flatten() * P_TO_D
        predicted_pixels = digits_knn.predict_array(K, Digit("", pixels), "pixels")
        predicted_pixels = predicted_pixels.reshape((
            PIXEL_HEIGHT, PIXEL_WIDTH)).transpose((1, 0)) * D_TO_P
        digit_pixels = np.stack((predicted_pixels, predicted_pixels,
                                predicted_pixels), axis=2)
```

The E key just erases the pixel array. The P key is the prediction part. First, we again convert the pixel array to a form the KNN class can use, as before. Next, we use the predict_array() method to get the predicted _pixels, which are the average of the pixels from the nine closest entries in our training set. We then convert those results back to a form that can be displayed in Pygame. This involves not only reshaping to a two-dimensional array but also changing to RGB format, where the same gray level is repeated in each of the three color channels. The reshape() and transpose() chains go from one to two dimensions, and the stack() call creates a third dimension that's all the same value—for example, a gray level of 128 becomes (128, 128, 128) for RGB.

The rest of the code draws white pixels anywhere the user clicks, exits when the user closes the window, and calls the run() function when *__main__.py* is executed:

```
        elif ((event.type == pygame.MOUSEBUTTONDOWN) or
            (event.type == pygame.MOUSEMOTION and pygame.mouse.get_pressed()[0])):
            x, y = event.pos
            if x < PIXEL_WIDTH and y < PIXEL_HEIGHT:
                digit_pixels[x][y] = WHITE
        elif event.type == pygame.QUIT:
            sys.exit()

if __name__ == "__main__":
    run()
```

It only takes about 50 lines of actual code to create a GUI-based handwritten digit recognizer using our existing KNN class. Python is so succinct! Try it out: it's not perfect, but it correctly recognizes the majority of my scrawls.

CODE MEETS LIFE

In 2016 I worked on a simple educational project called SwiftSimpleNeural Network[1] as preparation for a chapter about building neural networks from scratch in Swift for my second book, *Classic Computer Science Problems in Swift*. I implemented handwritten digit recognition using that framework, and it was extremely slow. To be fair, there were no optimizations at all, and the application was completely single threaded and CPU bound. Amazingly, the also unoptimized, but much simpler, KNN algorithm implementation in this chapter outperforms it in both speed and accuracy.

This anecdote speaks to two important lessons: the more complex algorithm isn't always the better algorithm for a particular application, and it's important to do some research to be well informed about what algorithms are used for what applications. That's why I've included a "Real-World Applications" section at the end of every chapter in this book.

Knowing your algorithmic options is important across many domains. To that end, one of the benefits of reading a survey book like this is that it introduces you to new algorithms and techniques that you may not have known about before. That way, when you encounter a problem that they're applicable to, you'll be ready.

Real-World Applications

KNN can be a great tool to start with when attempting to do regression, because it's so easy to use. There's very little tuning necessary, unlike with a neural network, and because there's effectively no training involved, a KNN-based application is trivial to stand up.

Researchers have really used KNN to predict hospital stay lengths, as described in the beginning of the chapter. Pei, Lin, and Chen found that KNN was approximately as accurate as more sophisticated techniques like logistic regression or random forest for predicting COVID-19 patients' hospital stay length.[2] I was able to find multiple other studies in the same domain that used KNN. KNN regression has also been used for applications in text mining, agriculture, and financial markets.[3] It makes intuitive sense—events or data points from the past that are most similar to what's currently happening are likely to be the most helpful in making predictions.

Due to performance issues, KNN doesn't work well when the data is noisy or the dataset is too large in terms of number of points and dimensionality. For most applications, however, it's a reasonable starting point to consider.

Exercises

1. Prove (or disprove) that KNN is effective for fish weight prediction by running it against the entire fish dataset and comparing the KNN results to the known weights from the dataset. On average, how accurate are the KNN predictions?

2. Change our digit recognizer program to use a larger grid, say 64×64 instead of 8×8. This will allow the user to draw more fluid digits. You'll need to find a way to accurately downscale the 64×64 drawings to 8×8 to utilize them with the training dataset.

3. Use either our implementation of KNN regression or that from a library like scikit-learn to try to make predictions using a dataset of your own interest.

Notes

1. See *https://github.com/davecom/SwiftSimpleNeuralNetwork*.

2. Jianing Pei, Xin Lin, and Qixuan Chen, "Prediction of Patients' Length of Stay at Hospital During COVID-19 Pandemic," *Journal of Physics: Conference Series* 1802 (March 2021): *https://doi.org/10.1088/1742-6596/ 1802/3/032038*.

3. Sadegh Bafandeh Imandoust and Mohammad Bolandraftar, "Application of K-Nearest Neighbor (KNN) Approach for Predicting Economic Events: Theoretical Background," *Journal of Engineering Research and Applications* 3, no. 5 (2013): 605–610, *https://www.ijera.com/papers/Vol3 _issue5/DI35605610.pdf*.

AFTERWORD

Thank you for reading *Computer Science from Scratch*. This afterword provides more resources for you based on the four themes of the book (interpreters, computational art, emulators, and machine learning). I've chosen to highlight nonacademic but highly regarded resources that I've personally found to be useful—there's no ivory tower here. But before we get to that, I have a few thoughts I'd like to share with you on what we've accomplished.

What We Did and What's Next

By working through the projects in this book, you were exposed to a broad survey of several different areas in computer science. Are you an expert on them now? Of course not. But you know enough to get started on a project of your own design in any of these four areas. More importantly, you're in a good position to learn more about these topics.

The interpreters we completed in Part I were simple, but NanoBASIC had the constituent parts of any real-world interpreter (tokenizer, parser, runtime environment). You could go build an interpreter for a more sophisticated language now without any further study. Where it gets tricky is when you want to make that language more performant. This may require more advanced techniques like implementing a VM or a compiler, or adding built-in runtime optimizations.

I'll share some more in-depth resources on interpreters later in this afterword, but the point is you can get started immediately. Have you ever wanted to create your own programming language? Now you can. I'm not necessarily saying that you should, but you can.

The computer art programs we developed in Part II introduced a hodgepodge of interesting algorithmic techniques, yet there wasn't really a unifying theme other than pixels. You know enough now to manipulate pixels. If you have an idea about how you want to make pixels change, you can probably do that. Computer graphics more generally is filled with much broader ideas and would be your next stop if you want to further explore manipulating pixels.

The NES emulator in Part III was by far the largest and most complex project in the book. A great next step would be to either add more compatibility to the emulator (as described in the Chapter 6 exercises) or try emulating another system. The Game Boy is of similar complexity, as is the Sega Master System. As discussed in the chapter, writing emulators in Python is challenging from a performance perspective. If you don't know C or C++, writing your next emulator may be a great opportunity to learn them.

In Part IV we took baby steps into the world of machine learning. KNN is perhaps the simplest algorithm in all of artificial intelligence. It works well for the right applications, but you'll want to learn several other techniques to know which ones to reach for in a given situation. Hopefully the super simple nature of Part IV made this area, which can often seem intimidating, feel more approachable to you. You don't need to be an expert on machine learning to use machine learning techniques. Today, everything is a library call away. You do, however, need to know which library call to make.

I hope you feel like you got a great start in all four of these areas by completing the projects in this book. Now it's up to you if you want to dive into your own projects or complete more training. In the rest of this afterword, I've suggested some more resources in each of these areas that I think will follow this book well. All of them have been vetted by me. I actually read the books that I'm recommending to you.

On Learning Computer Science

You don't need a formal university education to learn computer science. This book was a great start. Like almost all subjects, everything you need is available for free in a library and on the internet. It just requires perseverance (study time, project time).

I'm the type of person who likes to understand how things work at a fundamental level as much as possible. I've met other people like this, and it may just be a personality trait. Even if that's not you, let me try to convince you why there's a real benefit to learning some more computer science so that you can understand how things work "under the hood."

First, as programmers, computer science is fundamental to understanding the techniques we can use to solve the problems that our programs need to solve. Sure, if we're just building generic CRUD apps, it might not prove very useful, but if you want to do something novel or tricky, computer science really comes in handy.

Second, even if we can think of a way to solve a problem, is it the most efficient way? Does it create performance problems? Understanding some computer science fundamentals can really help you improve the performance of your code.

And finally, understanding computer science will help you in your career. You'll understand what your colleagues are talking about. You'll "get" software technology on a much more fundamental level. You'll become a better technical communicator. And it will help you with technical interviews. Unfortunately, far too many companies still require candidates to solve data structure and algorithm problems on a whiteboard. I don't agree with this practice, but there's no doubt that those who have studied computer science have a leg up in these interviews.

Computer science is a big subject. Don't be intimidated. Here are a couple friendly books that I think complement this book well if you're interested in furthering a general computer science education.

Grokking Algorithms, 2nd Edition, by Aditya Y. Bhargava

This is an eminently readable book on algorithms. It's much easier to consume than your average algorithms textbook. It's less math heavy and includes examples in Python to illustrate each concept. I use it myself instead of a traditional textbook when I teach a college-level data structures and algorithms class.

Classic Computer Science Problems in Python by David Kopec

I wrote *Classic Computer Science Problems* as a general overview of interesting algorithmic topics taught in a code-first, tutorial-like fashion. It covers everything from search algorithms to graph algorithms to even some introductory AI material. It's the perfect accompaniment to this book and there is zero content overlap between the two since they cover different areas of computer science. Whereas this book is composed of larger, entertaining projects, *Classic Computer Science Problems* is more about the algorithms themselves and the particular problems that are appropriate for them.

Interpreters

Ten years ago, there were very few nonacademic books that could be recommended on writing interpreters for a general programmer audience. Today, we're fortunate to have several great titles in this space, including two that I highly recommend:

Crafting Interpreters **by Robert Nystrom**
This is an absolutely wonderful book, in terms of both its pedagogy and its code. The older classic books on interpreters and compilers are extremely academic and even somewhat stuffy (like the so-called "Dragon Book"). *Crafting Interpreters* is a must-read book in this space if you want to write larger practical interpreters after having your interest piqued by the Brainfuck and NanoBASIC projects in this book.

Writing an Interpreter in Go **by Thorsten Ball**
I read this book myself in preparation for writing an interpreted programming language called SeaTurtle to help kids learn to code (see the "Code Meets Life" box in Chapter 2). It's less comprehensive than *Crafting Interpreters* and a little more niche, being written in Go. If you're interested in something more succinct or if you're a Go programmer, however, it's a great choice. It's well written, and the accompanying code is great.

Computational Art

I mostly learned about the techniques in the book's two computational art chapters from short online articles, so unfortunately I don't have any comprehensive resources to share, but I do want to mention Michael Fogleman's Primitive project. It was the inspiration for the Impressionist chapter (Chapter 4), although that program uses a different algorithm. The GitHub repository for Primitive (*https://github.com/fogleman/primitive*) has some easy-to-read Go source code, and Michael has a website for the project as well (*https://www.michaelfogleman.com/#primitive*).

Emulators

There may be good texts out there on writing emulators, but I'm personally not aware of them. Instead, I'm sharing a couple online resources that I've found to be helpful:

EmuDev
This subreddit (*https://www.reddit.com/r/EmuDev*) is one of the most vibrant communities that I've come across on emulator development,

where folks building every kind of emulator you can imagine go to share their insights. There's also an accompanying Discord that can be useful for getting questions answered live.

NesDev

The wiki documentation and forums at *https://www.nesdev.org* were invaluable to me both when developing my first NES emulator and when writing the emulator for this book. Unfortunately, despite NES emulation being a popular project, there are very few good tutorials or resources about it (which is part of how I got the idea to write this book). NesDev is the best resource that's out there, and if you want to further your NES development beyond what we did in Chapter 6 (like adding more mappers or a more accurate PPU), this site will be your go-to resource.

Machine Learning

There are so many resources on machine learning that it can be overwhelming to even decide which one to start with. That said, if you liked the simple algorithm presented in Chapters 7 and 8 and you liked the way that we developed it from scratch, then I have two particularly straightforward resources for learning about other machine learning algorithms that you can implement:

The Hundred-Page Machine Learning Book **by Andriy Burkov**

This book is straight to the point. You learn the algorithm with just enough theory and other information to implement it without any of the flowery trappings of some technical books. While it doesn't feature a lot of code, it's a great explainer that can be furthered by good online courses or YouTube channels.

Classic Computer Science Problems in Python **by David Kopec**

Yes, I'm recommending my own book a second time. That's a bit self-serving, but I wouldn't have written it if I didn't think it was truly a great resource. In fact, five of the nine chapters in the book could be said to be about artificial intelligence, and two of the chapters are specifically about machine learning. Do you want to learn how to write a neural network from scratch in Python (with no libraries)? Check out Chapter 7 of *Classic Computer Science Problems in Python*. You learned how to write a simple classifier and regressor using KNN in this book. In Chapter 6 of *Classic Computer Science Problems in Python*, you'll also learn how to build a clustering program using another simple algorithm, k-means.

FOLLOW ME ON SOCIAL MEDIA

- X: *https://x.com/davekopec*
- GitHub: *https://github.com/davecom*
- LinkedIn: *https://www.linkedin.com/in/dkopec*
- YouTube: *https://www.youtube.com/c/DavidKopec09*
- My website: *https://davekopec.com*
- *Kopec Explains Software*, a podcast: *http://kopec.live*

APPENDIX
BITWISE OPERATIONS

Low-level manipulation of bits is essential for half of the projects in this book. If you have no background in bitwise operations, this appendix provides an overview, including what the most essential bitwise operations do, how to use them in Python, and some examples of what they're used for.

A Review of Binary

I assume that most readers, as intermediate or advanced programmers, are familiar with binary. If that's you and you just want a quick refresher on bitwise operations, you can skip this section. However, if you're not familiar with binary, this section will get you started, although it's not comprehensive.

All information in computers is stored as 1s and 0s. This is convenient because the type of hardware used to build computers can physically represent 1s and 0s quite readily. For instance, if electricity (or a "signal") is present, we may say that represents a 1, while the absence of an electrical signal represents a 0. Binary also manifests itself physically in the now outdated technology of CDs and DVDs. Their readers have a laser that runs over the surface of the disc. When the laser doesn't reflect back because the disc has a microscopic pit, that represents a 0. If the laser does reflect back because there isn't a pit, that represents a 1. One final physical example is QR codes. The presence of a black dot can be a 1, and the absence can be a 0. There are many convenient physical manifestations of binary.

How are all those 1s and 0s converted into information? A sequence of 1s and 0s represents a number in binary. And once we have numbers, we can represent any other kind of information. A specific number can represent a specific letter in an electronic document. Or it can represent a specific color. Another number can represent where on the screen to place that color. Pretty soon we have pixels.

How does a sequence of 1s and 0s represent a number beyond 1 or 0, though? That's where the binary number system, also called *base 2*, comes into play.

Typical numbers in everyday use are in *base 10*, known as *decimal*. That means each digit in the number can have 10 different values (0–9), and each digit itself represents a power of 10. For instance, the number 427 is actually $(4 \times 10^2) + (2 \times 10^1) + (7 \times 10^0)$. Likewise, each digit in a binary number can have two different values (0 or 1), and each digit itself represents a power of 2. The number 427 is 110101011 in binary, which is $(1 \times 2^8) + (1 \times 2^7) + (0 \times 2^6) + (1 \times 2^5) + (0 \times 2^4) + (1 \times 2^3) + (0 \times 2^2) + (1 \times 2^1) + (1 \times 2^0)$. The 1s are powers of 2 that are "on" and the 0s are powers of 2 that are "off."

To test your understanding, try converting a few numbers from decimal to binary and vice versa. What's 73 in binary? What's 11000 in decimal? Try a few more that you pick. You can check your work with Python, where binary numbers are represented as literals by using the `0b` prefix, as in `0b11` for the decimal number 3:

```
>>> value = 0b11
>>> value
3
```

Meanwhile, Python's `bin()` function takes an integer and returns a string formatted as the binary equivalent:

```
>>> bin(3)
'0b11'
```

Each stored binary 1 or 0 is known in computing as a *bit*. And a standard *byte* is 8 bits. All modern computers use the 8-bit byte as their standard unit of storage. The maximum value a byte can hold (when representing an unsigned integer) is 255 because eight 1s, or 11111111 in binary, is 255 in decimal. That also means a byte can hold 256 different possible values (all the values from 0 to 255).

When a byte is written out, the *least-significant bit*—that is, the bit representing the smallest power of 2—is typically written all the way on the right (bit 0, representing 2^0). The *most-significant bit*—the one representing the largest power of 2—is typically written all the way to the left (bit 7 representing 2^7). In 10000000, for example, the 1 represents 2^7 being turned on, so the byte has a decimal value of 128. This assumes we're working with *unsigned* integers—integers that can't be negative. Signs are beyond the scope of this basic introduction to binary.

Some data types are represented using more than one byte. For instance, on a 64-bit microprocessor like the one probably powering your computer, integers are often stored using 64 bits (8 bytes). The maximum value of a 64-bit number in binary is:

1111111111111111111111111111111111111111111111111111111111111111

That translates to 18,446,744,073,709,551,615 in decimal.

For several projects in this book, we need to manipulate bytes at the bit level. The rest of this appendix covers some common operations for doing so.

Common Bitwise Operations

Bitwise operations manipulate a value at the level of individual binary digits. This means working with 1s and 0s. All microprocessors include instructions for performing bitwise operations, and Python has operators for tapping into these microprocessor instructions. *Truth tables*, which show the true/false outcome of logic functions based on different combinations of inputs, can be helpful in understanding bitwise operations. To make this more practical and applicable to our Python use of these operations, the tables accompanying each operation will show binary values instead of true and false.

Left Shift (<<)

Instead of thinking about our binary data as a number, for a minute just think about it as a collection of 1s and 0s. Imagine the 0s are empty spaces and the 1s are filled spaces. What if we want to move all the 1s to the left by one space? That's the job of a *left shift*, which in Python is represented with the << operator.

A left shift leaves a gap in the least-significant bit (bit position 0). With left shifts in Python, we fill that gap with a 0. Because Python integers are of arbitrary length (there's no maximum length), we can't move 1s off the end by moving them to the left. The number just grows by a digit. For example, 1010 shifted left by 1 becomes 10100, not 0100. We can also left shift by more than one place, so 1010 shifted to the left by three becomes 1010000. Table A-1 shows the results of some left shifts.

Table A-1: Left-Shift Examples

A	A << 1	A << 3
0	0	0
1	10	1000
1010	10100	1010000

In the first row of the table, where 0 is being shifted, you may think that it would become 00 and 0000, but in reality those are the same as 0. Instead, you can think of left shift as just moving the 1s. If there are no 1s, then the shift is essentially not doing anything.

Python's left-shift operator is preceded by the thing being shifted and followed by an integer indicating how many places to shift. Here's a quick example of using it:

```
>>> bin(0b1010 << 3)
'0b1010000'
```

Shift operators are typically used to move a bit or bits into alignment with another binary value in combination with other bitwise operators that we'll learn shortly.

Right Shift (>>)

A *right shift* is much like a left shift, except the 1s move to the right rather than the left. If a 1 moves off the end (past the 0-bit position), then it's "lost." There's no wrapping around. For example, 1001 shifted right by one becomes 100, not 1100. We can also right shift by more than one place, so 1001 shifted right by three becomes 1.

Python has the >> operator for performing right shifts. Table A-2 shows some example right shifts.

Table A-2: Right-Shift Examples

A	A >> 1	A >> 3
0	0	0
1	0	0
1010	101	1

In the second row of the table, the 1 is shifted "off the end" and there are no 1s left, so the result is 0.

OR (|)

With a *bitwise OR operation* between two values, if either value is a 1, then the result will be a 1. If neither value is a 1, then the result will be a 0. The operation is performed on the binary digits that are in the same digit places between the two values, one digit place at a time. Imagine the numbers are lined up, one below the other. Then, the OR operation is performed in each column, one column at a time, like this:

```
1010
0110
----
1110
```

Try calculating the final line on the bottom yourself by following the rules in the preceding paragraph. Those rules are also summarized in Table A-3.

Table A-3: OR Examples

A	B	A | B
0	0	0
0	1	1
1	0	1
1	1	1
1010	0110	1110

Python has the | operator for performing bitwise OR. Here's a quick example of using it on a couple binary numbers in Python:

```
>>> bin(0b1010 | 0b0110)
'0b1110'
```

One common use of the bitwise OR operation in low-level programming is to merge two values together in combination with the shift operators. For example, say we have one nibble (a *nibble* is 4 bits) that represents one-half of a byte and another nibble that represents the other half of the byte. We want to merge them together to produce the full byte. Perhaps nibble A is 1001 and nibble B is 0110, and we want nibble A to be the first half and nibble B the second half of the resulting byte. The code to merge them may look like this:

```
>>> a = 0b1001
>>> b = 0b0110
>>> c = (a << 4) | b
>>> bin(c)
'0b10010110'
```

With (a << 4) | b we shift a to the left 4 places and then OR its values with b. Remember that when we shift to the left, 0s fill in from the right, so a shifted to the left by 4 becomes 10010000. Then, if we line a and b up and OR them, we get:

```
10010000
    0110
--------
10010110
```

The resulting byte, 10010110, has the original a in the left four digits and the original b in the right four digits.

If you're seeing this for the first time, it may seem a little abstract. For instance, you may wonder why the numbers are being stored in just 4 bits to begin with. To give just one of several reasons, in the projects of this book we see several scenarios where we want to save space by combining values that need fewer than 8 bits into the same byte. For example, 8-bit microprocessors often had a 1-byte flags register where each individual bit represented a different flag that could be on or off. That's much more economical than using a separate byte for each flag. Likewise, some file formats store values that need less than 1 byte on the same byte to save disk space.

AND (&)

A *bitwise AND* returns a 1 if both operands are 1s; otherwise, it returns a 0. Here's an example using the same operands we looked at with bitwise OR:

```
1010
0110
----
0010
```

Only the bit that was lined up with two 1s resulted in a 1. Table A-4 summarizes how bitwise AND works.

Table A-4: AND Examples

A	B	A & B
0	0	0
0	1	0
1	0	0
1	1	1
1010	0110	0010

Python has the & operator for performing bitwise AND. Here's a quick example of using it on a couple binary numbers:

```
>>> bin(0b1010 & 0b0110)
'0b10'
```

Note that the output cuts off the leading 0s since they aren't needed to represent the resulting number (2 in decimal). In other words, 0010 in binary is 2 in decimal just as 10 in binary is 2 in decimal.

One common use of the bitwise AND operation in low-level programming is to ensure a final result only includes some of the bits from a prior result. For instance, suppose we only care about the rightmost 4 bits in the byte 10011110. We can AND the byte with 1111 to ensure only the rightmost 4 bits are in the final result. The code may look like this:

```
>>> a = 0b10011110
>>> b = 0b1111
>>> c = a & b
>>> bin(c)
'0b1110'
```

Let's see this operation with the bits lined up:

```
10011110
    1111
--------
    1110
```

We often use this technique with a single bit in our emulator projects when working with flags. We just need to know the single flag and whether it's 1 or 0 (true or false).

XOR (^)

A *bitwise XOR* ("exclusive or") returns a 1 if the operands are different (one 1 and one 0); otherwise, it returns a 0. Here's an example using the same operands we looked at with bitwise OR and AND:

```
1010
0110
----
1100
```

Table A-5 summarizes how XOR works.

Table A-5: XOR Examples

A	B	A ^ B
0	0	0
0	1	1
1	0	1
1	1	0
1010	0110	1100

Python has the ^ operator for performing bitwise XOR. Here's a quick example of using it on a couple binary numbers in Python:

```
>>> bin(0b1010 ^ 0b0110)
'0b1100'
```

XOR is a surprisingly powerful operation. It underlies the unbreakable encryption scheme known as a *one-time pad*. You can also flip bits by XOR-ing with 1: if you XOR a 1 with a 1, it becomes a 0, but if you XOR a 0 with a 1, it becomes a 1. Any bit you XOR with a 1 becomes the opposite of what it was before. This is how drawing on the screen works in the CHIP-8 project in Chapter 5.

Complement (~)

Complement is the simplest of all bitwise operations: it switches all 1s with 0s and all 0s with 1s, as shown in Table A-6.

Table A-6: Complement Examples

A	~A
1	0
0	1
1010	0101
011010	100101

Python has the ~ operator for taking a binary complement. We don't use complements much in this book, except for one small place in the NES emulator in Chapter 6.

INDEX

C

C (programming language), 6
cartridges (NES), 144, 148–152
characters in terminals and non-
        terminals, 29
CHIP-8, 115–140
    description of, 115–117
    history of, 116–117
    implementation of, 122–136
    instructions, 119–122
    memory and registers, 117–119
    playing games on, 137–138
    testing the virtual machine,
        136–137
CHR RAM (NES), 149, 177–178
CHR ROM (NES), 149, 177–178
classification
    of digits, 215–217
    of fish, 212–214
    with KNN, 205–219
CLC instruction (6502), 164
CLD instruction (6502), 164
CLI instruction (6502), 165
CLR (Common Language Runtime),
    139–140
CLV instruction (6502), 165
CMP instruction (6502), 165
collision detection (NES), 191
color dithering algorithms 63–72
    in MacPaint, 180–182
    in NES, 183–184
    in stochastic painting algorithm,
        90–95
Common Language Runtime (CLR),
    139–140
compilation, 17, 57
compilers, 17
complement (~) operator, 244
computational art, 63–112
    creating abstract impressions,
        89–112
consume() function, 42
COSMAC VIP, 117
Counter (Python), 211
CPM instruction (6502), 165
CPU (central processing unit) in NES,
    143, 152–176

CPX instruction (6502), 165
CPY instruction (6502), 165
cross validation, 218
CRT televisions, 147, 185
CSV files, 210, 212–213, 215

D

data fork, 80
DataPoint class, 209–211
data points, 209–211
DEC instruction (6502), 165
declaration vs. imperative
    languages, 23
DEFLATE algorithm, 86
DEX instruction (6502), 165
DEY instruction (6502), 165
digital art, 85
Digit class, 215–216
digits classification of, 215–217
    handwritten, 215–217, 224–228
    regression on, 224–228
Dijkstra, Edsger, 27, 48
dithering, 63–87
    algorithms for, 67–72
    Atkinson dithering, 67–72, 86
    explanation of, 64–65
    Floyd-Steinberg dithering,
        67–69, 86
DMA (direct memory access), 156, 174
domain-specific languages (DSLs), 57
drawing
    backgrounds (NES), 187–189
    using CHIP-8, 128–130
    using Pygame, 224–228
dynamic recompilation, 132

E

EOR instruction (6502), 165
error-diffusion dithering, 67–69
error handling
    in BASIC interpreter, 40–41
    in CHIP-8 VM, 126
esoteric programming languages, 3, 10
Euclidean distance, 206, 209, 211, 218

F

Fayzullin, Marat, 149
Fibonacci sequence, 27–28, 135

RETURN statement (BASIC), 26
ReturnStatement node, 39
RETURN_T token, 45
right-shift (>>) operator, 240
RLE (run-length encoding), 73–79
ROL instruction (6502), 167
ROM files, 122, 144–145, 149–152
ROR instruction (6502), 167
RTI instruction (6502), 167–168
RTS instruction (6502), 168
run-length encoding (RLE), 73–79

S

SBC instruction (6502), 168
scanlines, 147, 185
scrolling (NES), 201
SeaTurtle, 56, 234
SEC instruction (6502), 168
SED instruction (6502), 168
SEI instruction (6502), 168
setZN() method, 175
shunting yard algorithm, 48
6502 microprocessor, 143, 152–176
    addressing modes, 153–154,
        170–172
    CPU emulation, 152–176
    registers, 155–156
sound
    on CHIP-8, 125
    on NES, 143, 201
speed
    of NES emulator, 199–200
    of stochastic painting, 95
sprites
    on CHIP-8, 129–130
    on NES, 177, 189–191
stack, 155, 175
stack pointer, 156
STA instruction (6502), 168
standard library, 11, 71
Statement node, 37
static type checking, 12
status register (6502), 156, 175–176
step() method, 132, 169, 187
stochastic optimization, 111
stochastic painting, 89–112
    algorithm explanation, 98–99

implementation of, 99–107
    results of, 107–110
strings, escaping, 58
struct module, 150
STX instruction (6502), 168
STY instruction (6502), 168
SVG (Scalable Vector Graphics),
    97–98
switch statement, 131
System 1 (Mac OS), 84

T

take_same() function, 76–77
TAX instruction (6502), 168
TAY instruction (6502), 169
terminal, 29
testing
    Brainfuck interpreter, 15–16
    CHIP-8 VM, 136–137
    dithering, 78–79
    NanoBASIC interpreter, 53–57
    NES emulator, 194–197
    OCR with KNN, 216–217
text processing, 229
Thwaite (game), 182
tiles (NES), 178–180
timers
    in CHIP-8, 118, 125
    in NES, 185
tokenizer, 9, 33–36
Torvalds, Linus, 22
transpiler, 18
TSX instruction (6502), 169
TXA instruction (6502), 169
TXS instruction (6502), 169
TYA instruction (6502), 169
type hints, 12, 35

U

under-fitting, 218
unit tests, 15–16, 78–79, 194–197,
    213–217, 224
unpack() function, 150

V

variables in BASIC, 25
variable table, 49–51

Computer Science from Scratch is set in New Baskerville, Futura, Dogma, and TheSansMono Condensed.

RESOURCES

Visit *https://nostarch.com/computer-science-from-scratch* for errata and more information.

More no-nonsense books from **NO STARCH PRESS**

PRACTICAL DEEP LEARNING, 2ND EDITION
A Python-Based Introduction
BY RONALD T. KNEUSEL
584 PP., $69.99
ISBN 978-1-7185-0420-2

OBJECT-ORIENTED PYTHON
Master OOP by Building Games and GUIs
BY IRV KALB
416 PP., $44.99
ISBN 978-1-7185-0206-2

PYTHON PLAYGROUND, 2ND EDITION
Geeky Projects for the Curious Programmer
BY MAHESH VENKITACHALAM
448 PP., $44.99
ISBN 978-1-7185-0304-5

STRANGE CODE
Esoteric Languages That Make Programming Fun Again
BY RONALD T. KNEUSEL
496 PP., $49.99
ISBN 978-1-7185-0240-6

ALGORITHMIC THINKING, 2ND EDITION
Learn Algorithms to Level Up Your Coding Skills
BY DANIEL ZINGARO
480 PP., $49.99
ISBN 978-1-7185-0322-9

THE RECURSIVE BOOK OF RECURSION
Ace the Coding Interview with Python and JavaScript
BY AL SWEIGART
328 PP., $39.99
ISBN 978-1-7185-0202-4

PHONE:
800.420.7240 OR
415.863.9900

EMAIL:
SALES@NOSTARCH.COM

WEB:
WWW.NOSTARCH.COM

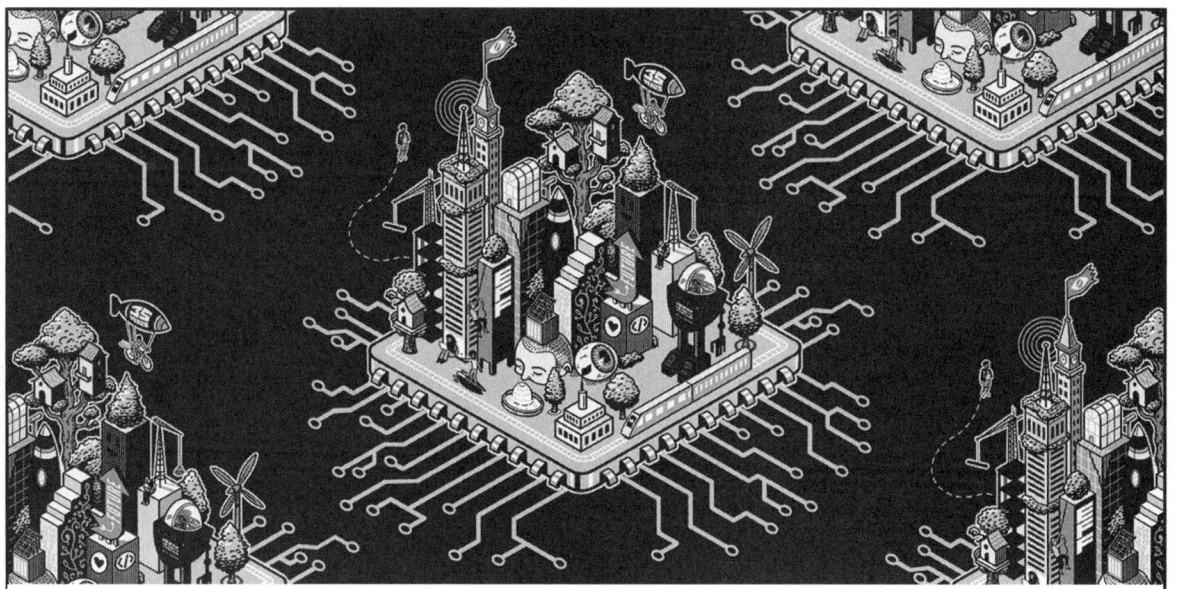

Never before has the world relied so heavily on the internet to stay connected and informed. That makes the Electronic Frontier Foundation's mission—to ensure that technology supports freedom, justice, and innovation for all people—more urgent than ever.

For over 35 years, EFF has fought for your rights through activism, in the courts, and by developing software because we believe in a better future—one where your device is truly yours, you can speak without being surveilled, and technology helps you connect with the people you care about. With your help, we can realize that vision for a brighter world together.